INVINCIBLE
IRON MAN

THE WAR MACHINES

BRIAN MICHAEL BENDIS
WRITER

MIKE DEODATO JR.
ARTIST

FRANK MARTIN
COLOR ARTIST

VC'S CLAYTON COWLES
LETTERER

MIKE DEODATO JR. (#6-9, #11)
WITH **FRANK MARTIN** (#6, #8-9),
DEAN WHITE (#7) &
RAIN BEREDO (#11)
AND **KATE NIEMCZYK** (#10)
COVER ART

ALANNA SMITH
ASSISTANT EDITOR

TOM BREVOORT
EDITOR

IRON MAN CREATED BY STAN LEE, LARRY LIEBER, DON HECK & JACK KIRBY

COLLECTION EDITOR: JENNIFER GRÜNWALD
ASSISTANT EDITOR: CAITLIN O'CONNELL
ASSOCIATE MANAGING EDITOR: KATERI WOODY
EDITOR, SPECIAL PROJECTS: MARK D. BEAZLEY
VP PRODUCTION & SPECIAL PROJECTS: JEFF YOUNGQUIST
SVP PRINT, SALES & MARKETING: DAVID GABRIEL
BOOK DESIGNER: JAY BOWEN

EDITOR IN CHIEF: AXEL ALONSO
CHIEF CREATIVE OFFICER: JOE QUESADA
PRESIDENT: DAN BUCKLEY
EXECUTIVE PRODUCER: ALAN FINE

...IBLE IRON MAN VOL. 2: THE WAR MACHINES. Contains material originally published in magazine form as INVINCIBLE IRON MAN #6-11. First printing 2017. ISBN# 978-0-7851-9941-0. Published by MARVEL WORLDWIDE, INC., a
...ry of MARVEL ENTERTAINMENT, LLC. OFFICE OF PUBLICATION: 135 West 50th Street, New York, NY 10020. Copyright © 2017 MARVEL. No similarity between any of the names, characters, persons, and/or institutions in this magazine
...se of any living or dead person or institution is intended, and any such similarity which may exist is purely coincidental. **Printed in the U.S.A.** DAN BUCKLEY, President, Marvel Entertainment; JOE QUESADA, Chief Creative Officer;
...REVOORT, SVP of Publishing; DAVID BOGART, SVP of Business Affairs & Operations, Publishing & Partnership; C.B. CEBULSKI, VP of Brand Management & Development, Asia; DAVID GABRIEL, SVP of Sales & Marketing, Publishing; JEFF
...QUIST, VP of Production & Special Projects; DAN CARR, Executive Director of Publishing Technology; ALEX MORALES, Director of Publishing Operations; SUSAN CRESPI, Production Manager; STAN LEE, Chairman Emeritus. For information
...n advertising in Marvel Comics or on Marvel.com, please contact Vit DeBellis, Integrated Sales Manager, at vdebellis@marvel.com. For Marvel subscription inquiries, please call 888-511-5480. **Manufactured between 2/24/2017**

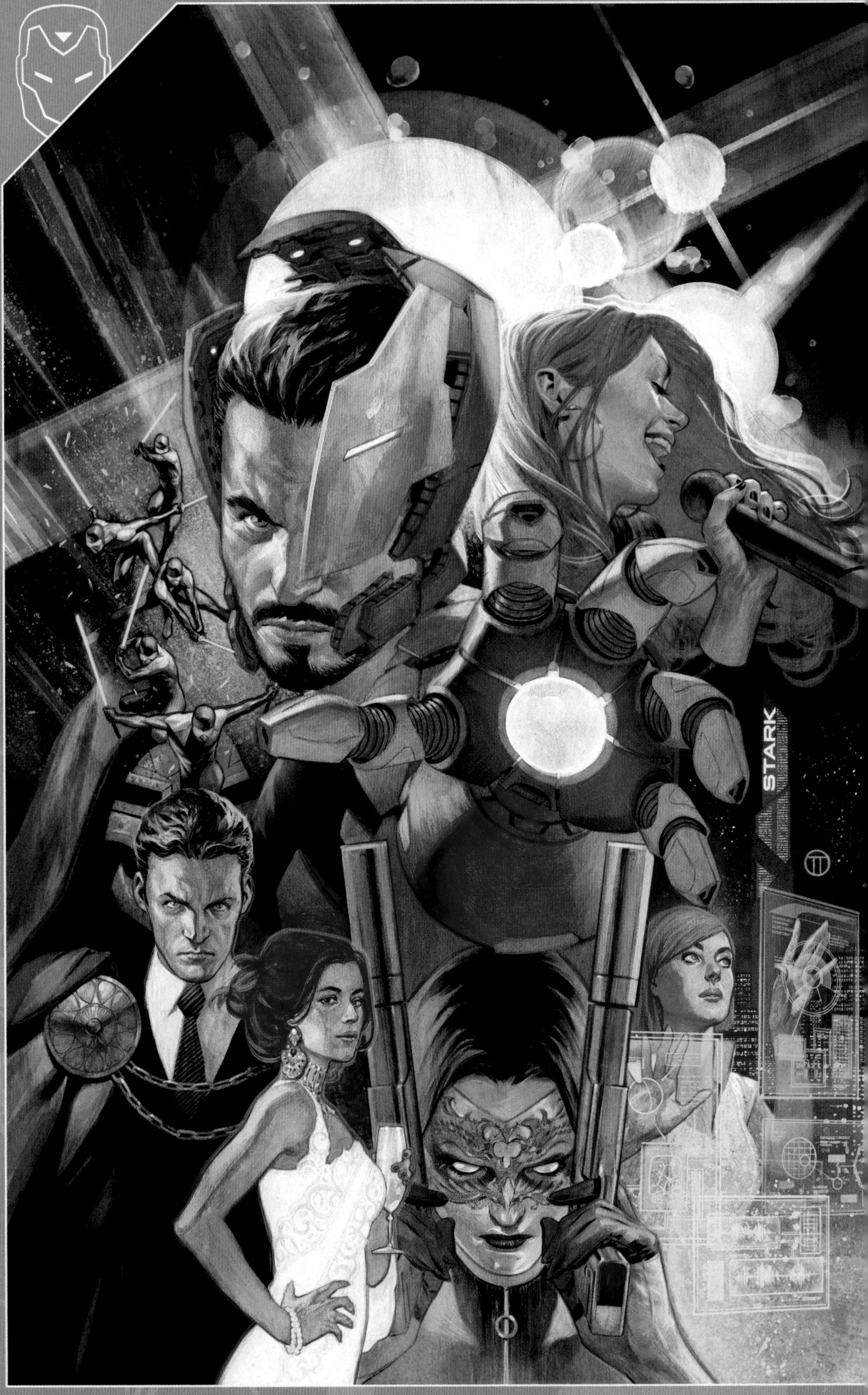
STARK

#6 STORY THUS FAR VARIANT BY JULIAN TOTINO TEDESCO

#6

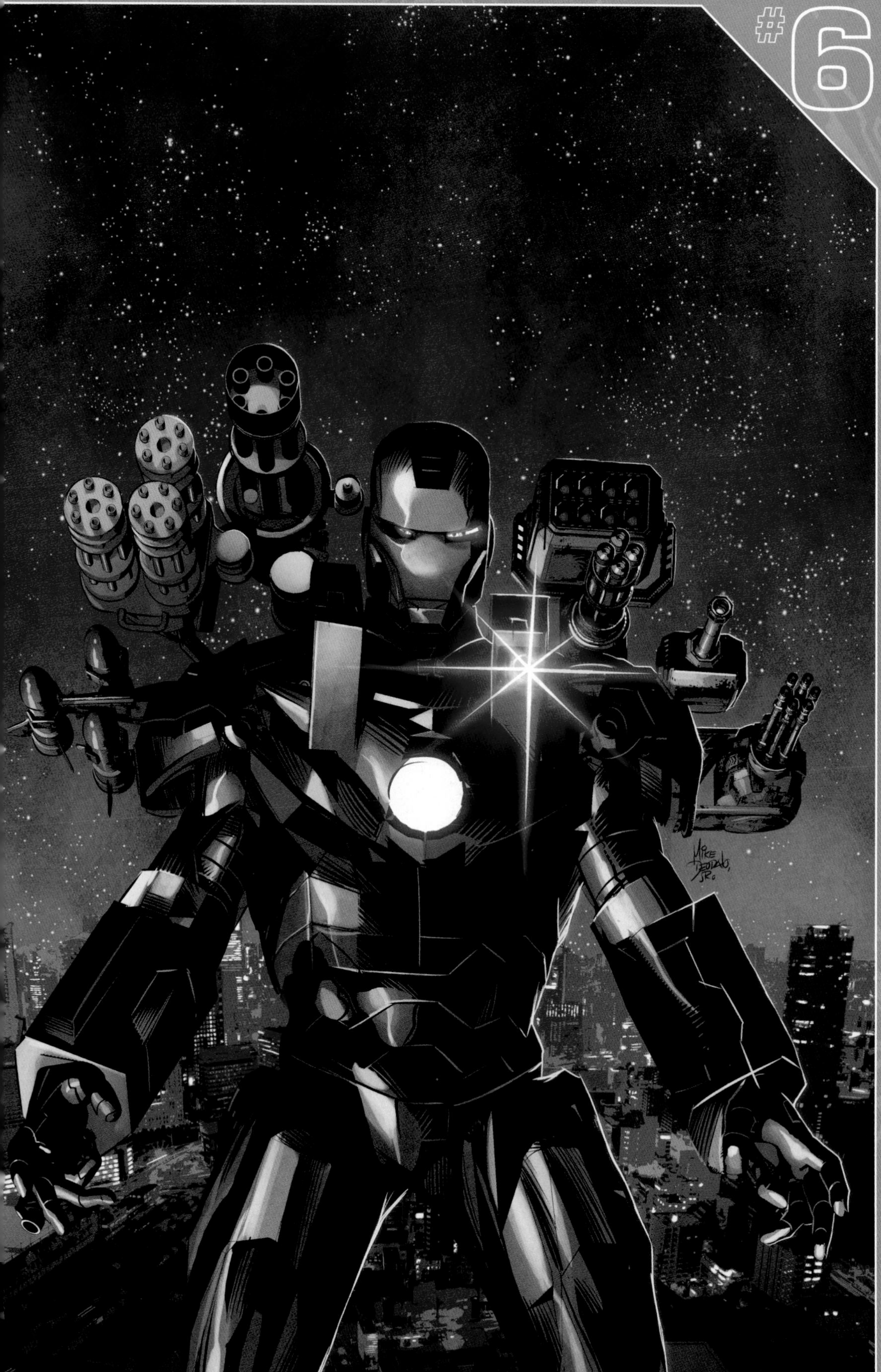

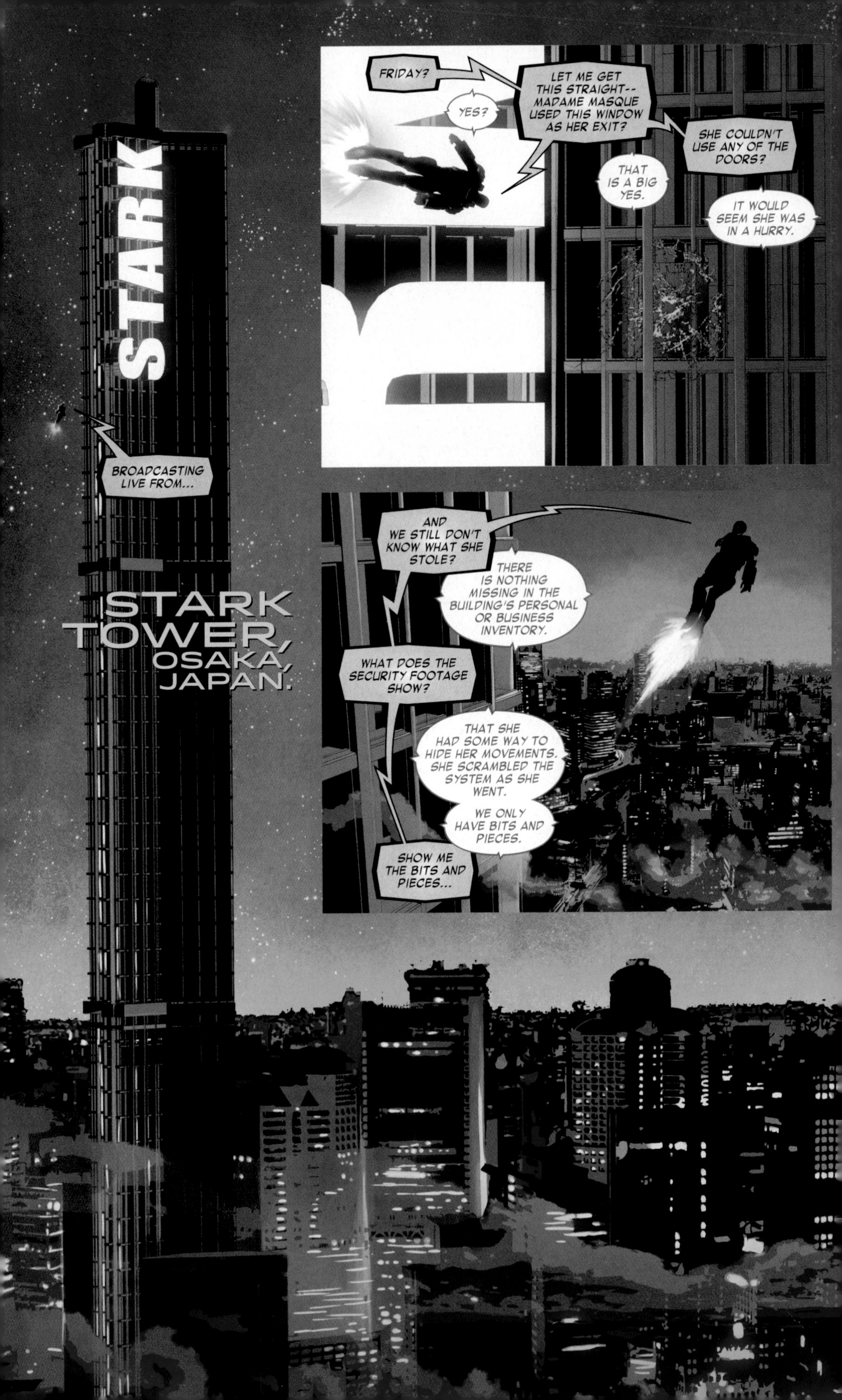
STARK
BROADCASTING LIVE FROM...
STARK TOWER, OSAKA, JAPAN.
FRIDAY?
YES?
LET ME GET THIS STRAIGHT-- MADAME MASQUE USED THIS WINDOW AS HER EXIT?
THAT IS A BIG YES.
SHE COULDN'T USE ANY OF THE DOORS?
IT WOULD SEEM SHE WAS IN A HURRY.
AND WE STILL DON'T KNOW WHAT SHE STOLE?
THERE IS NOTHING MISSING IN THE BUILDING'S PERSONAL OR BUSINESS INVENTORY.
WHAT DOES THE SECURITY FOOTAGE SHOW?
THAT SHE HAD SOME WAY TO HIDE HER MOVEMENTS. SHE SCRAMBLED THE SYSTEM AS SHE WENT.
WE ONLY HAVE BITS AND PIECES.
SHOW ME THE BITS AND PIECES...

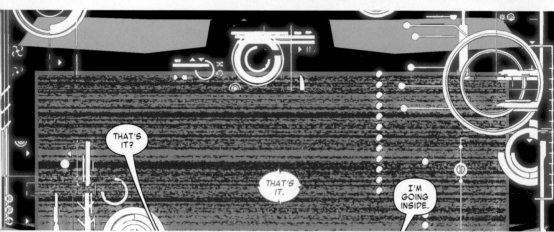

THAT'S IT?

THAT'S IT.

I'M GOING INSIDE.

YOU SCANNING THE ROOM FOR ME, FRIDAY?

FULL ENVIRONMENTAL SCAN.

I'M PICKING UP VERY THIN TRACES OF ENERGY SIGNATURE RESIDUE THAT MATCHES THE BIOHACK NINJAS FROM THE BEACH ATTACK THE OTHER NIGHT.

CAN YOU TRACE IT?

NOT ENOUGH TO TRACE.

I COULD MATCH IT IF I EVER CAME ACROSS IT AGAIN.

AND THERE WERE HOW MANY OF THESE--?

<WHO ARE YOU?>*

*TRANSLATED FROM JAPANESE.

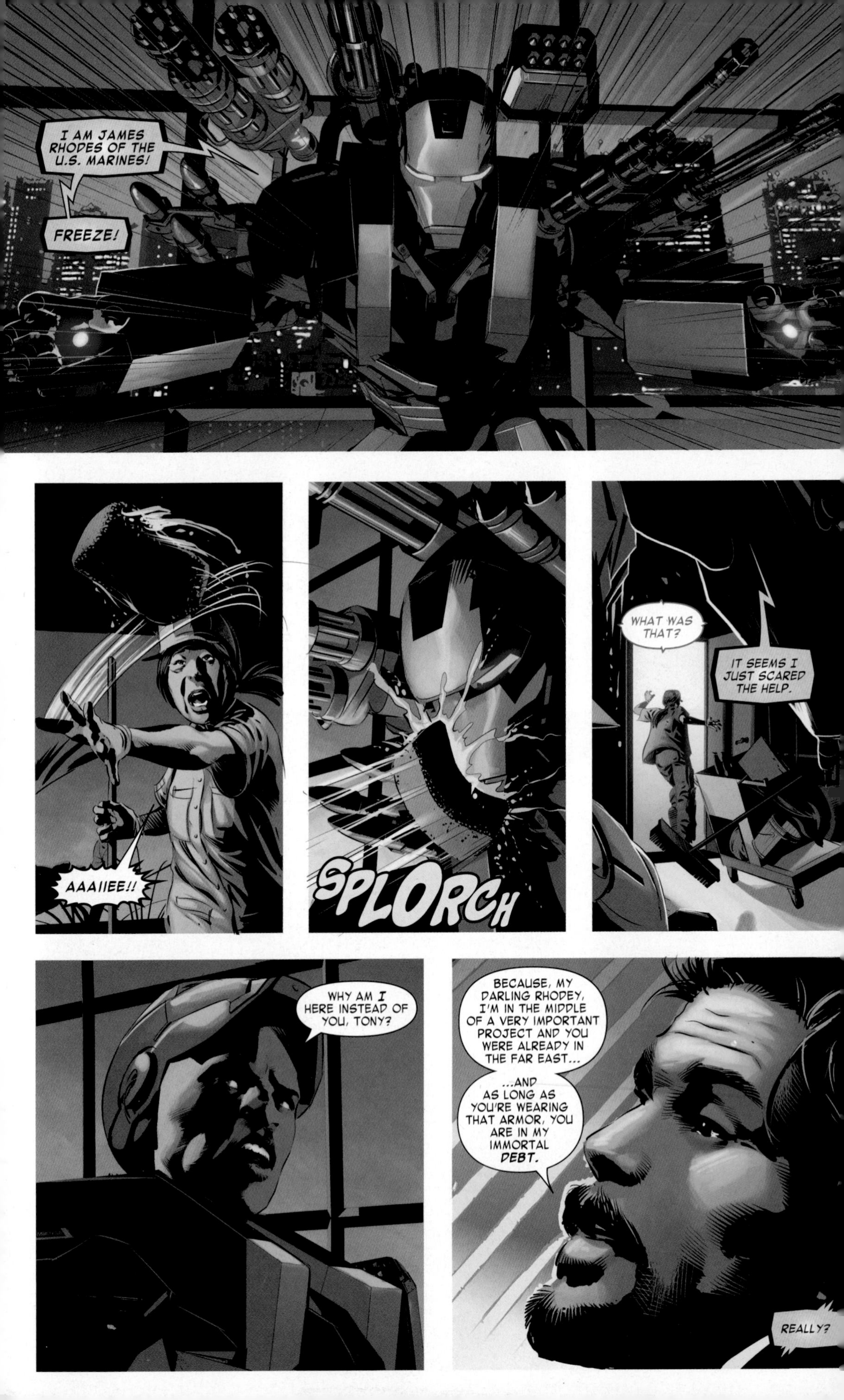
I AM JAMES RHODES OF THE U.S. MARINES!
FREEZE!
AAAIIEE!!
SPLORCH
WHAT WAS THAT?
IT SEEMS I JUST SCARED THE HELP.
WHY AM I HERE INSTEAD OF YOU, TONY?
BECAUSE, MY DARLING RHODEY, I'M IN THE MIDDLE OF A VERY IMPORTANT PROJECT AND YOU WERE ALREADY IN THE FAR EAST...
...AND AS LONG AS YOU'RE WEARING THAT ARMOR, YOU ARE IN MY IMMORTAL DEBT.
REALLY?

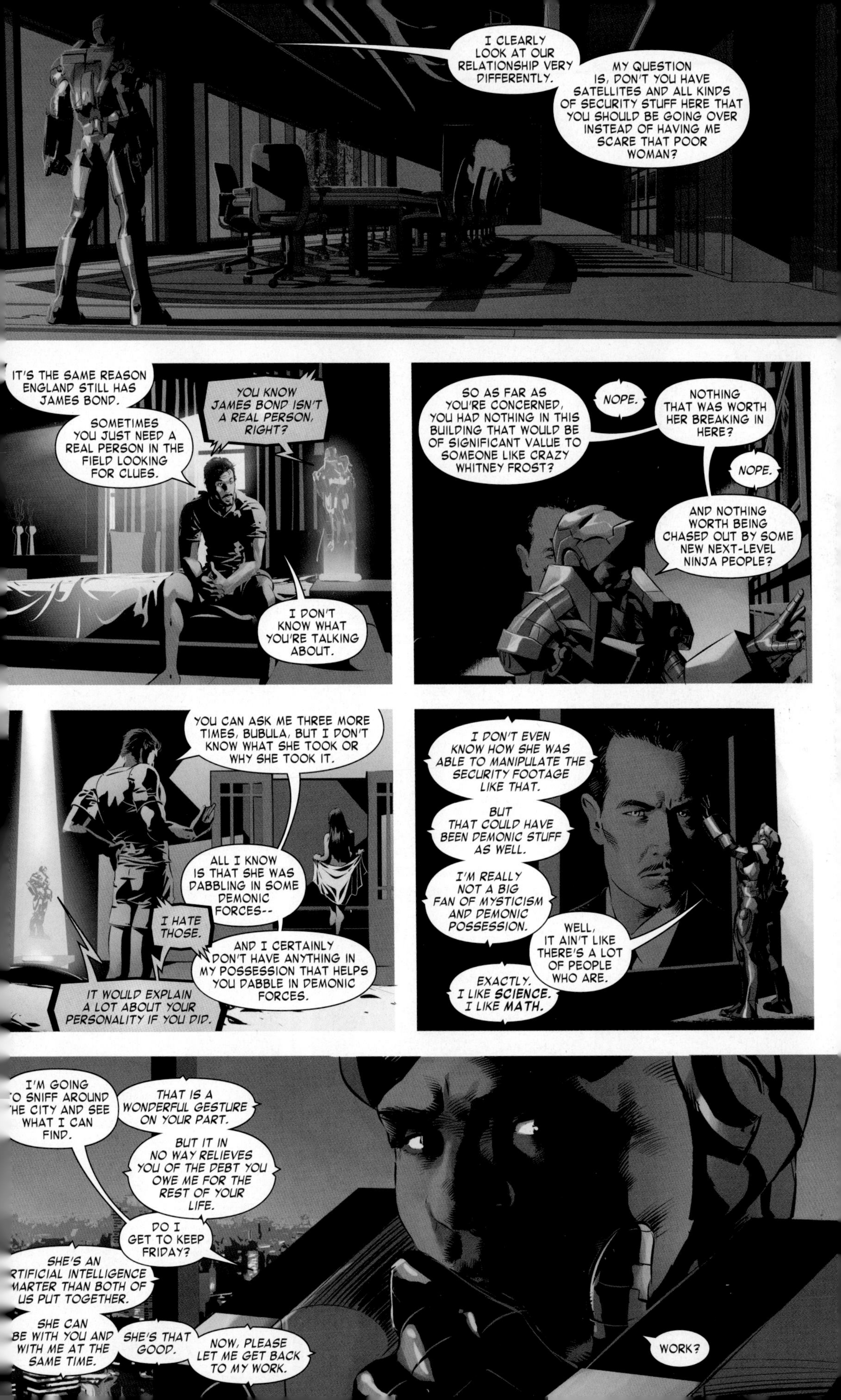
I CLEARLY LOOK AT OUR RELATIONSHIP VERY DIFFERENTLY.
MY QUESTION IS, DON'T YOU HAVE SATELLITES AND ALL KINDS OF SECURITY STUFF HERE THAT YOU SHOULD BE GOING OVER INSTEAD OF HAVING ME SCARE THAT POOR WOMAN?
IT'S THE SAME REASON ENGLAND STILL HAS JAMES BOND.
SOMETIMES YOU JUST NEED A REAL PERSON IN THE FIELD LOOKING FOR CLUES.
YOU KNOW JAMES BOND ISN'T A REAL PERSON, RIGHT?
I DON'T KNOW WHAT YOU'RE TALKING ABOUT.
SO AS FAR AS YOU'RE CONCERNED, YOU HAD NOTHING IN THIS BUILDING THAT WOULD BE OF SIGNIFICANT VALUE TO SOMEONE LIKE CRAZY WHITNEY FROST?
NOPE.
NOTHING THAT WAS WORTH HER BREAKING IN HERE?
NOPE.
AND NOTHING WORTH BEING CHASED OUT BY SOME NEW NEXT-LEVEL NINJA PEOPLE?
YOU CAN ASK ME THREE MORE TIMES, BUBULA, BUT I DON'T KNOW WHAT SHE TOOK OR WHY SHE TOOK IT.
ALL I KNOW IS THAT SHE WAS DABBLING IN SOME DEMONIC FORCES--
I HATE THOSE.
AND I CERTAINLY DON'T HAVE ANYTHING IN MY POSSESSION THAT HELPS YOU DABBLE IN DEMONIC FORCES.
IT WOULD EXPLAIN A LOT ABOUT YOUR PERSONALITY IF YOU DID.
I DON'T EVEN KNOW HOW SHE WAS ABLE TO MANIPULATE THE SECURITY FOOTAGE LIKE THAT.
BUT THAT COULD HAVE BEEN DEMONIC STUFF AS WELL.
I'M REALLY NOT A BIG FAN OF MYSTICISM AND DEMONIC POSSESSION.
WELL, IT AIN'T LIKE THERE'S A LOT OF PEOPLE WHO ARE.
EXACTLY. I LIKE SCIENCE. I LIKE MATH.
I'M GOING TO SNIFF AROUND THE CITY AND SEE WHAT I CAN FIND.
THAT IS A WONDERFUL GESTURE ON YOUR PART.
BUT IT IN NO WAY RELIEVES YOU OF THE DEBT YOU OWE ME FOR THE REST OF YOUR LIFE.
DO I GET TO KEEP FRIDAY?
SHE'S AN ARTIFICIAL INTELLIGENCE SMARTER THAN BOTH OF US PUT TOGETHER.
SHE CAN BE WITH YOU AND WITH ME AT THE SAME TIME.
SHE'S THAT GOOD.
NOW, PLEASE LET ME GET BACK TO MY WORK.
WORK?

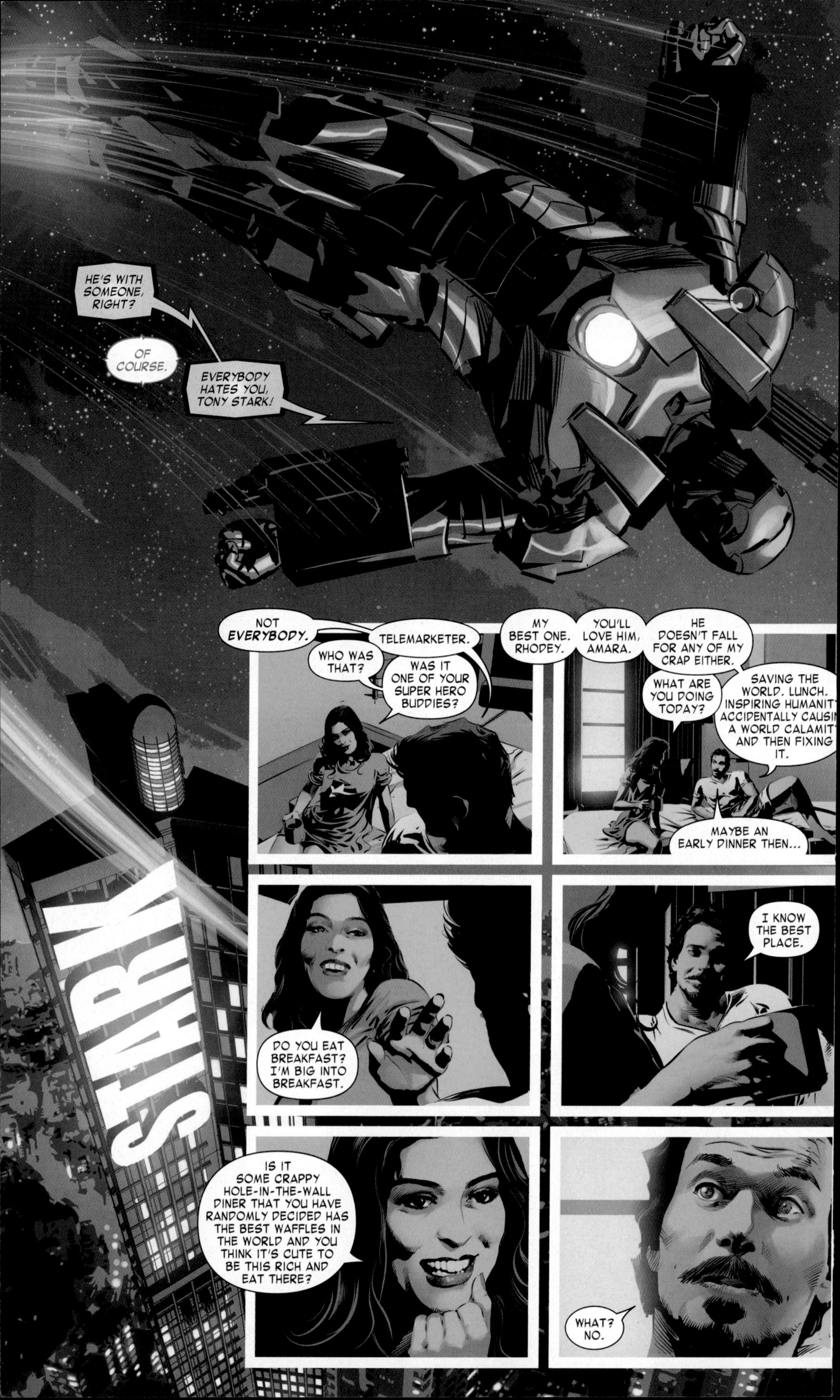

HE'S WITH SOMEONE, RIGHT?
OF COURSE.
EVERYBODY HATES YOU, TONY STARK!
NOT EVERYBODY.
TELEMARKETER.
WHO WAS THAT?
WAS IT ONE OF YOUR SUPER HERO BUDDIES?
MY BEST ONE. RHODEY.
YOU'LL LOVE HIM, AMARA.
HE DOESN'T FALL FOR ANY OF MY CRAP EITHER.
WHAT ARE YOU DOING TODAY?
SAVING THE WORLD. LUNCH. INSPIRING HUMANIT ACCIDENTALLY CAUSIN A WORLD CALAMIT AND THEN FIXING IT.
MAYBE AN EARLY DINNER THEN...
STARK
DO YOU EAT BREAKFAST? I'M BIG INTO BREAKFAST.
I KNOW THE BEST PLACE.
IS IT SOME CRAPPY HOLE-IN-THE-WALL DINER THAT YOU HAVE RANDOMLY DECIDED HAS THE BEST WAFFLES IN THE WORLD AND YOU THINK IT'S CUTE TO BE THIS RICH AND EAT THERE?
WHAT? NO.

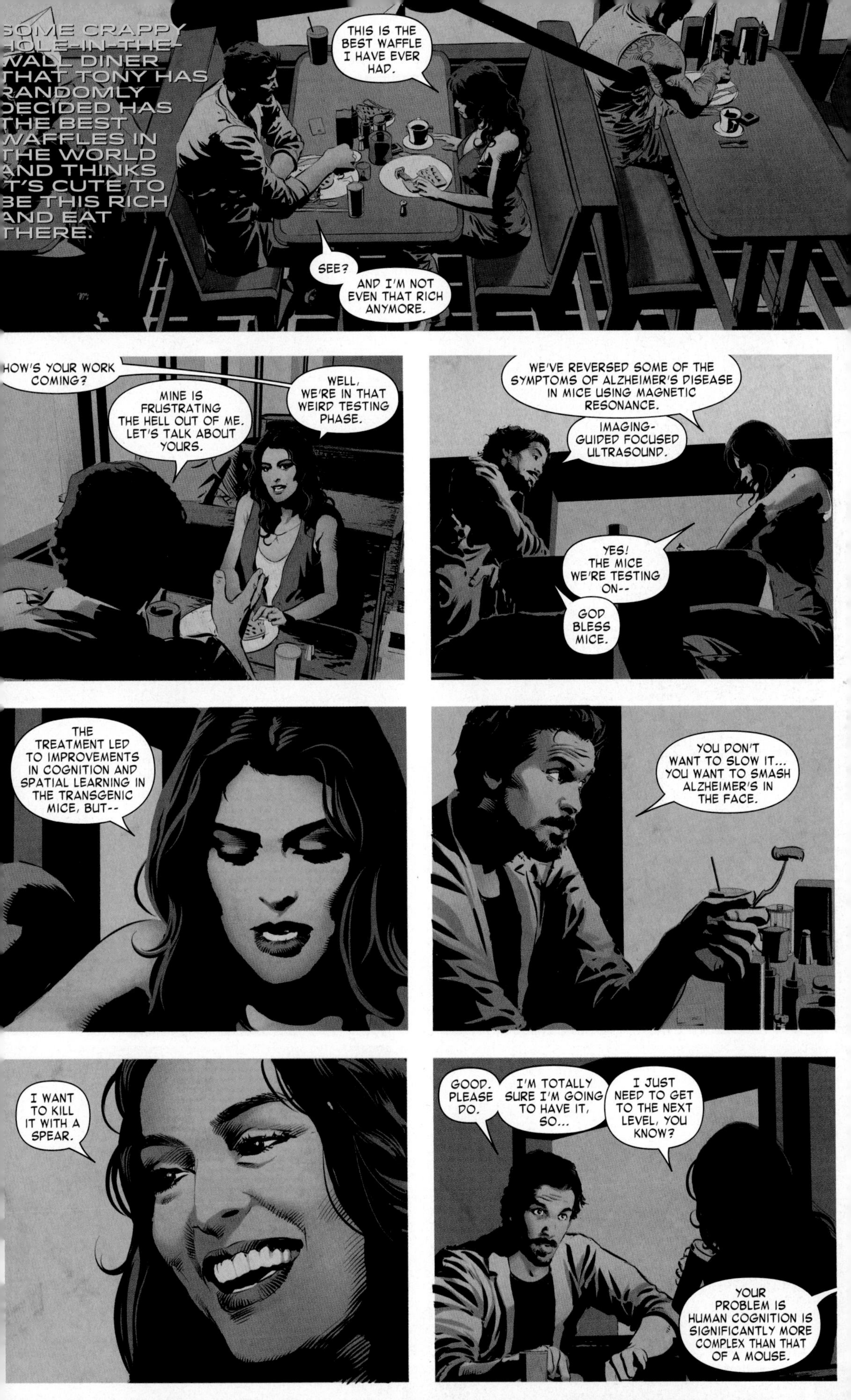
SOME CRAPPY HOLE-IN-THE-WALL DINER THAT TONY HAS RANDOMLY DECIDED HAS THE BEST WAFFLES IN THE WORLD AND THINKS IT'S CUTE TO BE THIS RICH AND EAT THERE.
THIS IS THE BEST WAFFLE I HAVE EVER HAD.
SEE?
AND I'M NOT EVEN THAT RICH ANYMORE.
HOW'S YOUR WORK COMING?
MINE IS FRUSTRATING THE HELL OUT OF ME. LET'S TALK ABOUT YOURS.
WELL, WE'RE IN THAT WEIRD TESTING PHASE.
WE'VE REVERSED SOME OF THE SYMPTOMS OF ALZHEIMER'S DISEASE IN MICE USING MAGNETIC RESONANCE.
IMAGING-GUIDED FOCUSED ULTRASOUND.
YES! THE MICE WE'RE TESTING ON--
GOD BLESS MICE.
THE TREATMENT LED TO IMPROVEMENTS IN COGNITION AND SPATIAL LEARNING IN THE TRANSGENIC MICE, BUT--
YOU DON'T WANT TO SLOW IT... YOU WANT TO SMASH ALZHEIMER'S IN THE FACE.
I WANT TO KILL IT WITH A SPEAR.
GOOD. PLEASE DO.
I'M TOTALLY SURE I'M GOING TO HAVE IT, SO...
I JUST NEED TO GET TO THE NEXT LEVEL, YOU KNOW?
YOUR PROBLEM IS HUMAN COGNITION IS SIGNIFICANTLY MORE COMPLEX THAN THAT OF A MOUSE.

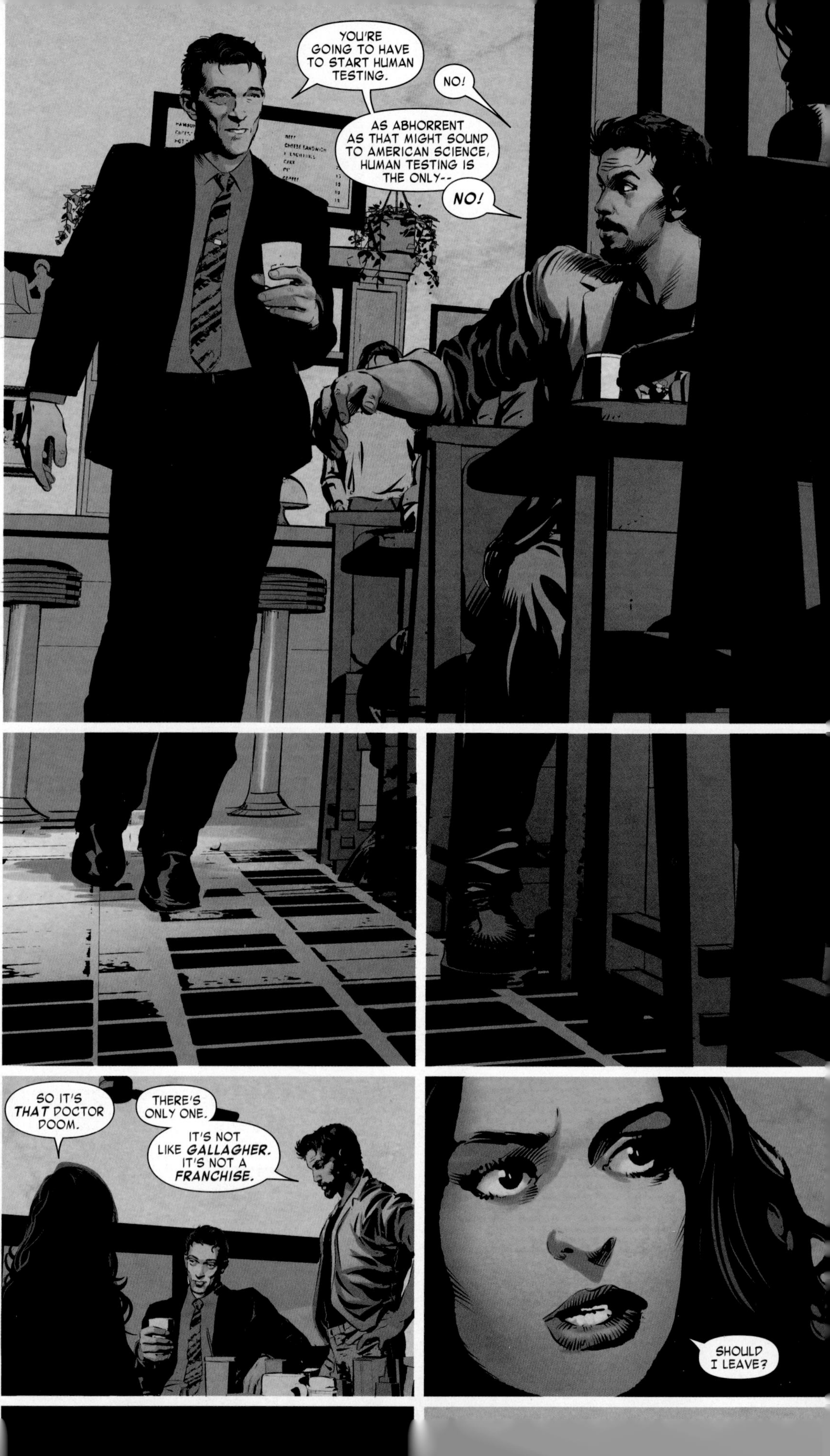
YOU'RE GOING TO HAVE TO START HUMAN TESTING.
NO!
AS ABHORRENT AS THAT MIGHT SOUND TO AMERICAN SCIENCE, HUMAN TESTING IS THE ONLY--
NO!
SO IT'S THAT DOCTOR DOOM.
THERE'S ONLY ONE.
IT'S NOT LIKE GALLAGHER. IT'S NOT A FRANCHISE.
SHOULD I LEAVE?

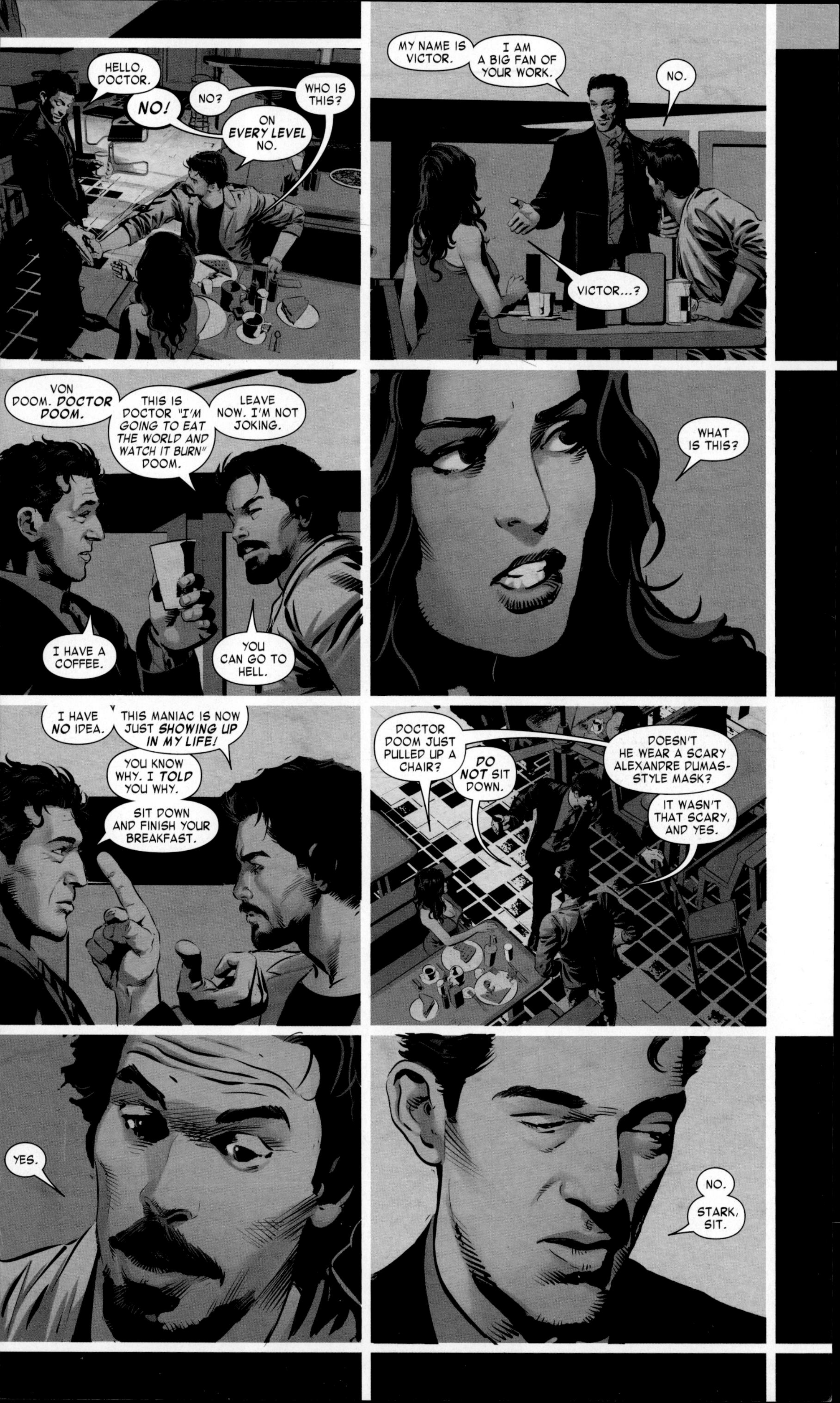
HELLO, DOCTOR.
NO!
NO?
WHO IS THIS?
ON EVERY LEVEL NO.
MY NAME IS VICTOR.
I AM A BIG FAN OF YOUR WORK.
NO.
VICTOR...?
VON DOOM. DOCTOR DOOM.
THIS IS DOCTOR "I'M GOING TO EAT THE WORLD AND WATCH IT BURN" DOOM.
LEAVE NOW. I'M NOT JOKING.
I HAVE A COFFEE.
YOU CAN GO TO HELL.
WHAT IS THIS?
I HAVE NO IDEA.
THIS MANIAC IS NOW JUST SHOWING UP IN MY LIFE!
YOU KNOW WHY. I TOLD YOU WHY.
SIT DOWN AND FINISH YOUR BREAKFAST.
DOCTOR DOOM JUST PULLED UP A CHAIR?
DO NOT SIT DOWN.
DOESN'T HE WEAR A SCARY ALEXANDRE DUMAS-STYLE MASK?
IT WASN'T THAT SCARY, AND YES.
YES.
NO.
STARK, SIT.

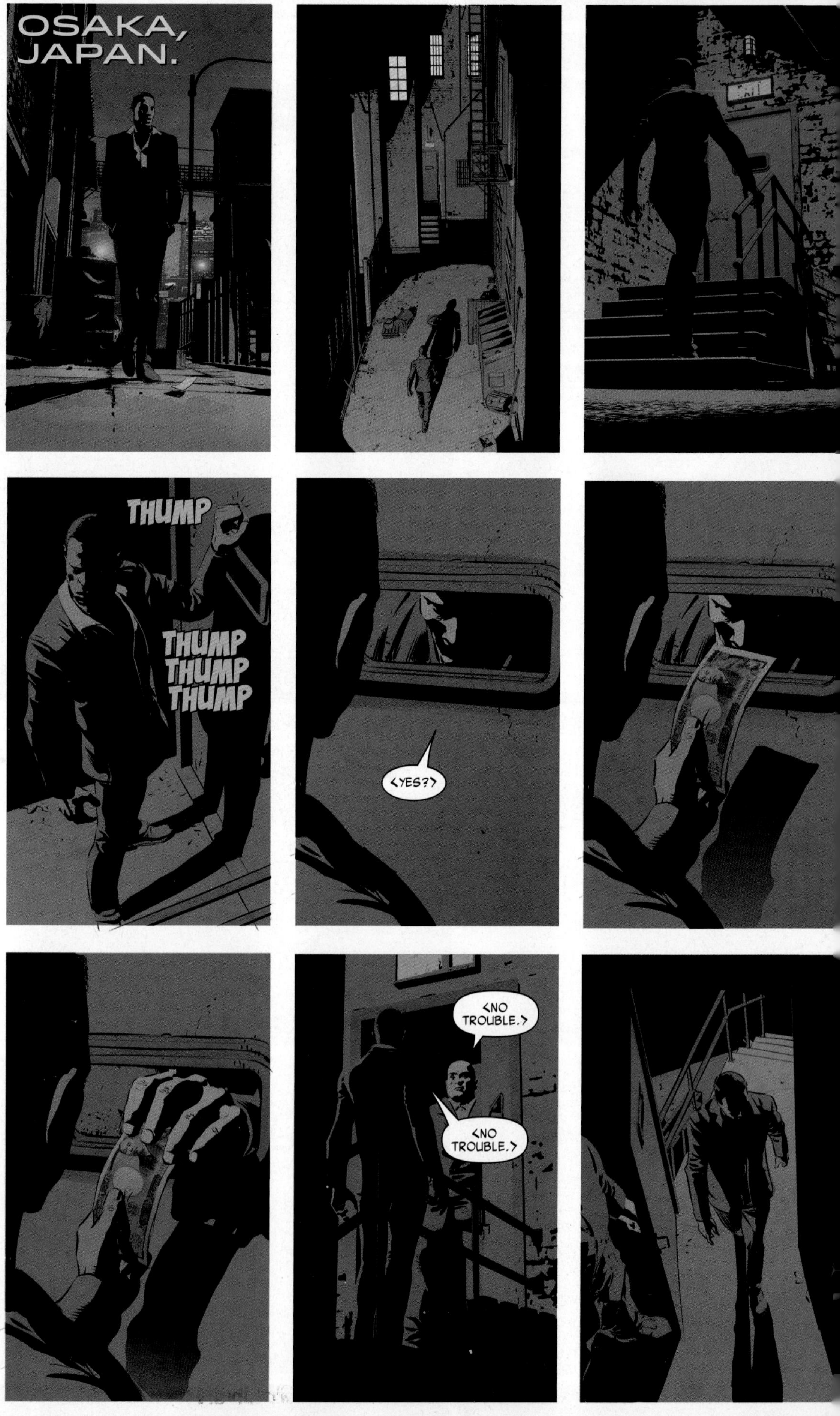
OSAKA, JAPAN.
THUMP
THUMP THUMP THUMP
<YES?>
<NO TROUBLE.>
<NO TROUBLE.>

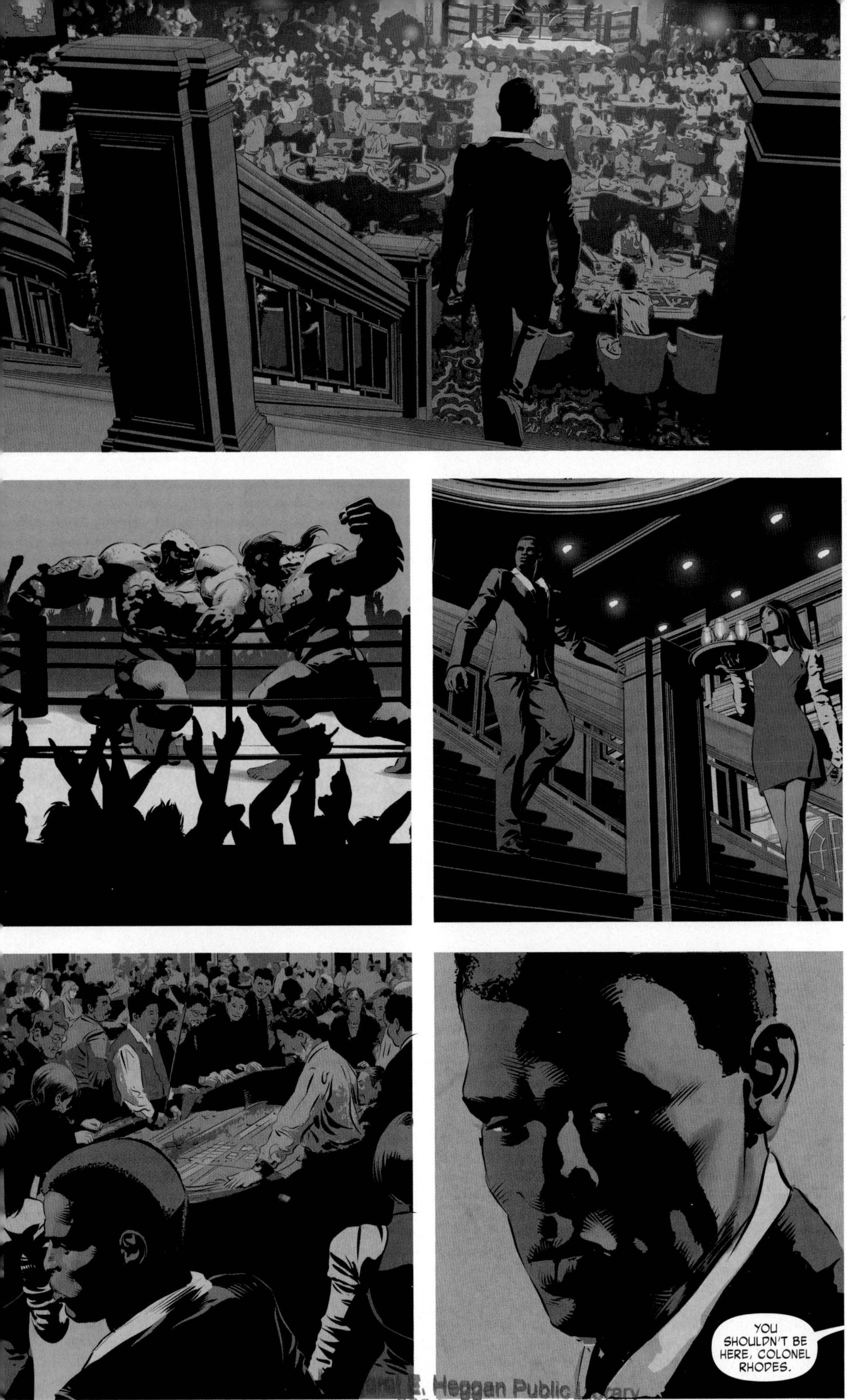
YOU SHOULDN'T BE HERE, COLONEL RHODES.

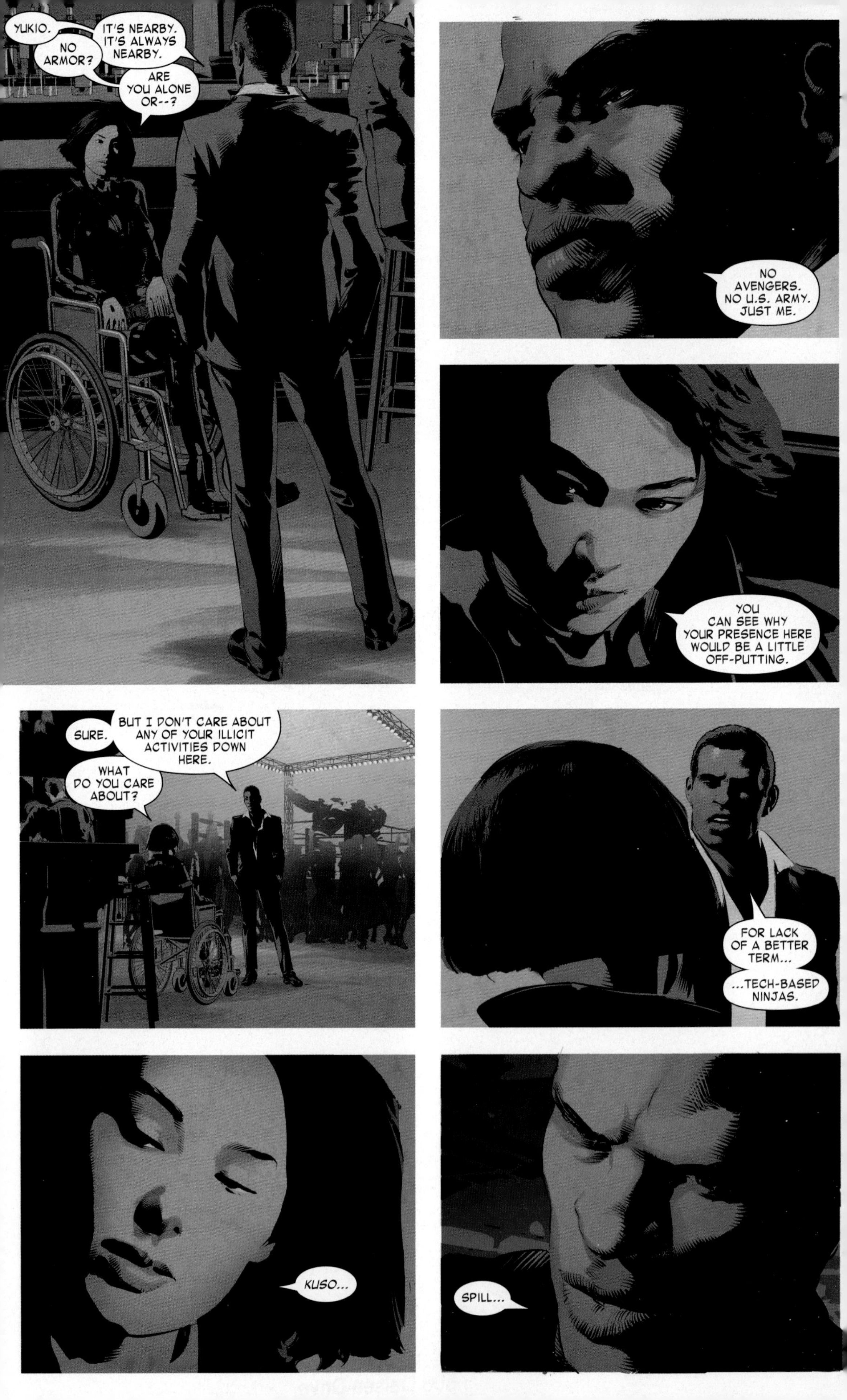
YUKIO.
IT'S NEARBY. IT'S ALWAYS NEARBY.
NO ARMOR?
ARE YOU ALONE OR--?
NO AVENGERS. NO U.S. ARMY. JUST ME.
YOU CAN SEE WHY YOUR PRESENCE HERE WOULD BE A LITTLE OFF-PUTTING.
SURE.
BUT I DON'T CARE ABOUT ANY OF YOUR ILLICIT ACTIVITIES DOWN HERE.
WHAT DO YOU CARE ABOUT?
FOR LACK OF A BETTER TERM...
...TECH-BASED NINJAS.
KUSO...
SPILL...

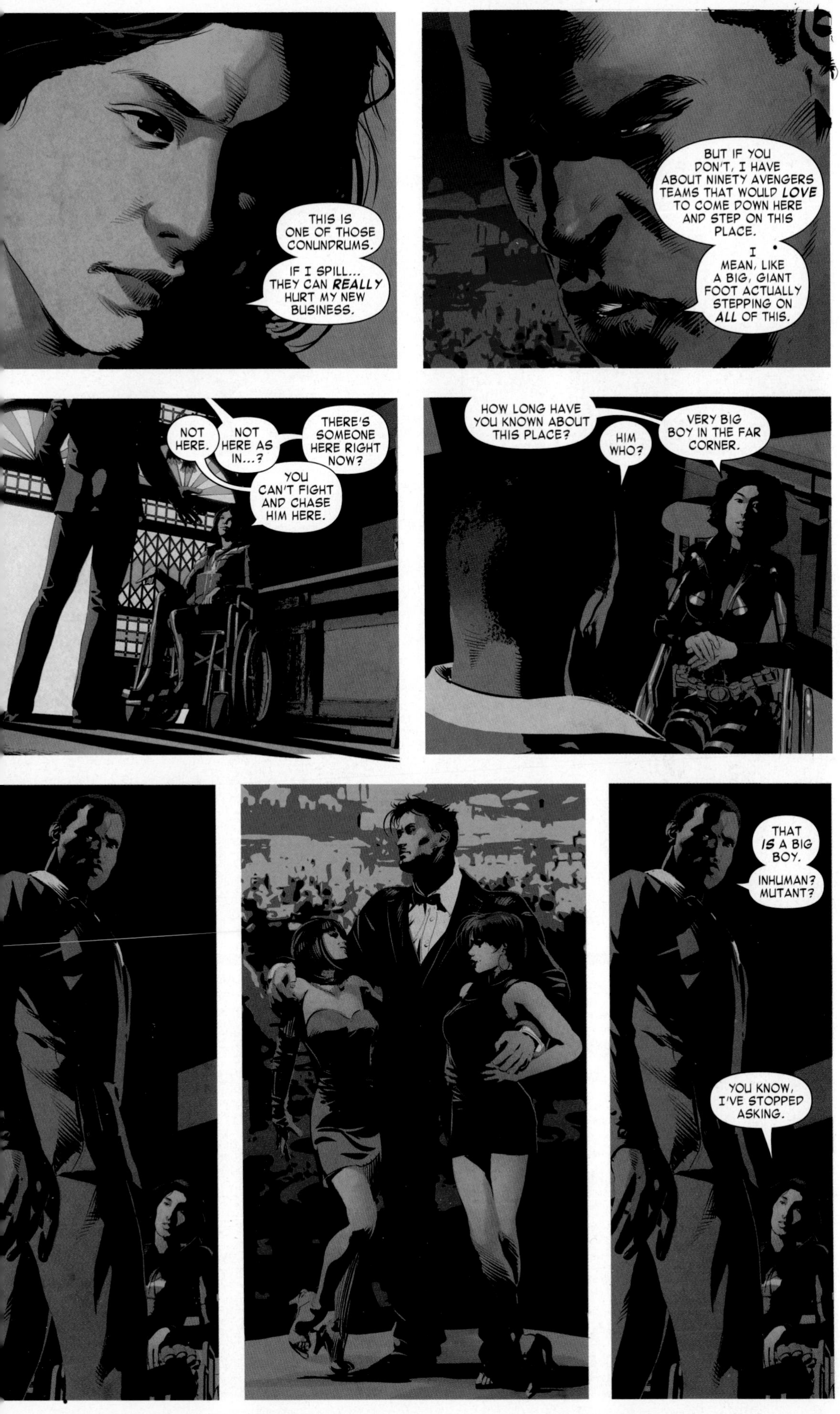

THIS IS ONE OF THOSE CONUNDRUMS.
IF I SPILL... THEY CAN REALLY HURT MY NEW BUSINESS.
BUT IF YOU DON'T, I HAVE ABOUT NINETY AVENGERS TEAMS THAT WOULD LOVE TO COME DOWN HERE AND STEP ON THIS PLACE.
I MEAN, LIKE A BIG, GIANT FOOT ACTUALLY STEPPING ON ALL OF THIS.
THERE'S SOMEONE HERE RIGHT NOW?
NOT HERE AS IN...?
NOT HERE.
YOU CAN'T FIGHT AND CHASE HIM HERE.
HOW LONG HAVE YOU KNOWN ABOUT THIS PLACE?
VERY BIG BOY IN THE FAR CORNER.
HIM WHO?
THAT IS A BIG BOY.
INHUMAN? MUTANT?
YOU KNOW, I'VE STOPPED ASKING.

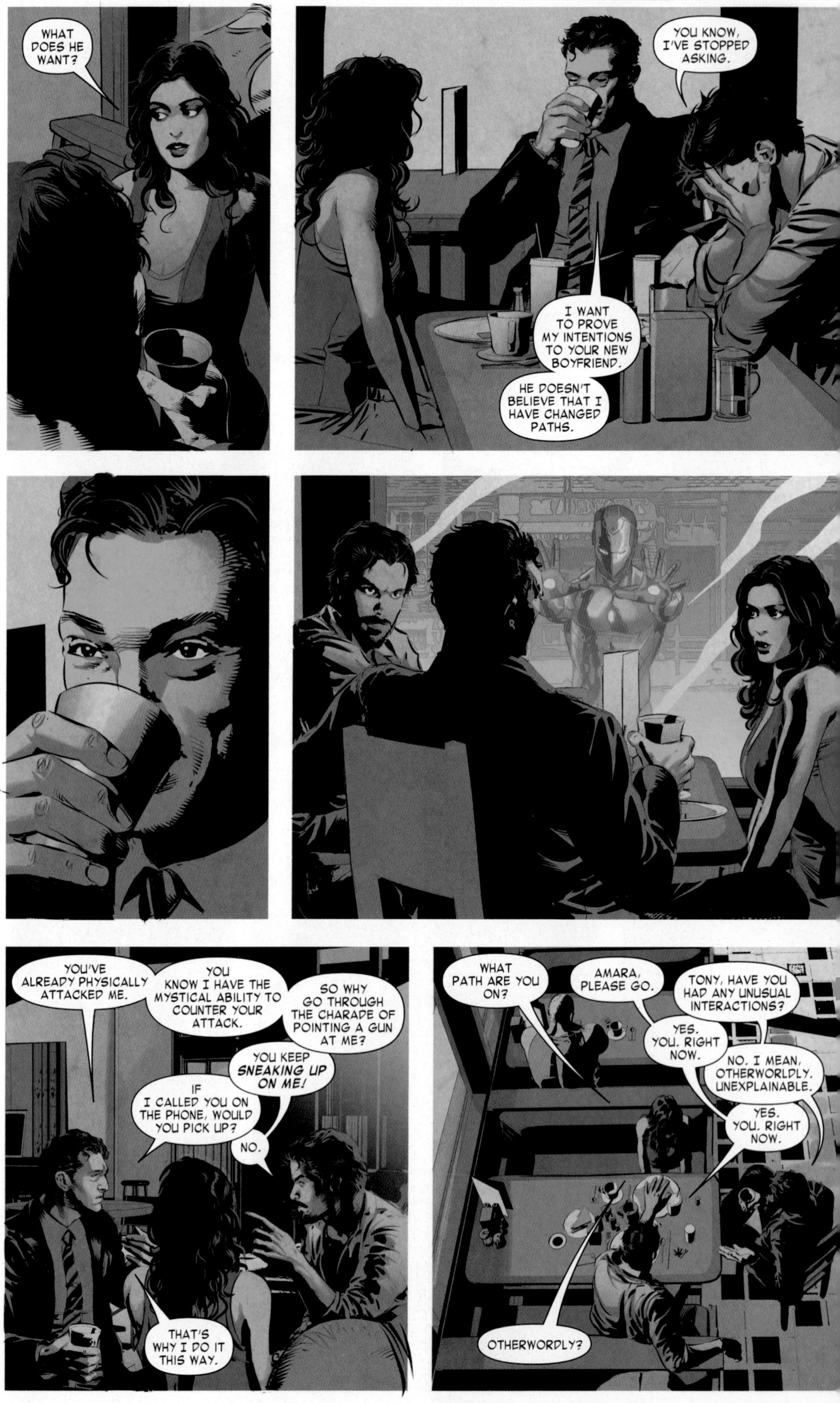
WHAT DOES HE WANT?
YOU KNOW, I'VE STOPPED ASKING.
I WANT TO PROVE MY INTENTIONS TO YOUR NEW BOYFRIEND.
HE DOESN'T BELIEVE THAT I HAVE CHANGED PATHS.
YOU'VE ALREADY PHYSICALLY ATTACKED ME.
YOU KNOW I HAVE THE MYSTICAL ABILITY TO COUNTER YOUR ATTACK.
SO WHY GO THROUGH THE CHARADE OF POINTING A GUN AT ME?
YOU KEEP *SNEAKING UP ON ME!*
IF I CALLED YOU ON THE PHONE, WOULD YOU PICK UP?
NO.
THAT'S WHY I DO IT THIS WAY.
WHAT PATH ARE YOU ON?
AMARA, PLEASE GO.
TONY, HAVE YOU HAD ANY UNUSUAL INTERACTIONS?
YES. YOU. RIGHT NOW.
NO. I MEAN, OTHERWORLDLY. UNEXPLAINABLE.
YES. YOU. RIGHT NOW.
OTHERWORDLY?

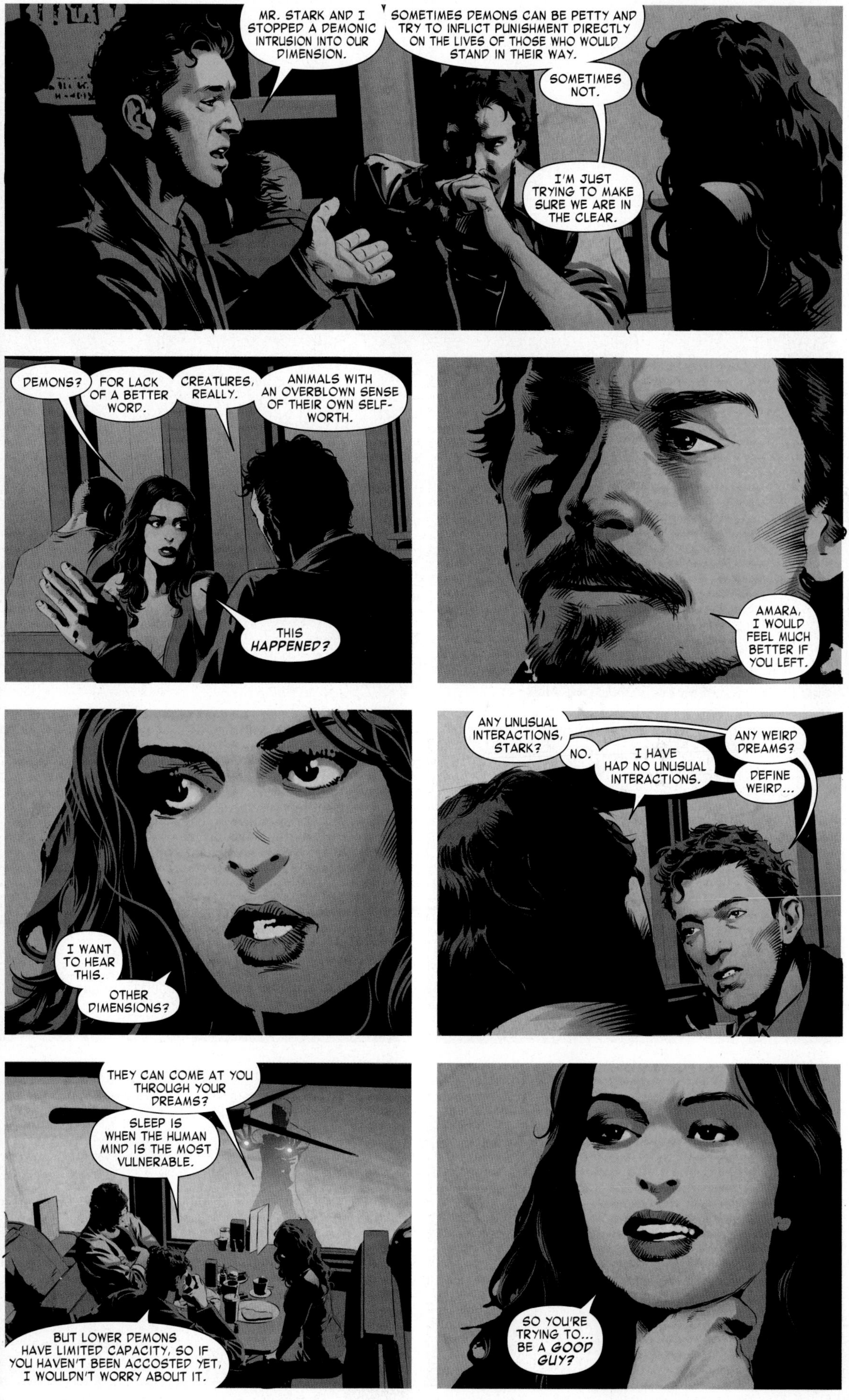

MR. STARK AND I STOPPED A DEMONIC INTRUSION INTO OUR DIMENSION.
SOMETIMES DEMONS CAN BE PETTY AND TRY TO INFLICT PUNISHMENT DIRECTLY ON THE LIVES OF THOSE WHO WOULD STAND IN THEIR WAY.
SOMETIMES NOT.
I'M JUST TRYING TO MAKE SURE WE ARE IN THE CLEAR.
DEMONS?
FOR LACK OF A BETTER WORD.
CREATURES, REALLY.
ANIMALS WITH AN OVERBLOWN SENSE OF THEIR OWN SELF-WORTH.
THIS HAPPENED?
AMARA, I WOULD FEEL MUCH BETTER IF YOU LEFT.
I WANT TO HEAR THIS.
OTHER DIMENSIONS?
ANY UNUSUAL INTERACTIONS, STARK?
NO.
I HAVE HAD NO UNUSUAL INTERACTIONS.
ANY WEIRD DREAMS?
DEFINE WEIRD...
THEY CAN COME AT YOU THROUGH YOUR DREAMS?
SLEEP IS WHEN THE HUMAN MIND IS THE MOST VULNERABLE.
BUT LOWER DEMONS HAVE LIMITED CAPACITY, SO IF YOU HAVEN'T BEEN ACCOSTED YET, I WOULDN'T WORRY ABOUT IT.
SO YOU'RE TRYING TO... BE A GOOD GUY?

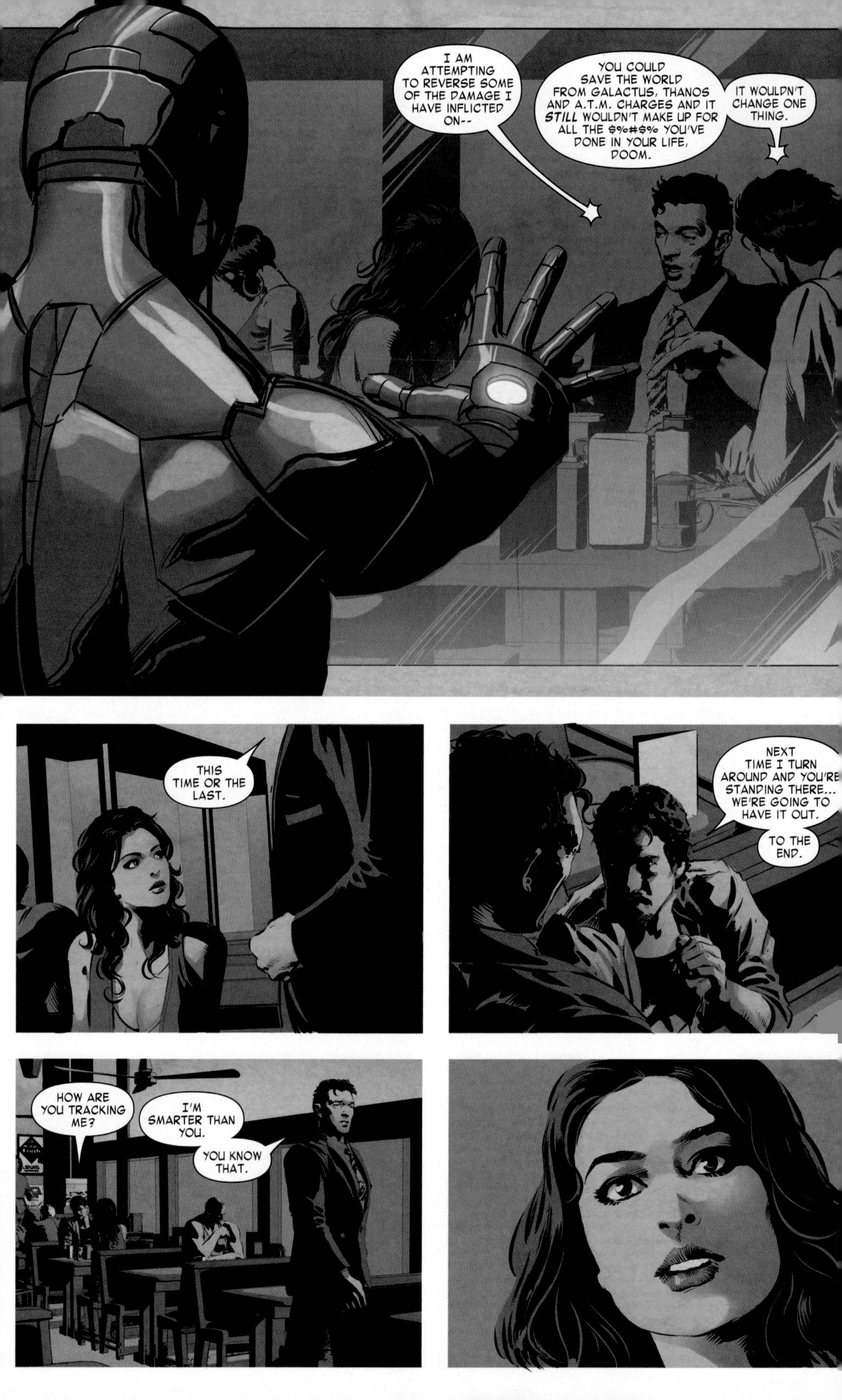
I AM ATTEMPTING TO REVERSE SOME OF THE DAMAGE I HAVE INFLICTED ON--
YOU COULD SAVE THE WORLD FROM GALACTUS, THANOS AND A.T.M. CHARGES AND IT *STILL* WOULDN'T MAKE UP FOR ALL THE $%#$% YOU'VE DONE IN YOUR LIFE, DOOM.
IT WOULDN'T CHANGE ONE THING.
THIS TIME OR THE LAST.
NEXT TIME I TURN AROUND AND YOU'RE STANDING THERE... WE'RE GOING TO HAVE IT OUT.
TO THE END.
HOW ARE YOU TRACKING ME?
I'M SMARTER THAN YOU.
YOU KNOW THAT.

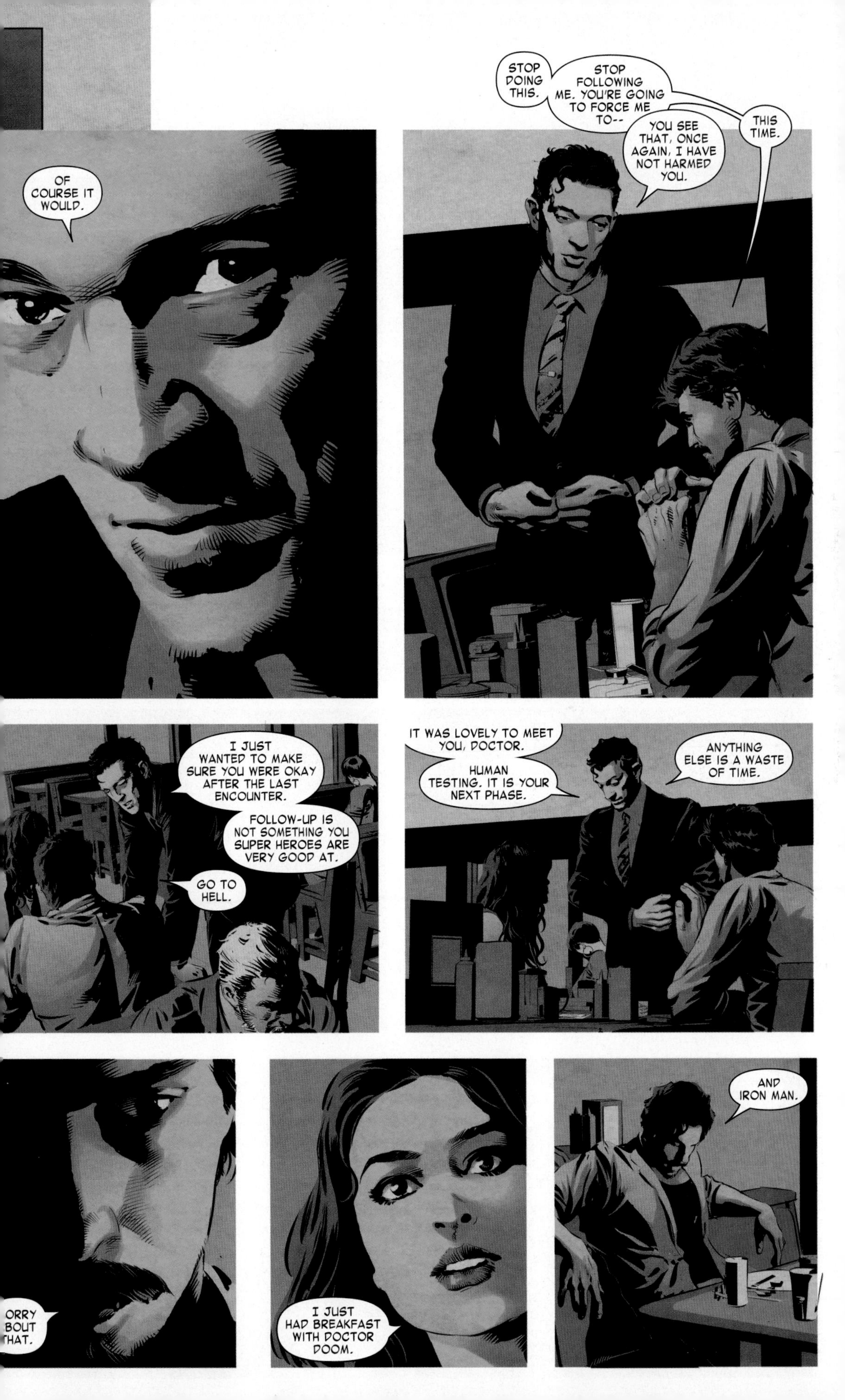
OF COURSE IT WOULD.
STOP DOING THIS.
STOP FOLLOWING ME. YOU'RE GOING TO FORCE ME TO--
THIS TIME.
YOU SEE THAT, ONCE AGAIN, I HAVE NOT HARMED YOU.
I JUST WANTED TO MAKE SURE YOU WERE OKAY AFTER THE LAST ENCOUNTER.
FOLLOW-UP IS NOT SOMETHING YOU SUPER HEROES ARE VERY GOOD AT.
GO TO HELL.
IT WAS LOVELY TO MEET YOU, DOCTOR.
HUMAN TESTING. IT IS YOUR NEXT PHASE.
ANYTHING ELSE IS A WASTE OF TIME.
ORRY BOUT THAT.
I JUST HAD BREAKFAST WITH DOCTOR DOOM.
AND IRON MAN.

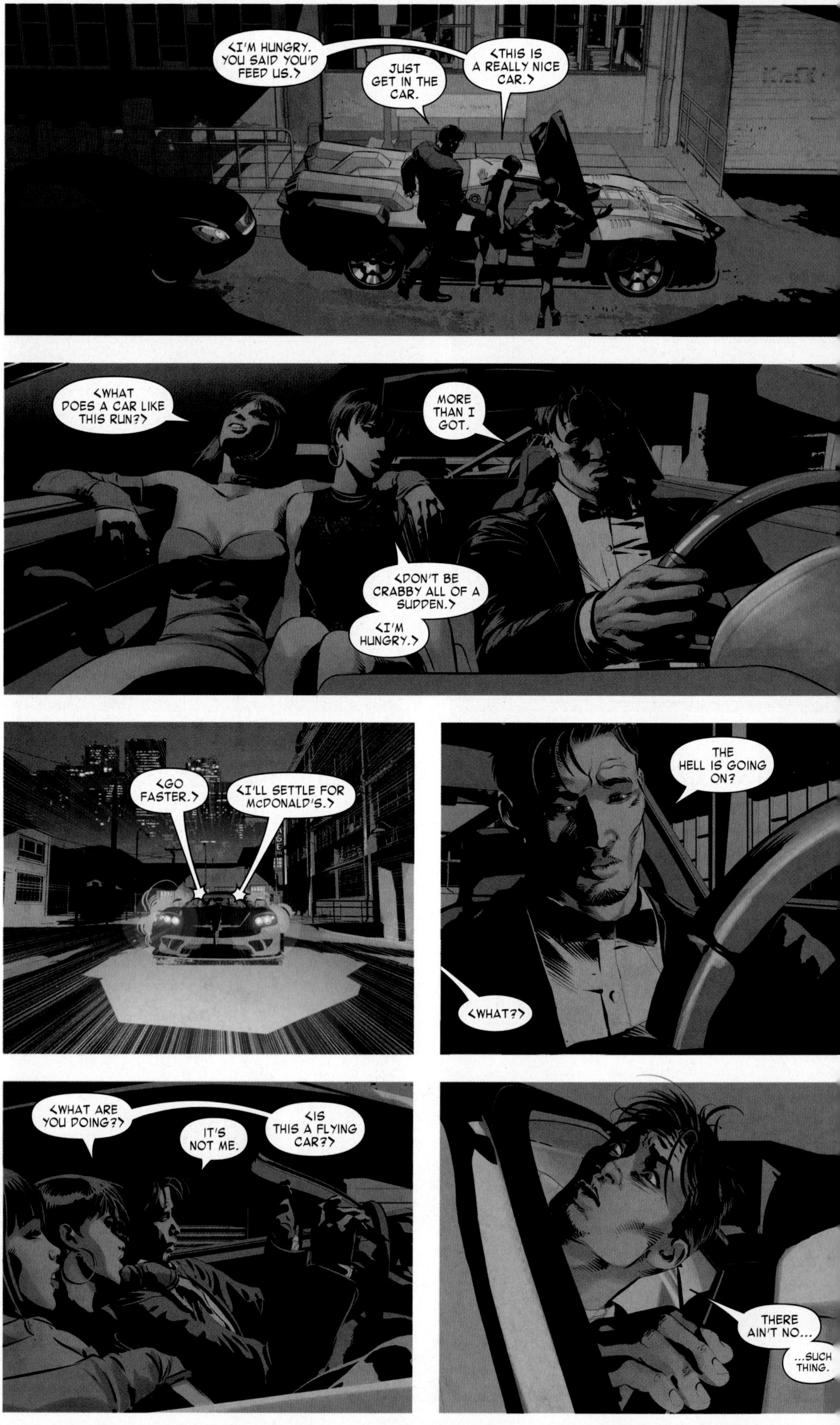
<I'M HUNGRY. YOU SAID YOU'D FEED US.>
JUST GET IN THE CAR.
<THIS IS A REALLY NICE CAR.>
<WHAT DOES A CAR LIKE THIS RUN?>
MORE THAN I GOT.
<DON'T BE CRABBY ALL OF A SUDDEN.>
<I'M HUNGRY.>
<GO FASTER.>
<I'LL SETTLE FOR McDONALD'S.>
THE HELL IS GOING ON?
<WHAT?>
<WHAT ARE YOU DOING?>
IT'S NOT ME.
<IS THIS A FLYING CAR?>
THERE AIN'T NO...
...SUCH THING.

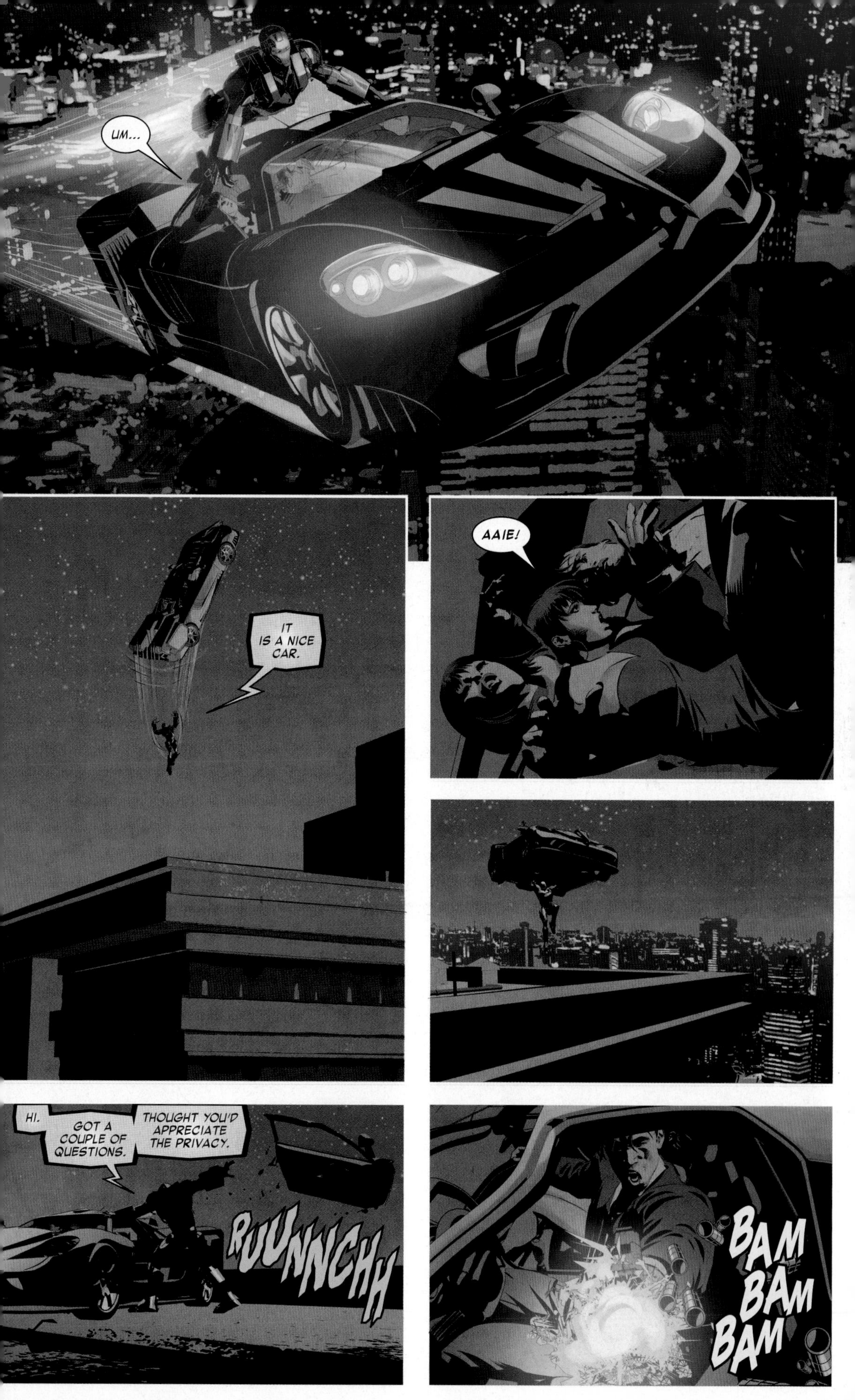
UM...
IT IS A NICE CAR.
AAIE!
HI.
GOT A COUPLE OF QUESTIONS.
THOUGHT YOU'D APPRECIATE THE PRIVACY.
RUUNNCHH
BAM BAM BAM

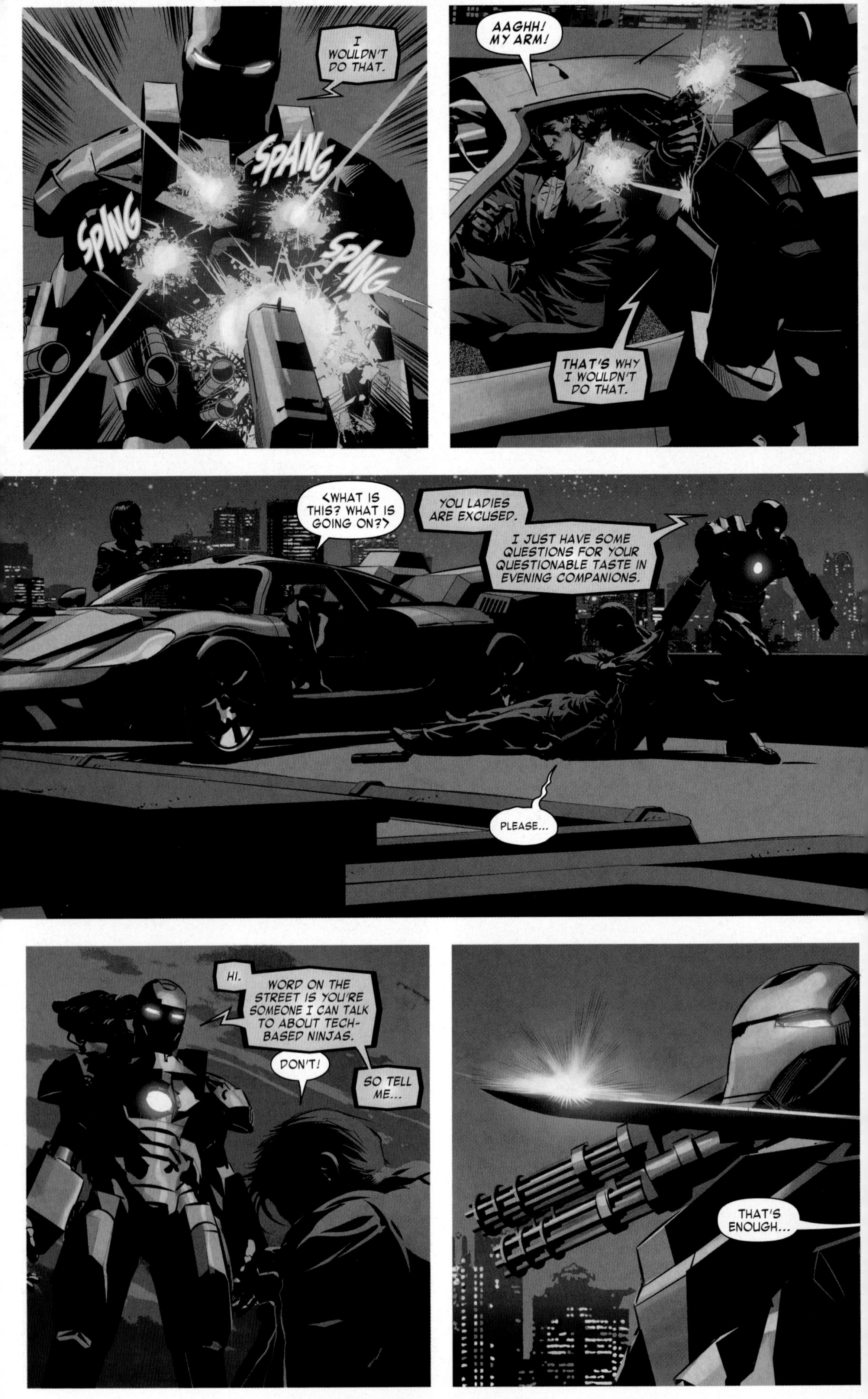
I WOULDN'T DO THAT.
SPANG
SPING
SPING
AAGHH! MY ARM!
THAT'S WHY I WOULDN'T DO THAT.
<WHAT IS THIS? WHAT IS GOING ON?>
YOU LADIES ARE EXCUSED.
I JUST HAVE SOME QUESTIONS FOR YOUR QUESTIONABLE TASTE IN EVENING COMPANIONS.
PLEASE...
HI.
WORD ON THE STREET IS YOU'RE SOMEONE I CAN TALK TO ABOUT TECH-BASED NINJAS.
DON'T!
SO TELL ME...
THAT'S ENOUGH...

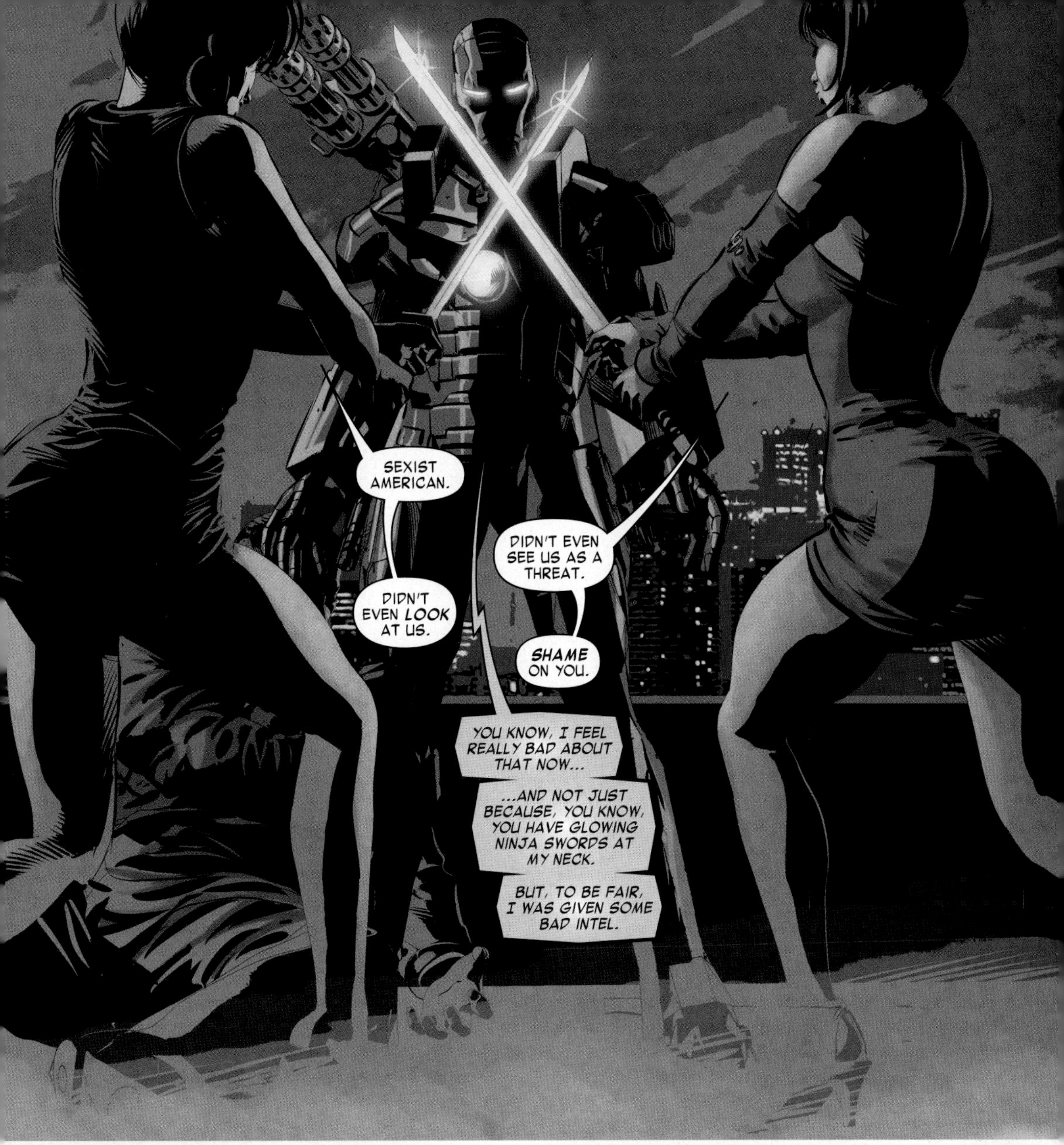
SEXIST AMERICAN.
DIDN'T EVEN LOOK AT US.
DIDN'T EVEN SEE US AS A THREAT.
SHAME ON YOU.
YOU KNOW, I FEEL REALLY BAD ABOUT THAT NOW...
...AND NOT JUST BECAUSE, YOU KNOW, YOU HAVE GLOWING NINJA SWORDS AT MY NECK.
BUT, TO BE FAIR, I WAS GIVEN SOME BAD INTEL.

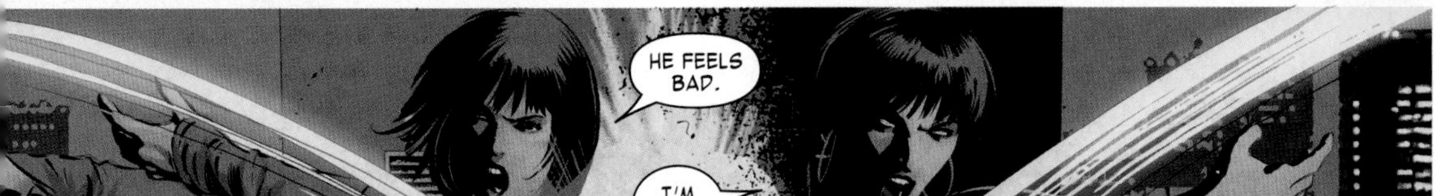
HE FEELS BAD.
I'M SURE.

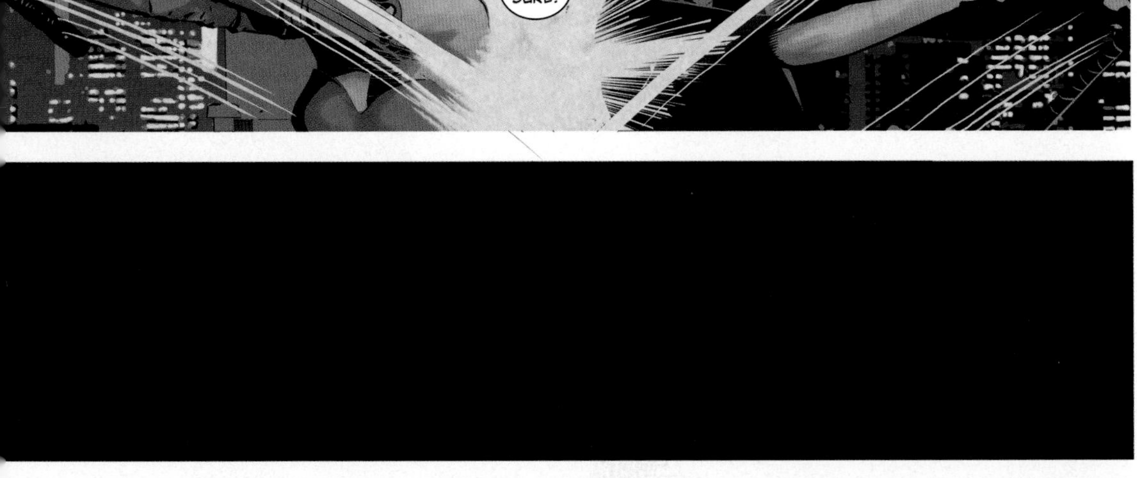

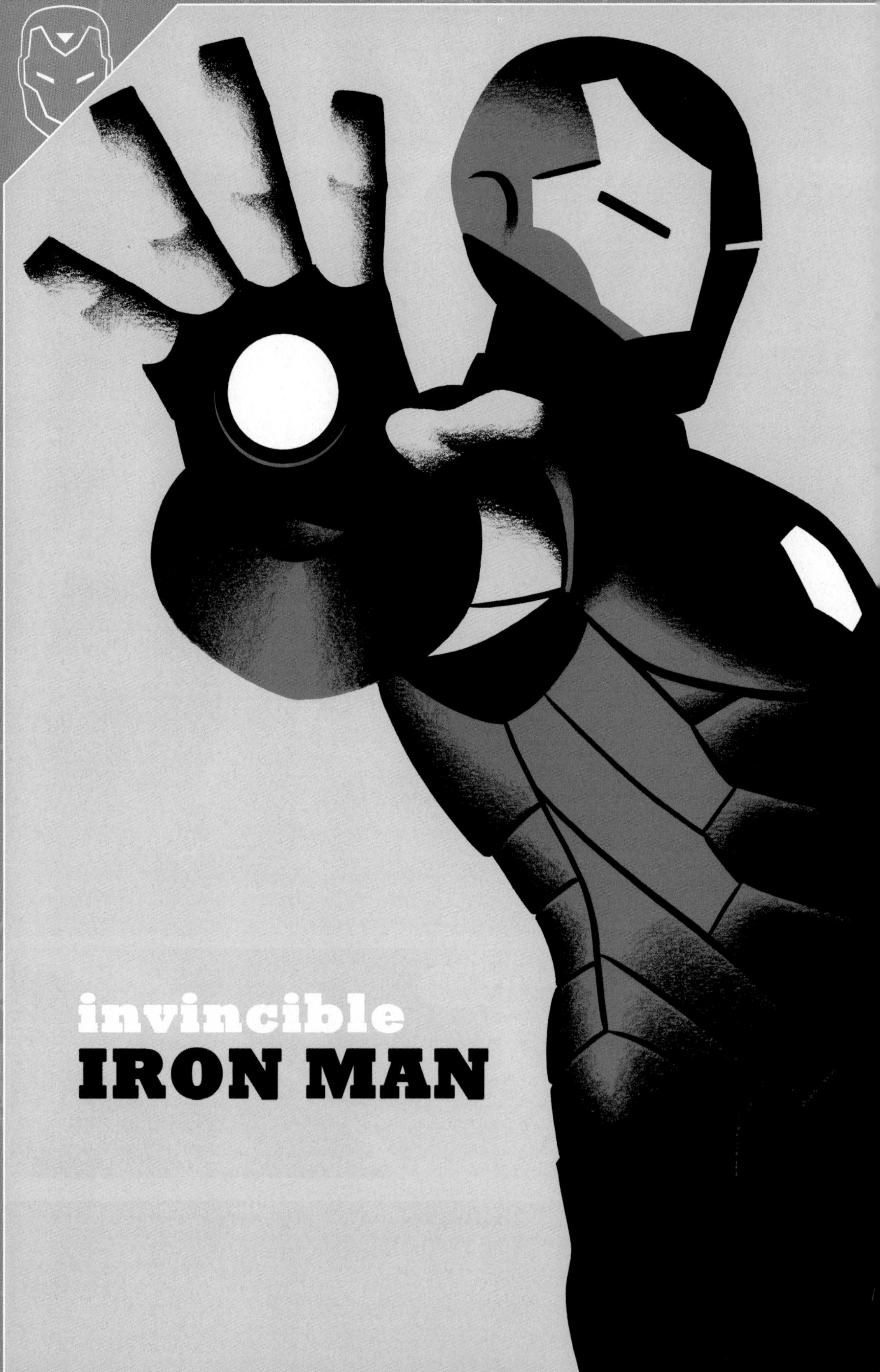
invincible
IRON MAN

#6 VARIANT BY MICHAEL CHO

#7

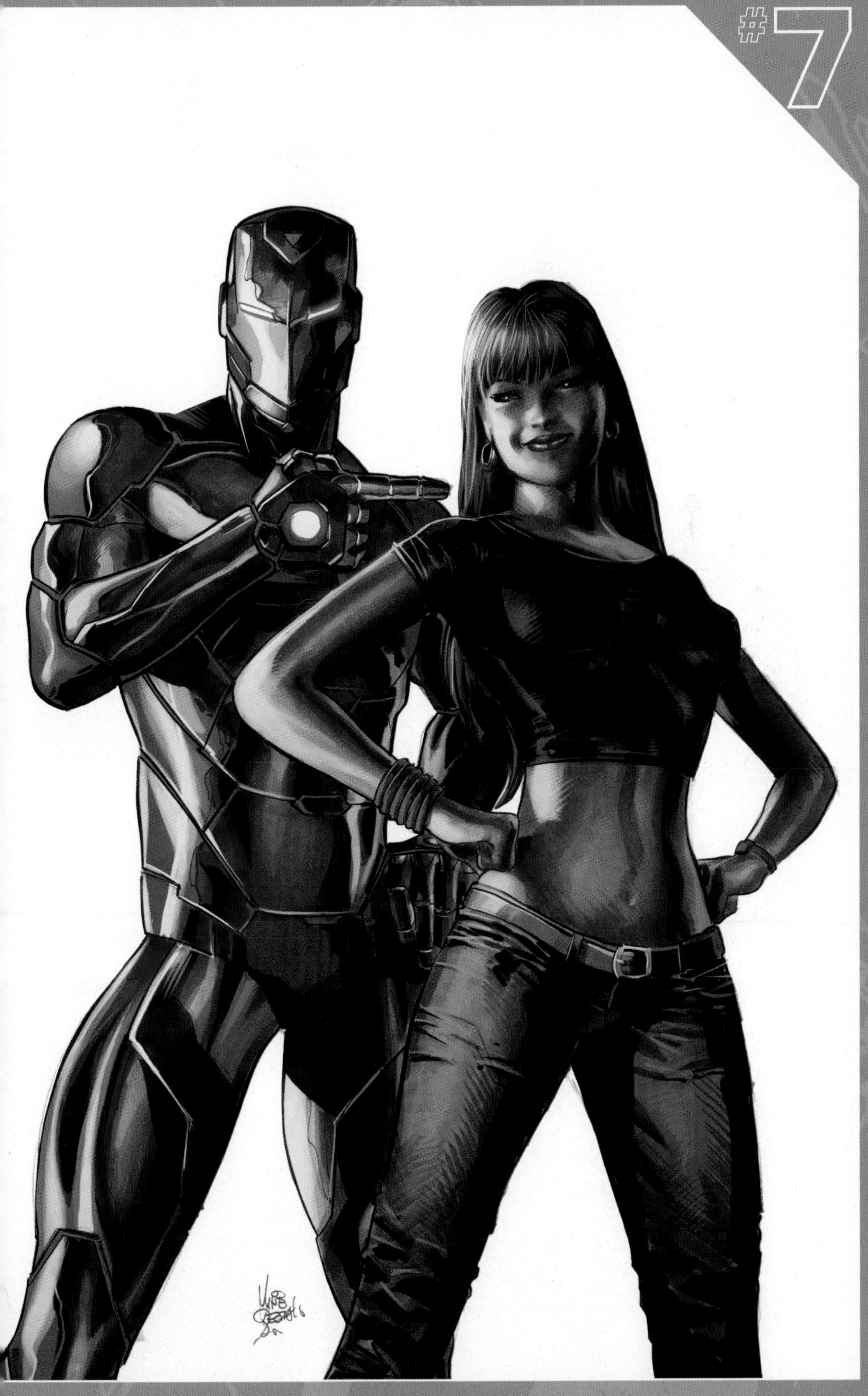

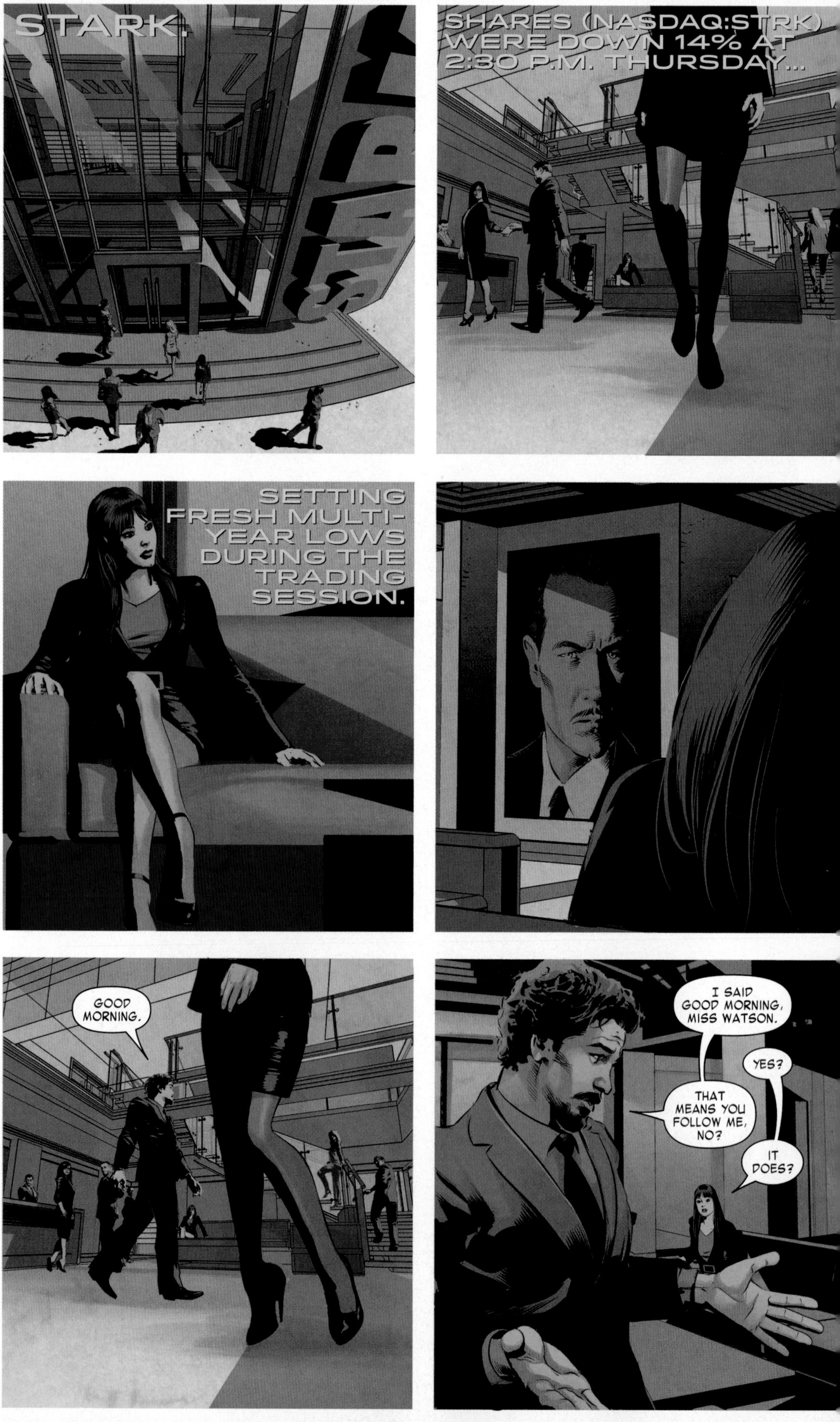
STARK.
SHARES (NASDAQ:STRK) WERE DOWN 14% AT 2:30 P.M. THURSDAY...
SETTING FRESH MULTI-YEAR LOWS DURING THE TRADING SESSION.
GOOD MORNING.
I SAID GOOD MORNING, MISS WATSON.
YES?
THAT MEANS YOU FOLLOW ME, NO?
IT DOES?

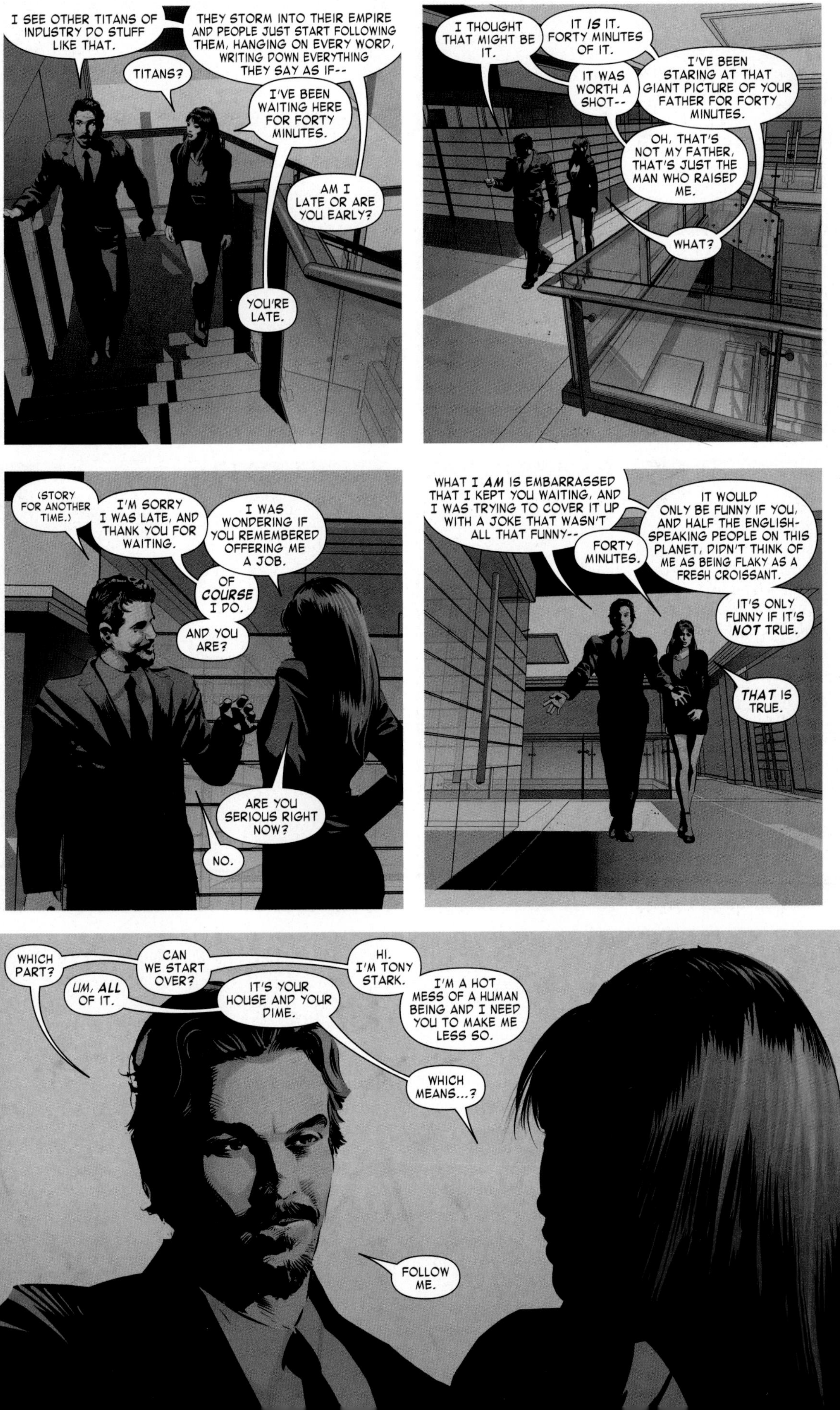
I SEE OTHER TITANS OF INDUSTRY DO STUFF LIKE THAT.
THEY STORM INTO THEIR EMPIRE AND PEOPLE JUST START FOLLOWING THEM, HANGING ON EVERY WORD, WRITING DOWN EVERYTHING THEY SAY AS IF--
TITANS?
I'VE BEEN WAITING HERE FOR FORTY MINUTES.
AM I LATE OR ARE YOU EARLY?
YOU'RE LATE.
I THOUGHT THAT MIGHT BE IT.
IT *IS* IT. FORTY MINUTES OF IT.
IT WAS WORTH A SHOT--
I'VE BEEN STARING AT THAT GIANT PICTURE OF YOUR FATHER FOR FORTY MINUTES.
OH, THAT'S NOT MY FATHER, THAT'S JUST THE MAN WHO RAISED ME.
WHAT?
(STORY FOR ANOTHER TIME.)
I'M SORRY I WAS LATE, AND THANK YOU FOR WAITING.
I WAS WONDERING IF YOU REMEMBERED OFFERING ME A JOB.
OF *COURSE* I DO.
AND YOU ARE?
ARE YOU SERIOUS RIGHT NOW?
NO.
WHAT I *AM* IS EMBARRASSED THAT I KEPT YOU WAITING, AND I WAS TRYING TO COVER IT UP WITH A JOKE THAT WASN'T ALL THAT FUNNY--
FORTY MINUTES.
IT WOULD ONLY BE FUNNY IF YOU, AND HALF THE ENGLISH-SPEAKING PEOPLE ON THIS PLANET, DIDN'T THINK OF ME AS BEING FLAKY AS A FRESH CROISSANT.
IT'S ONLY FUNNY IF IT'S *NOT* TRUE.
THAT IS TRUE.
WHICH PART?
UM, *ALL* OF IT.
CAN WE START OVER?
IT'S YOUR HOUSE AND YOUR DIME.
HI. I'M TONY STARK.
I'M A HOT MESS OF A HUMAN BEING AND I NEED YOU TO MAKE ME LESS SO.
WHICH MEANS...?
FOLLOW ME.

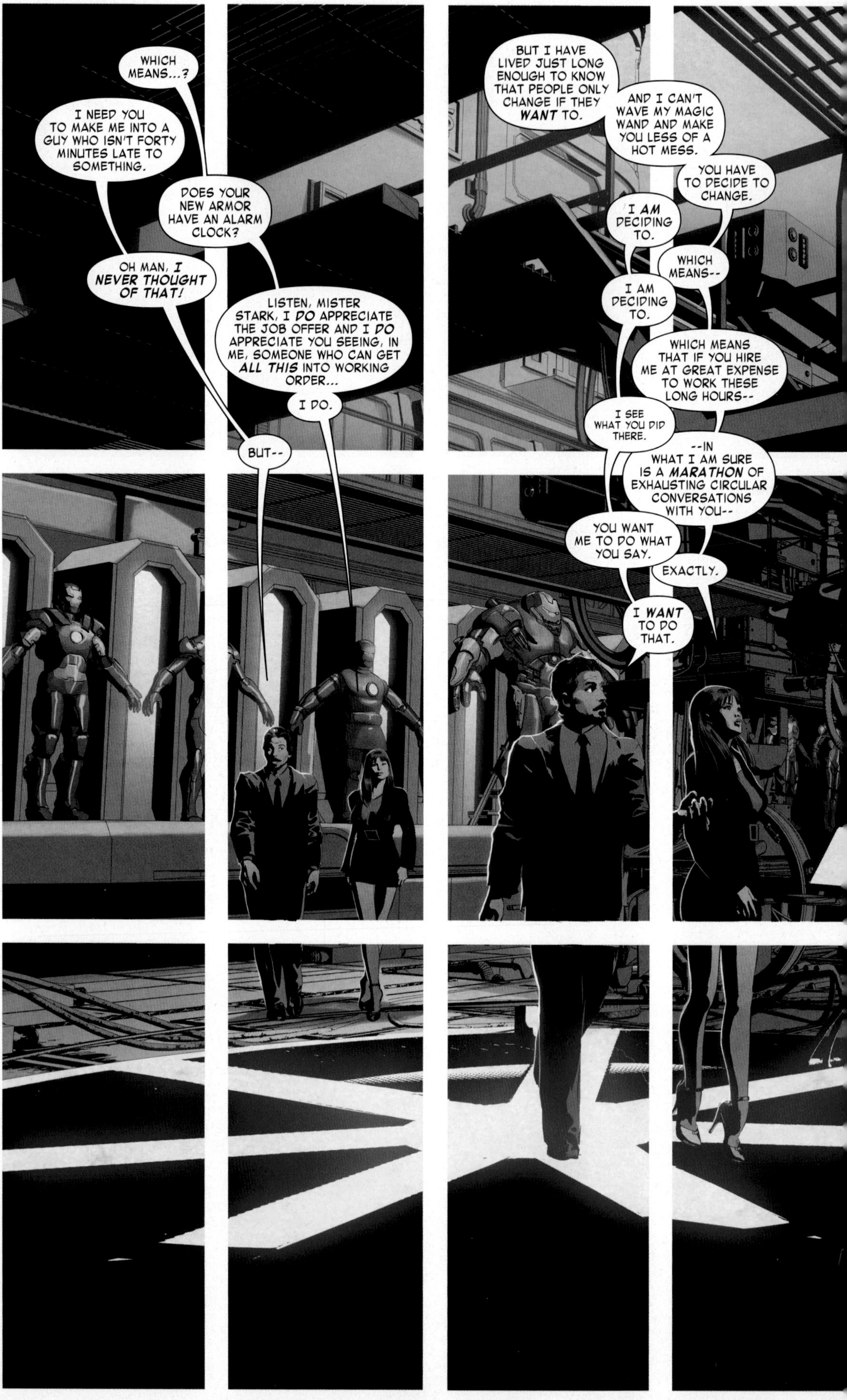

WHICH MEANS...?
I NEED YOU TO MAKE ME INTO A GUY WHO ISN'T FORTY MINUTES LATE TO SOMETHING.
DOES YOUR NEW ARMOR HAVE AN ALARM CLOCK?
OH MAN, I NEVER THOUGHT OF THAT!
LISTEN, MISTER STARK, I DO APPRECIATE THE JOB OFFER AND I DO APPRECIATE YOU SEEING, IN ME, SOMEONE WHO CAN GET ALL THIS INTO WORKING ORDER...
I DO.
BUT--
BUT I HAVE LIVED JUST LONG ENOUGH TO KNOW THAT PEOPLE ONLY CHANGE IF THEY WANT TO.
AND I CAN'T WAVE MY MAGIC WAND AND MAKE YOU LESS OF A HOT MESS.
YOU HAVE TO DECIDE TO CHANGE.
I AM DECIDING TO.
WHICH MEANS--
I AM DECIDING TO.
WHICH MEANS THAT IF YOU HIRE ME AT GREAT EXPENSE TO WORK THESE LONG HOURS--
I SEE WHAT YOU DID THERE.
--IN WHAT I AM SURE IS A MARATHON OF EXHAUSTING CIRCULAR CONVERSATIONS WITH YOU--
YOU WANT ME TO DO WHAT YOU SAY.
EXACTLY.
I WANT TO DO THAT.

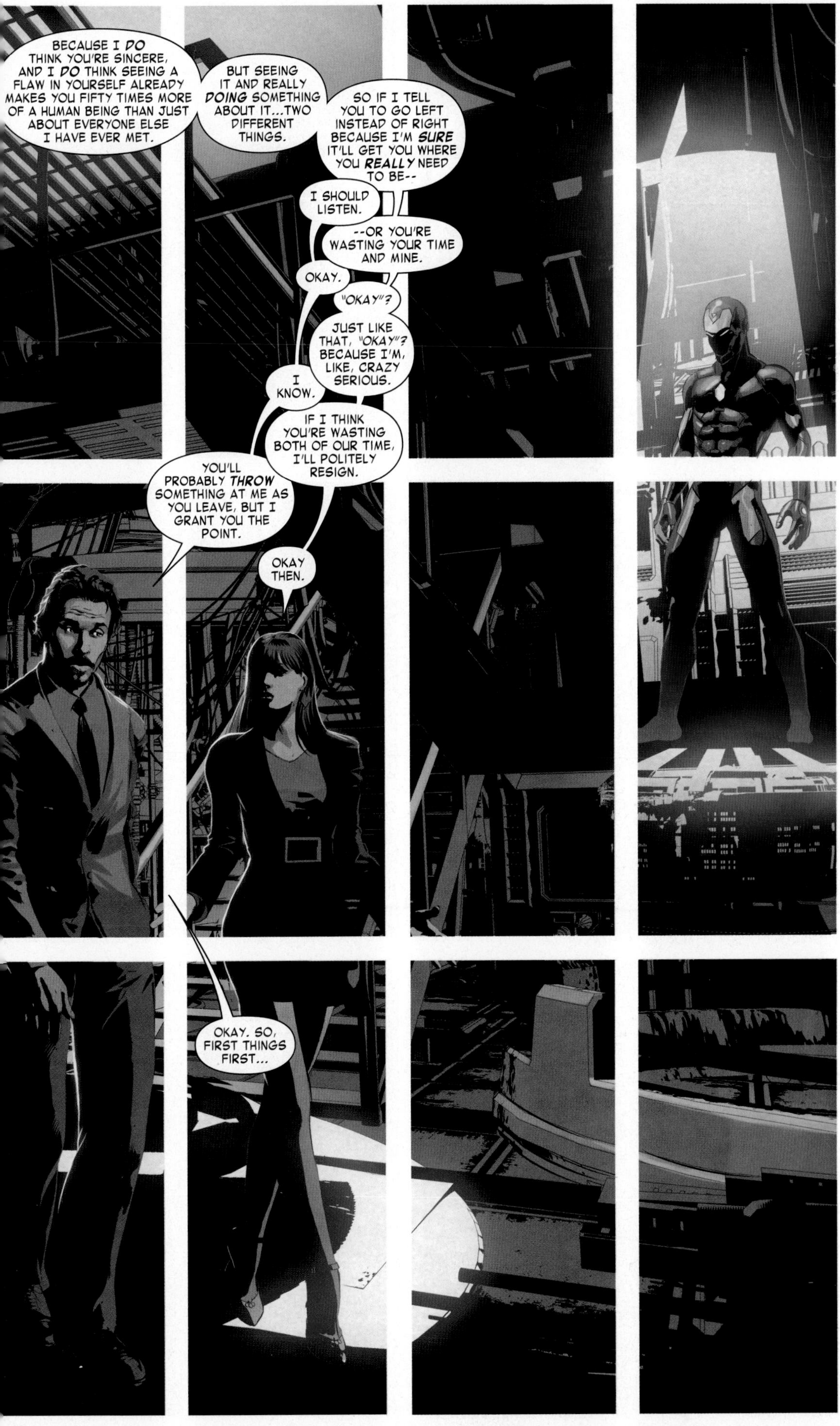
BECAUSE I *DO* THINK YOU'RE SINCERE, AND I *DO* THINK SEEING A FLAW IN YOURSELF ALREADY MAKES YOU FIFTY TIMES MORE OF A HUMAN BEING THAN JUST ABOUT EVERYONE ELSE I HAVE EVER MET.
BUT SEEING IT AND REALLY *DOING* SOMETHING ABOUT IT...TWO DIFFERENT THINGS.
SO IF I TELL YOU TO GO LEFT INSTEAD OF RIGHT BECAUSE I'M *SURE* IT'LL GET YOU WHERE YOU *REALLY* NEED TO BE--
I SHOULD LISTEN.
--OR YOU'RE WASTING YOUR TIME AND MINE.
OKAY.
"OKAY"?
JUST LIKE THAT, "OKAY"? BECAUSE I'M, LIKE, CRAZY SERIOUS.
I KNOW.
IF I THINK YOU'RE WASTING BOTH OF OUR TIME, I'LL POLITELY RESIGN.
YOU'LL PROBABLY *THROW* SOMETHING AT ME AS YOU LEAVE, BUT I GRANT YOU THE POINT.
OKAY THEN.
OKAY. SO, FIRST THINGS FIRST...

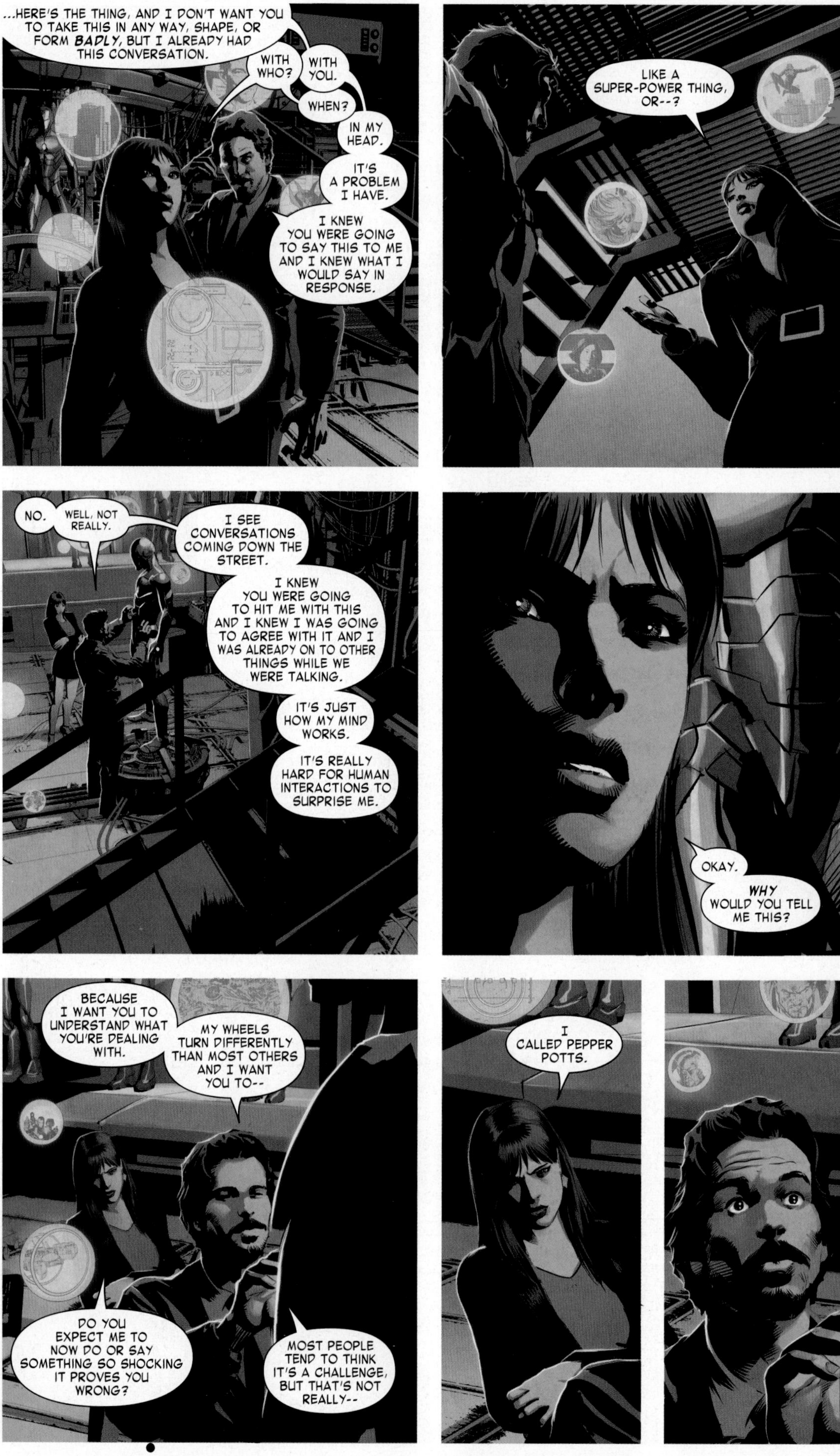
...HERE'S THE THING, AND I DON'T WANT YOU TO TAKE THIS IN ANY WAY, SHAPE, OR FORM BADLY, BUT I ALREADY HAD THIS CONVERSATION.
WITH WHO?
WITH YOU.
WHEN?
IN MY HEAD.
IT'S A PROBLEM I HAVE.
I KNEW YOU WERE GOING TO SAY THIS TO ME AND I KNEW WHAT I WOULD SAY IN RESPONSE.
LIKE A SUPER-POWER THING, OR--?
NO.
WELL, NOT REALLY.
I SEE CONVERSATIONS COMING DOWN THE STREET.
I KNEW YOU WERE GOING TO HIT ME WITH THIS AND I KNEW I WAS GOING TO AGREE WITH IT AND I WAS ALREADY ON TO OTHER THINGS WHILE WE WERE TALKING.
IT'S JUST HOW MY MIND WORKS.
IT'S REALLY HARD FOR HUMAN INTERACTIONS TO SURPRISE ME.
OKAY.
WHY WOULD YOU TELL ME THIS?
BECAUSE I WANT YOU TO UNDERSTAND WHAT YOU'RE DEALING WITH.
MY WHEELS TURN DIFFERENTLY THAN MOST OTHERS AND I WANT YOU TO--
DO YOU EXPECT ME TO NOW DO OR SAY SOMETHING SO SHOCKING IT PROVES YOU WRONG?
MOST PEOPLE TEND TO THINK IT'S A CHALLENGE, BUT THAT'S NOT REALLY--
I CALLED PEPPER POTTS.

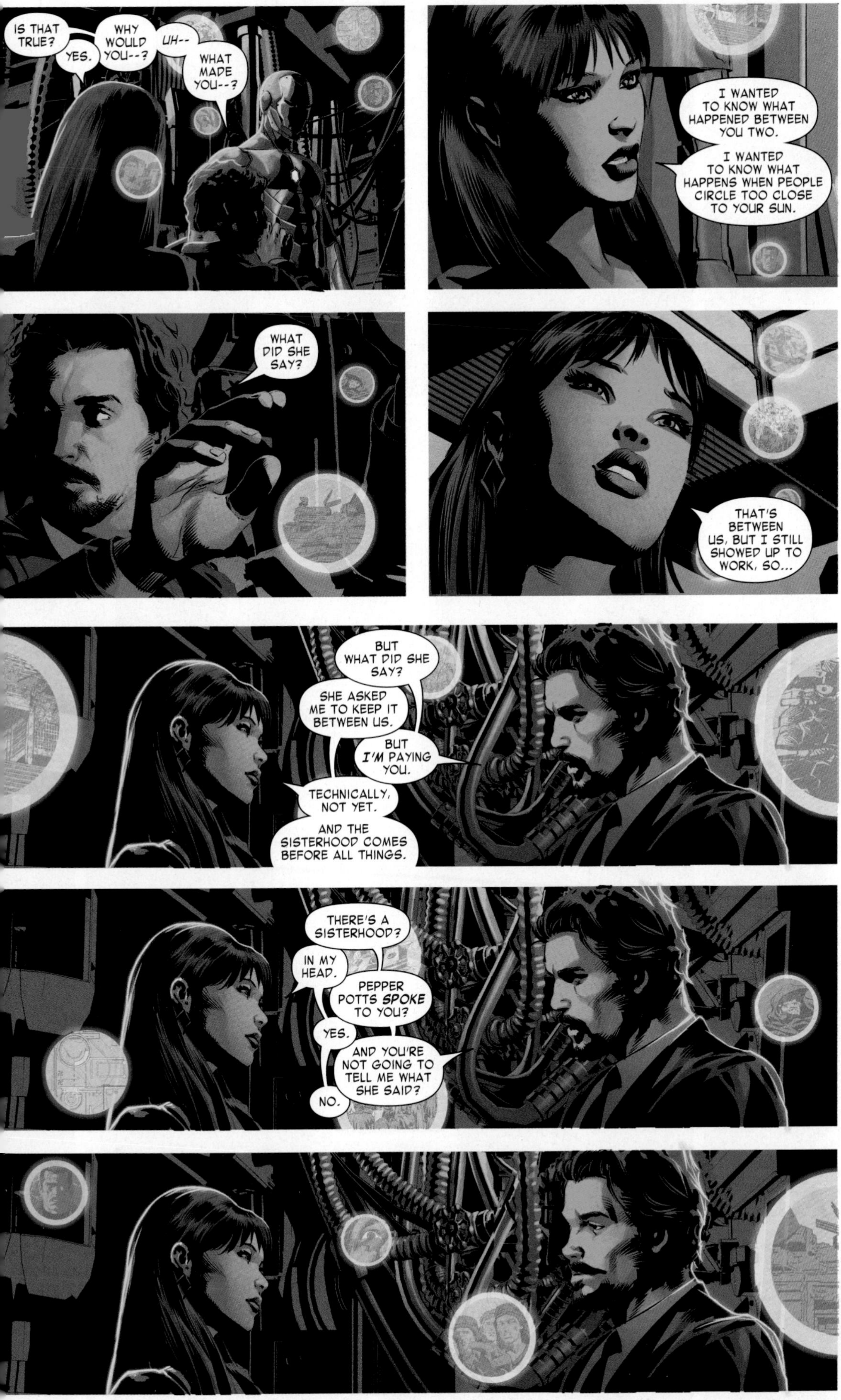
IS THAT TRUE?
YES.
WHY WOULD YOU--?
UH--
WHAT MADE YOU--?
I WANTED TO KNOW WHAT HAPPENED BETWEEN YOU TWO.
I WANTED TO KNOW WHAT HAPPENS WHEN PEOPLE CIRCLE TOO CLOSE TO YOUR SUN.
WHAT DID SHE SAY?
THAT'S BETWEEN US, BUT I STILL SHOWED UP TO WORK, SO...
BUT WHAT DID SHE SAY?
SHE ASKED ME TO KEEP IT BETWEEN US.
BUT I'M PAYING YOU.
TECHNICALLY, NOT YET.
AND THE SISTERHOOD COMES BEFORE ALL THINGS.
THERE'S A SISTERHOOD?
IN MY HEAD.
PEPPER POTTS SPOKE TO YOU?
YES.
AND YOU'RE NOT GOING TO TELL ME WHAT SHE SAID?
NO.

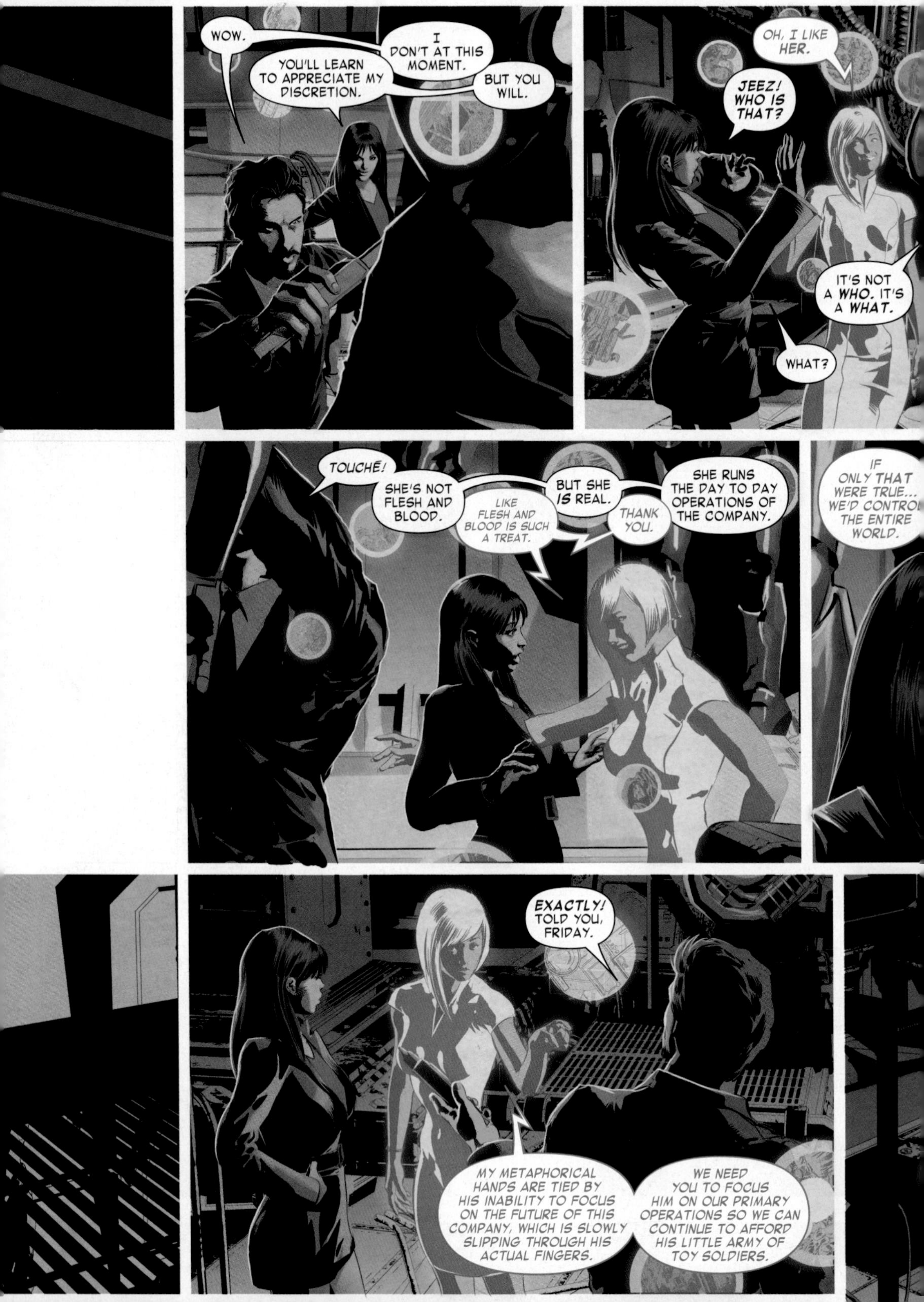
WOW.
I DON'T AT THIS MOMENT.
YOU'LL LEARN TO APPRECIATE MY DISCRETION.
BUT YOU WILL.
OH, I LIKE HER.
JEEZ! WHO IS THAT?
IT'S NOT A WHO. IT'S A WHAT.
WHAT?
TOUCHÉ!
SHE'S NOT FLESH AND BLOOD.
LIKE FLESH AND BLOOD IS SUCH A TREAT.
BUT SHE IS REAL.
THANK YOU.
SHE RUNS THE DAY TO DAY OPERATIONS OF THE COMPANY.
IF ONLY THAT WERE TRUE... WE'D CONTROL THE ENTIRE WORLD.
EXACTLY! TOLD YOU, FRIDAY.
MY METAPHORICAL HANDS ARE TIED BY HIS INABILITY TO FOCUS ON THE FUTURE OF THIS COMPANY, WHICH IS SLOWLY SLIPPING THROUGH HIS ACTUAL FINGERS.
WE NEED YOU TO FOCUS HIM ON OUR PRIMARY OPERATIONS SO WE CAN CONTINUE TO AFFORD HIS LITTLE ARMY OF TOY SOLDIERS.

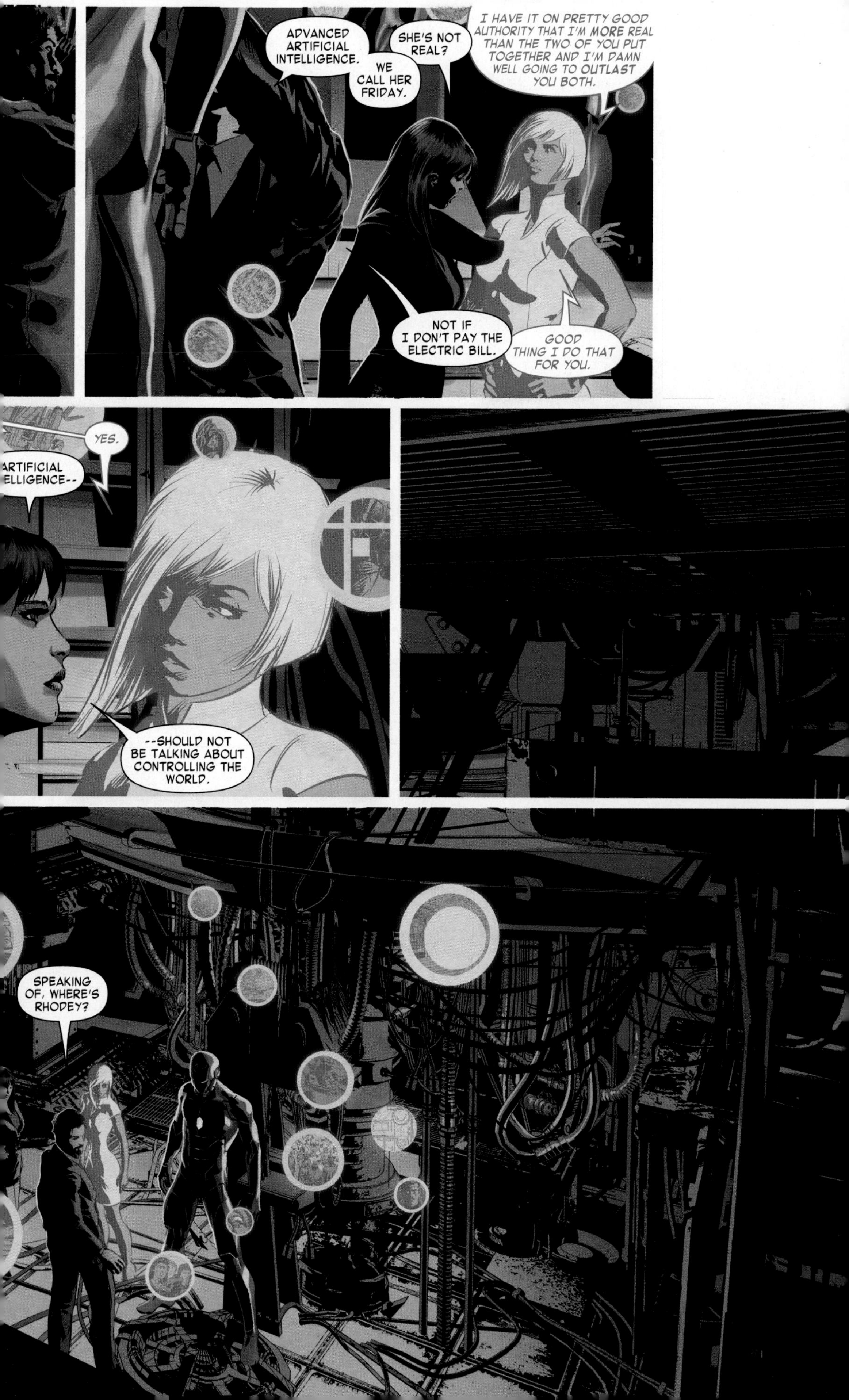
ADVANCED ARTIFICIAL INTELLIGENCE.
WE CALL HER FRIDAY.
SHE'S NOT REAL?
I HAVE IT ON PRETTY GOOD AUTHORITY THAT I'M MORE REAL THAN THE TWO OF YOU PUT TOGETHER AND I'M DAMN WELL GOING TO OUTLAST YOU BOTH.
NOT IF I DON'T PAY THE ELECTRIC BILL.
GOOD THING I DO THAT FOR YOU.
ARTIFICIAL ELLIGENCE--
YES.
--SHOULD NOT BE TALKING ABOUT CONTROLLING THE WORLD.
SPEAKING OF, WHERE'S RHODEY?

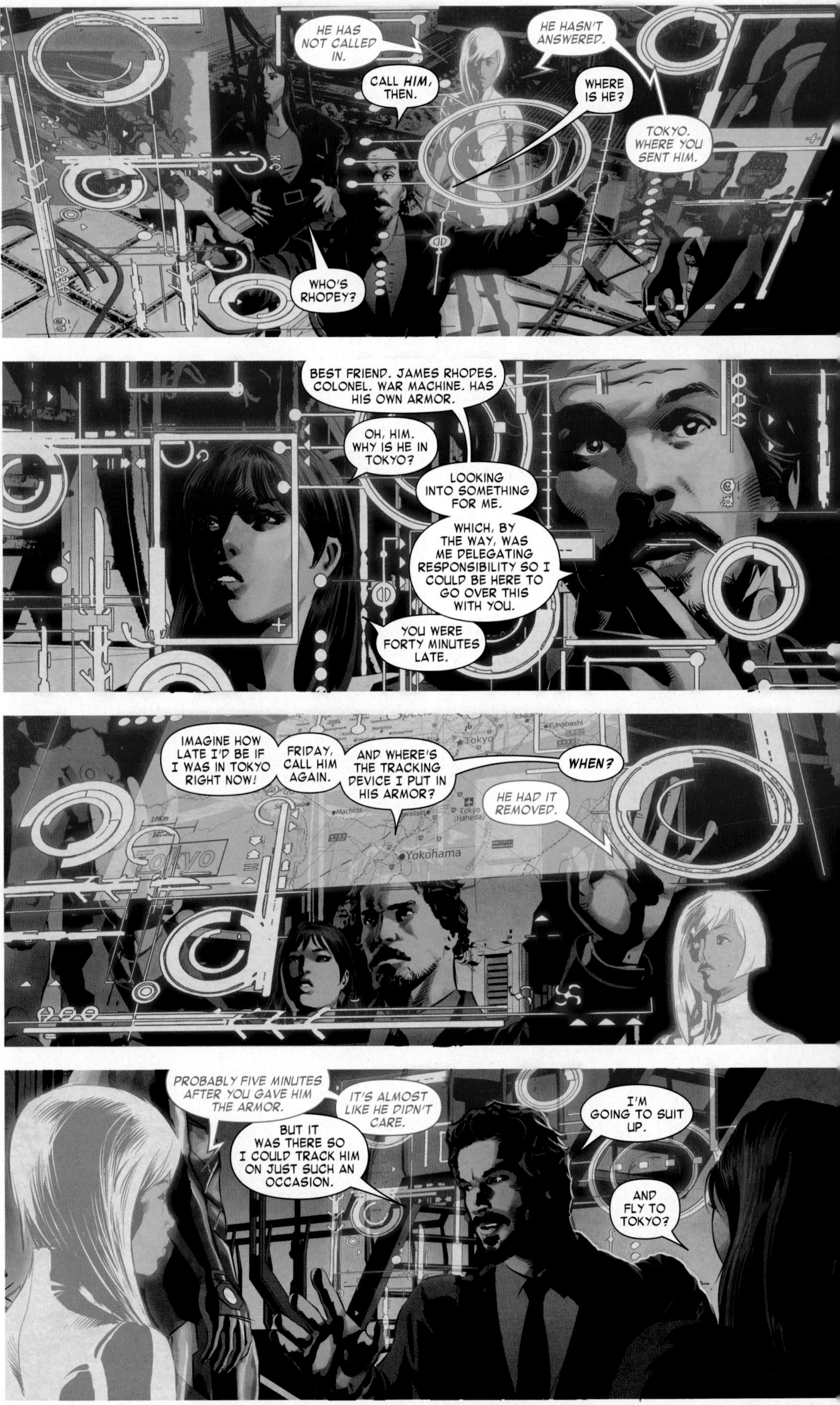

HE HAS NOT CALLED IN.
HE HASN'T ANSWERED.
CALL *HIM*, THEN.
WHERE IS HE?
TOKYO. WHERE YOU SENT HIM.
WHO'S RHODEY?
BEST FRIEND. JAMES RHODES. COLONEL. WAR MACHINE. HAS HIS OWN ARMOR.
OH, HIM. WHY IS HE IN TOKYO?
LOOKING INTO SOMETHING FOR ME.
WHICH, BY THE WAY, WAS ME DELEGATING RESPONSIBILITY SO I COULD BE HERE TO GO OVER THIS WITH YOU.
YOU WERE FORTY MINUTES LATE.
IMAGINE HOW LATE I'D BE IF I WAS IN TOKYO RIGHT NOW!
FRIDAY, CALL HIM AGAIN.
AND WHERE'S THE TRACKING DEVICE I PUT IN HIS ARMOR?
WHEN?
HE HAD IT REMOVED.
Tokyo
Funabashi
Machida
Tokyo (Haneda)
Yokohama
10Km
PROBABLY FIVE MINUTES AFTER YOU GAVE HIM THE ARMOR.
IT'S ALMOST LIKE HE DIDN'T CARE.
BUT IT WAS THERE SO I COULD TRACK HIM ON JUST SUCH AN OCCASION.
I'M GOING TO SUIT UP.
AND FLY TO TOKYO?

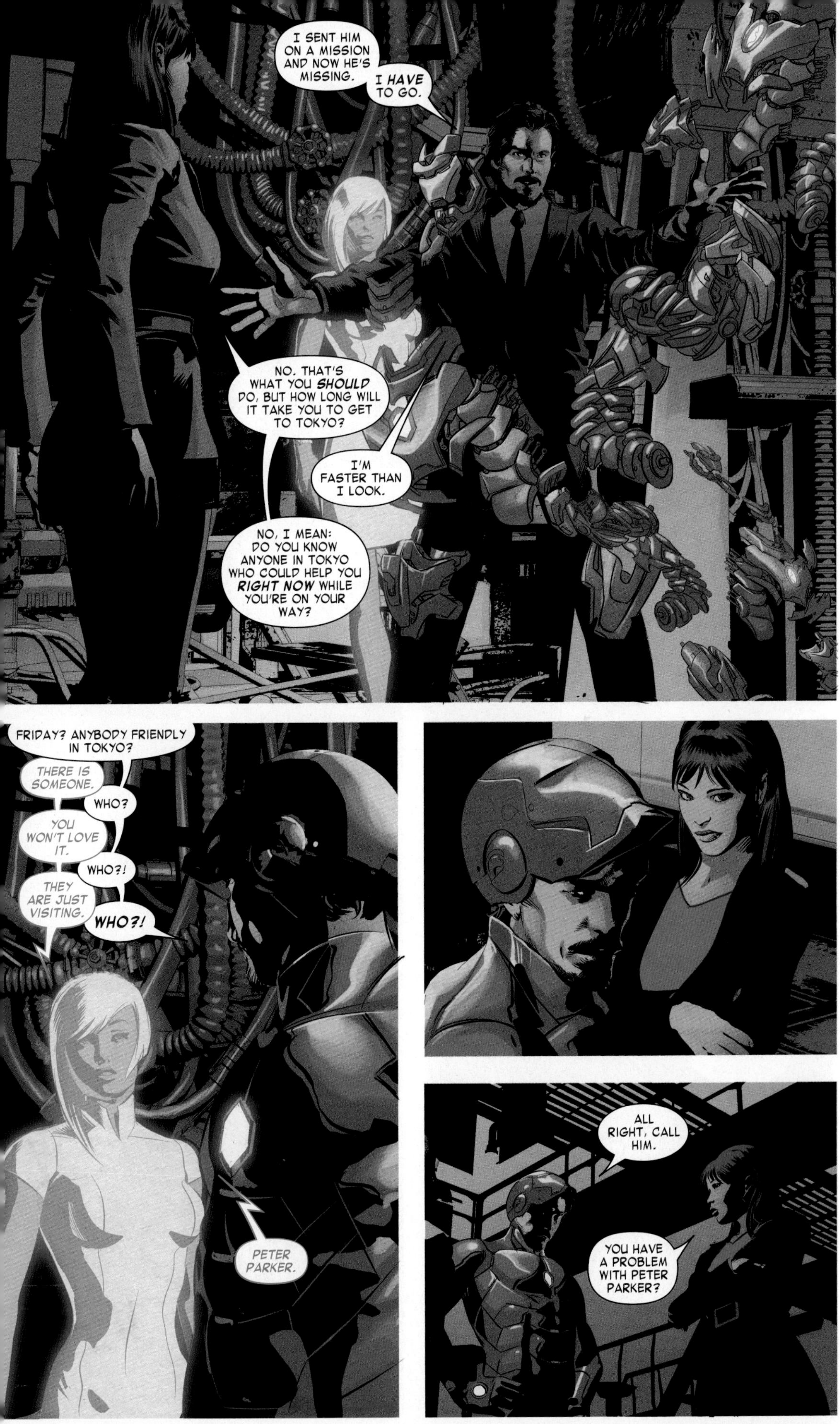
I SENT HIM ON A MISSION AND NOW HE'S MISSING.
I *HAVE* TO GO.
NO. THAT'S WHAT YOU *SHOULD* DO, BUT HOW LONG WILL IT TAKE YOU TO GET TO TOKYO?
I'M FASTER THAN I LOOK.
NO, I MEAN: DO YOU KNOW ANYONE IN TOKYO WHO COULD HELP YOU *RIGHT NOW* WHILE YOU'RE ON YOUR WAY?
FRIDAY? ANYBODY FRIENDLY IN TOKYO?
THERE IS SOMEONE.
WHO?
YOU WON'T LOVE IT.
WHO?!
THEY ARE JUST VISITING.
WHO?!
PETER PARKER.
ALL RIGHT, CALL HIM.
YOU HAVE A PROBLEM WITH PETER PARKER?

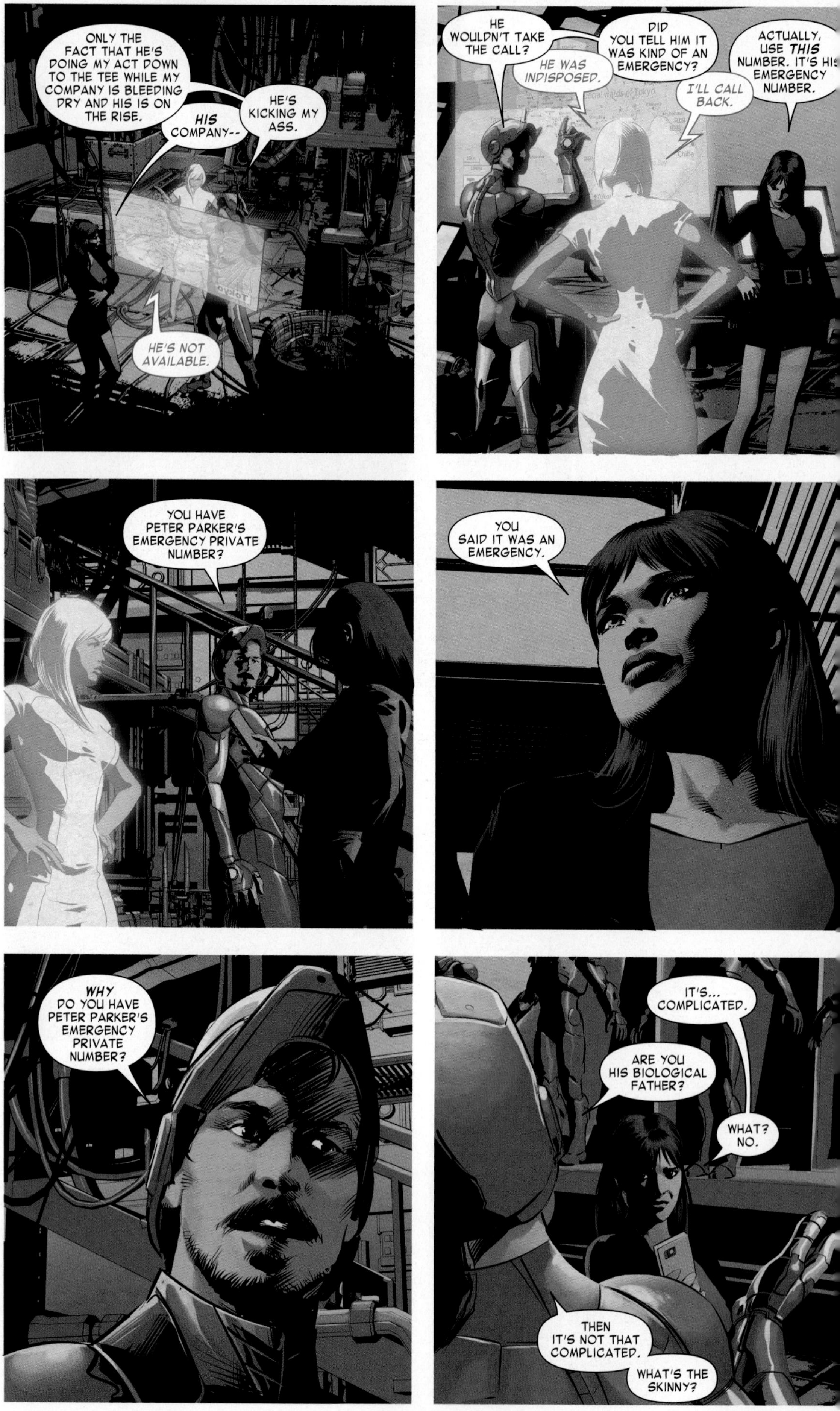

ONLY THE FACT THAT HE'S DOING MY ACT DOWN TO THE TEE WHILE MY COMPANY IS BLEEDING DRY AND HIS IS ON THE RISE.
HE'S KICKING MY ASS.
HIS COMPANY--
HE'S NOT AVAILABLE.
HE WOULDN'T TAKE THE CALL?
HE WAS INDISPOSED.
DID YOU TELL HIM IT WAS KIND OF AN EMERGENCY?
I'LL CALL BACK.
ACTUALLY, USE THIS NUMBER. IT'S HIS EMERGENCY NUMBER.
YOU HAVE PETER PARKER'S EMERGENCY PRIVATE NUMBER?
YOU SAID IT WAS AN EMERGENCY.
WHY DO YOU HAVE PETER PARKER'S EMERGENCY PRIVATE NUMBER?
IT'S... COMPLICATED.
ARE YOU HIS BIOLOGICAL FATHER?
WHAT? NO.
THEN IT'S NOT THAT COMPLICATED.
WHAT'S THE SKINNY?

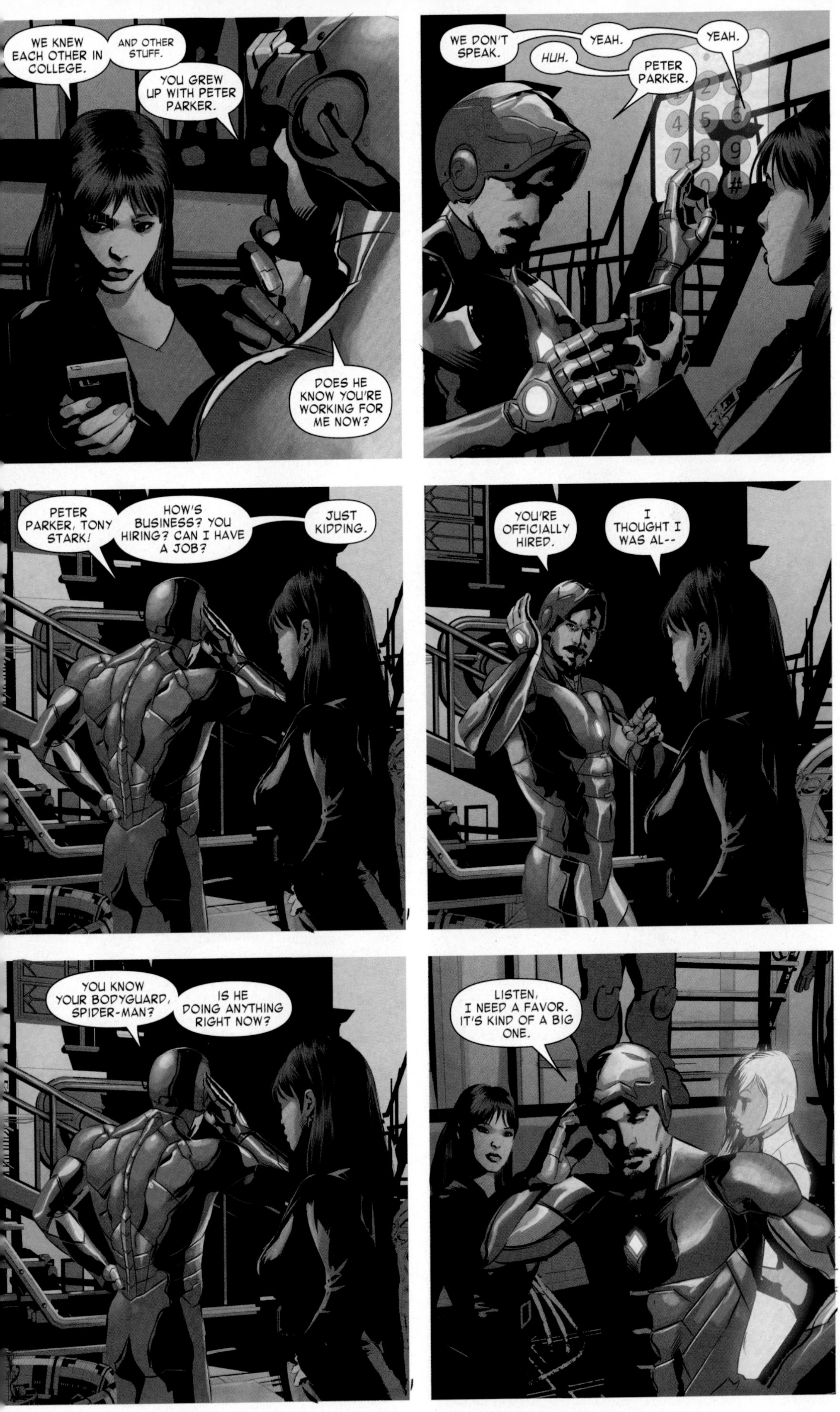
WE KNEW EACH OTHER IN COLLEGE.
AND OTHER STUFF.
YOU GREW UP WITH PETER PARKER.
DOES HE KNOW YOU'RE WORKING FOR ME NOW?
WE DON'T SPEAK.
YEAH.
HUH.
YEAH.
PETER PARKER.
PETER PARKER, TONY STARK!
HOW'S BUSINESS? YOU HIRING? CAN I HAVE A JOB?
JUST KIDDING.
YOU'RE OFFICIALLY HIRED.
I THOUGHT I WAS AL--
YOU KNOW YOUR BODYGUARD, SPIDER-MAN?
IS HE DOING ANYTHING RIGHT NOW?
LISTEN, I NEED A FAVOR. IT'S KIND OF A BIG ONE.

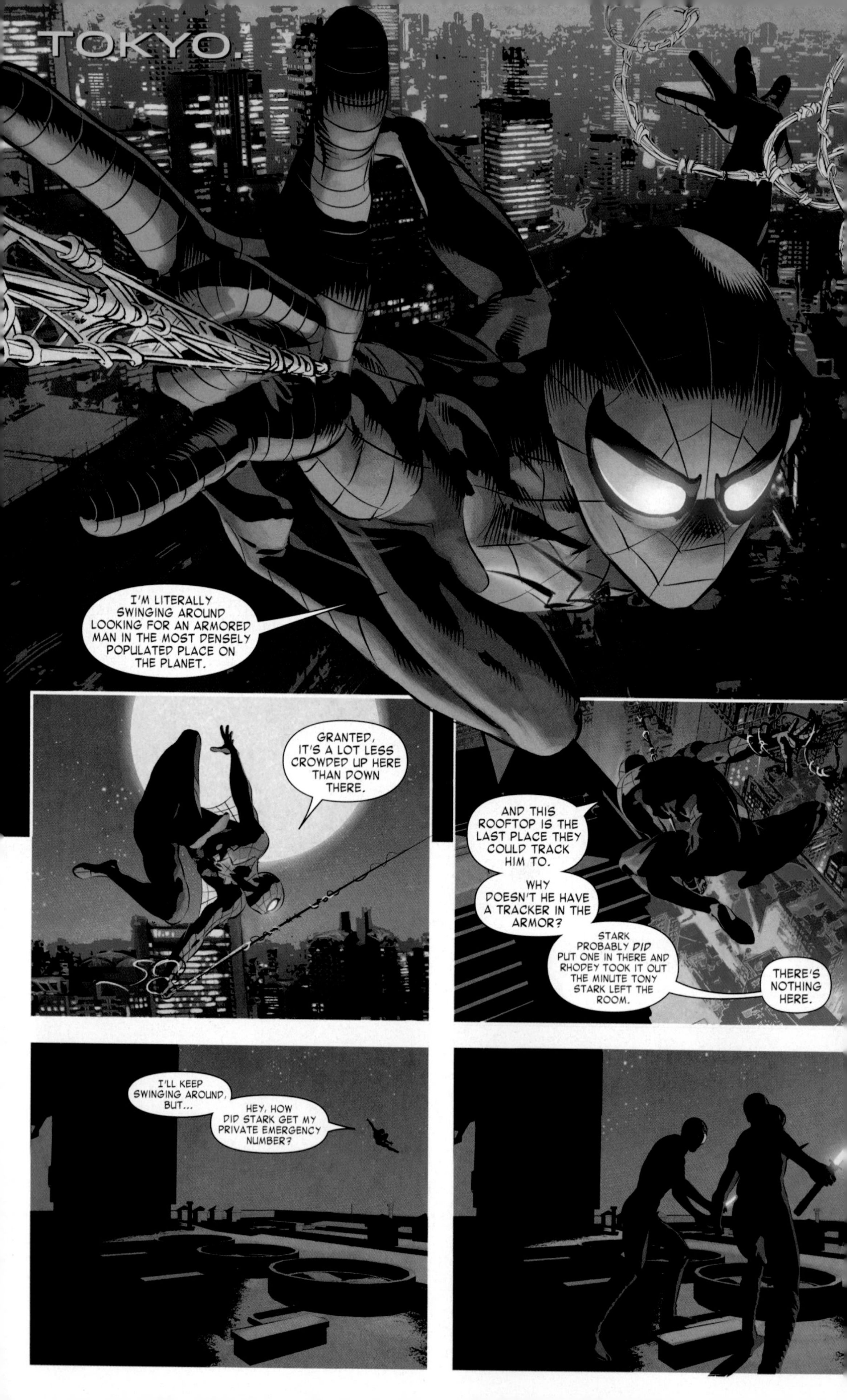
TOKYO.
I'M LITERALLY SWINGING AROUND LOOKING FOR AN ARMORED MAN IN THE MOST DENSELY POPULATED PLACE ON THE PLANET.
GRANTED, IT'S A LOT LESS CROWDED UP HERE THAN DOWN THERE.
AND THIS ROOFTOP IS THE LAST PLACE THEY COULD TRACK HIM TO.
WHY DOESN'T HE HAVE A TRACKER IN THE ARMOR?
STARK PROBABLY *DID* PUT ONE IN THERE AND RHODEY TOOK IT OUT THE MINUTE TONY STARK LEFT THE ROOM.
THERE'S NOTHING HERE.
I'LL KEEP SWINGING AROUND, BUT...
HEY, HOW DID STARK GET MY PRIVATE EMERGENCY NUMBER?

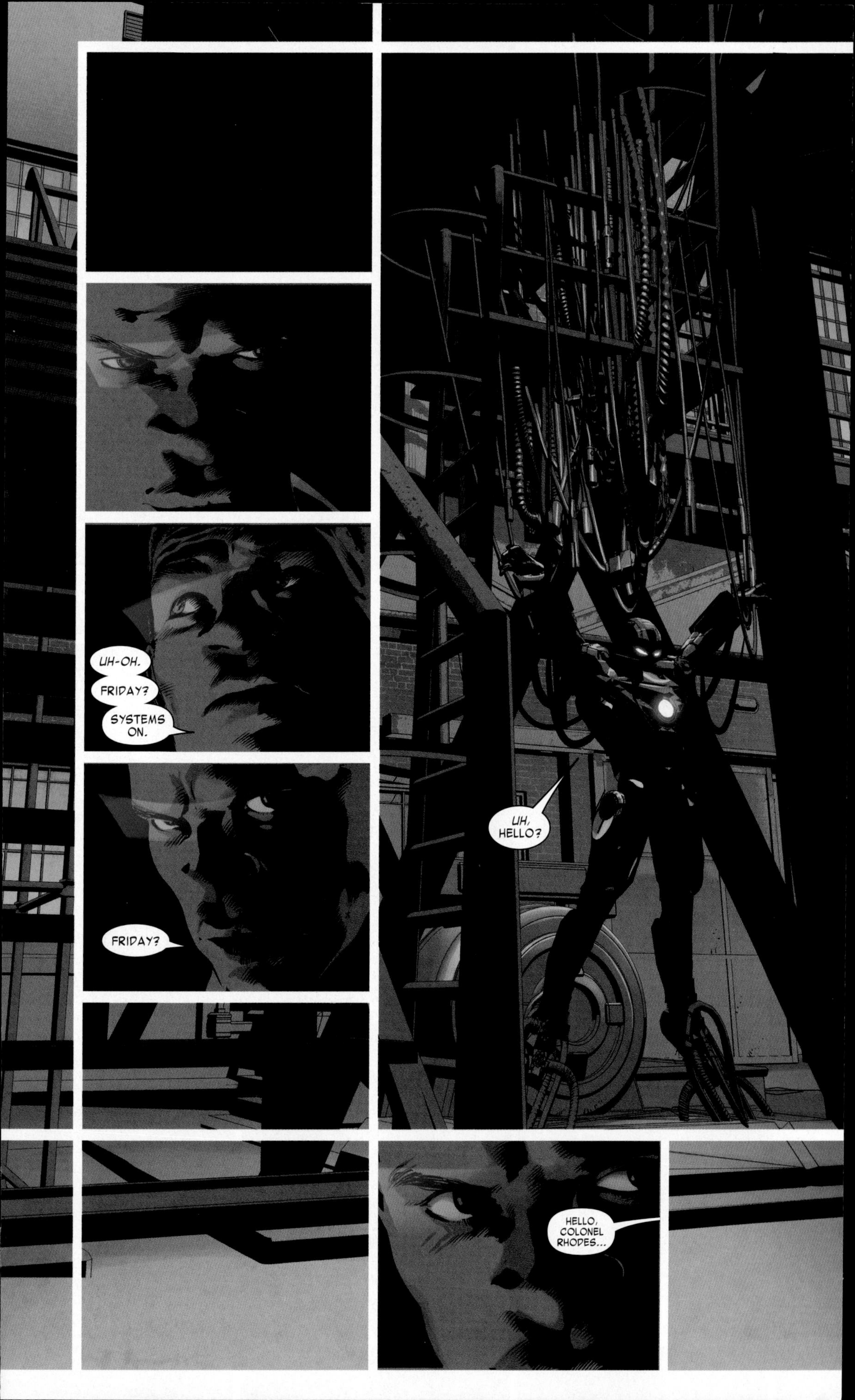
UH-OH.
FRIDAY?
SYSTEMS ON.
FRIDAY?
UH, HELLO?
HELLO, COLONEL RHODES...

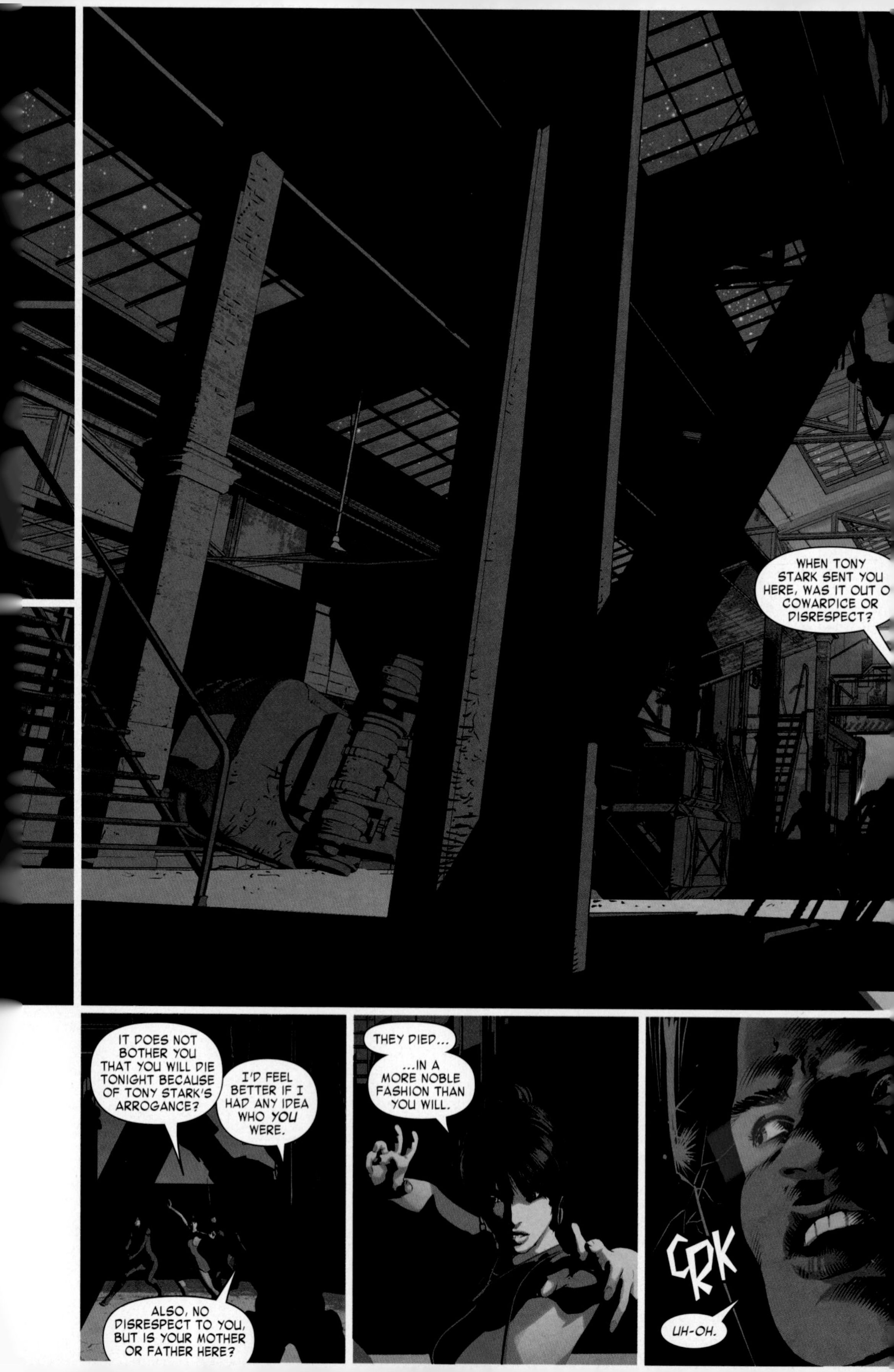
WHEN TONY STARK SENT YOU HERE, WAS IT OUT O COWARDICE OR DISRESPECT?
IT DOES NOT BOTHER YOU THAT YOU WILL DIE TONIGHT BECAUSE OF TONY STARK'S ARROGANCE?
I'D FEEL BETTER IF I HAD ANY IDEA WHO YOU WERE.
ALSO, NO DISRESPECT TO YOU, BUT IS YOUR MOTHER OR FATHER HERE?
THEY DIED...
...IN A MORE NOBLE FASHION THAN YOU WILL.
CRK
UH-OH.

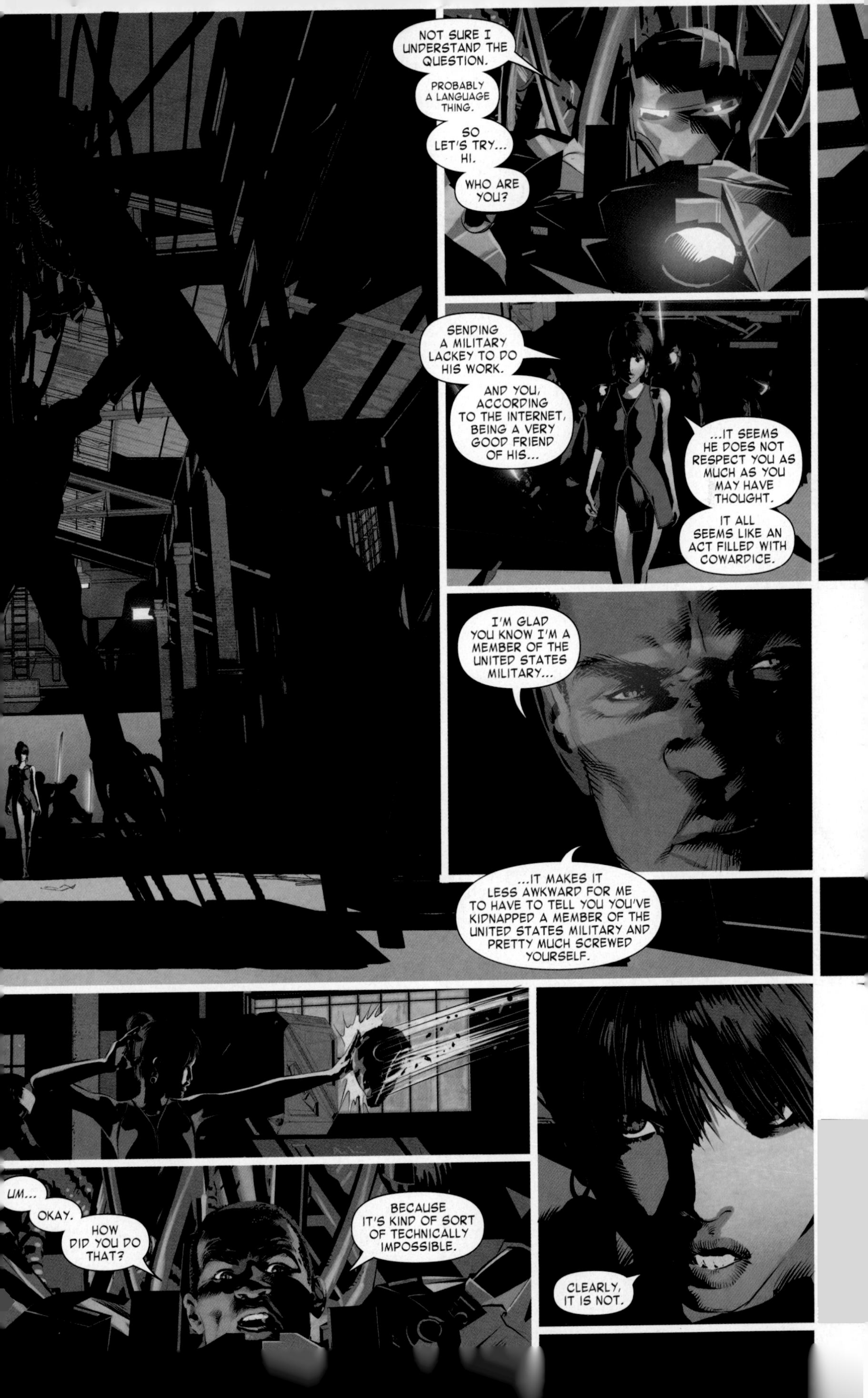
NOT SURE I UNDERSTAND THE QUESTION.
PROBABLY A LANGUAGE THING.
SO LET'S TRY... HI.
WHO ARE YOU?
SENDING A MILITARY LACKEY TO DO HIS WORK.
AND YOU, ACCORDING TO THE INTERNET, BEING A VERY GOOD FRIEND OF HIS...
...IT SEEMS HE DOES NOT RESPECT YOU AS MUCH AS YOU MAY HAVE THOUGHT.
IT ALL SEEMS LIKE AN ACT FILLED WITH COWARDICE.
I'M GLAD YOU KNOW I'M A MEMBER OF THE UNITED STATES MILITARY...
...IT MAKES IT LESS AWKWARD FOR ME TO HAVE TO TELL YOU YOU'VE KIDNAPPED A MEMBER OF THE UNITED STATES MILITARY AND PRETTY MUCH SCREWED YOURSELF.
UM...
OKAY.
HOW DID YOU DO THAT?
BECAUSE IT'S KIND OF SORT OF TECHNICALLY IMPOSSIBLE.
CLEARLY, IT IS NOT.

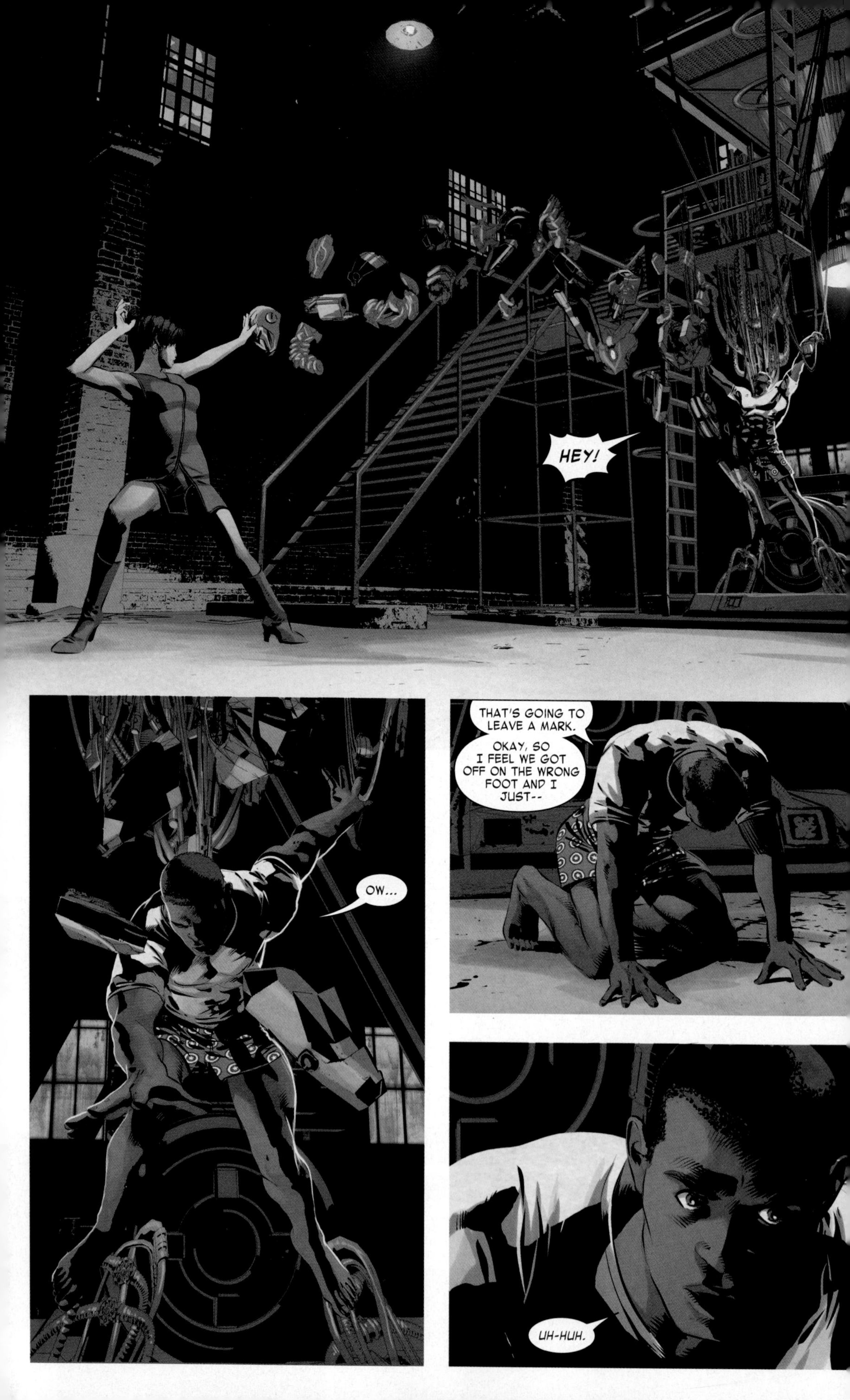
HEY!
OW...
THAT'S GOING TO LEAVE A MARK.
OKAY, SO I FEEL WE GOT OFF ON THE WRONG FOOT AND I JUST--
UH-HUH.

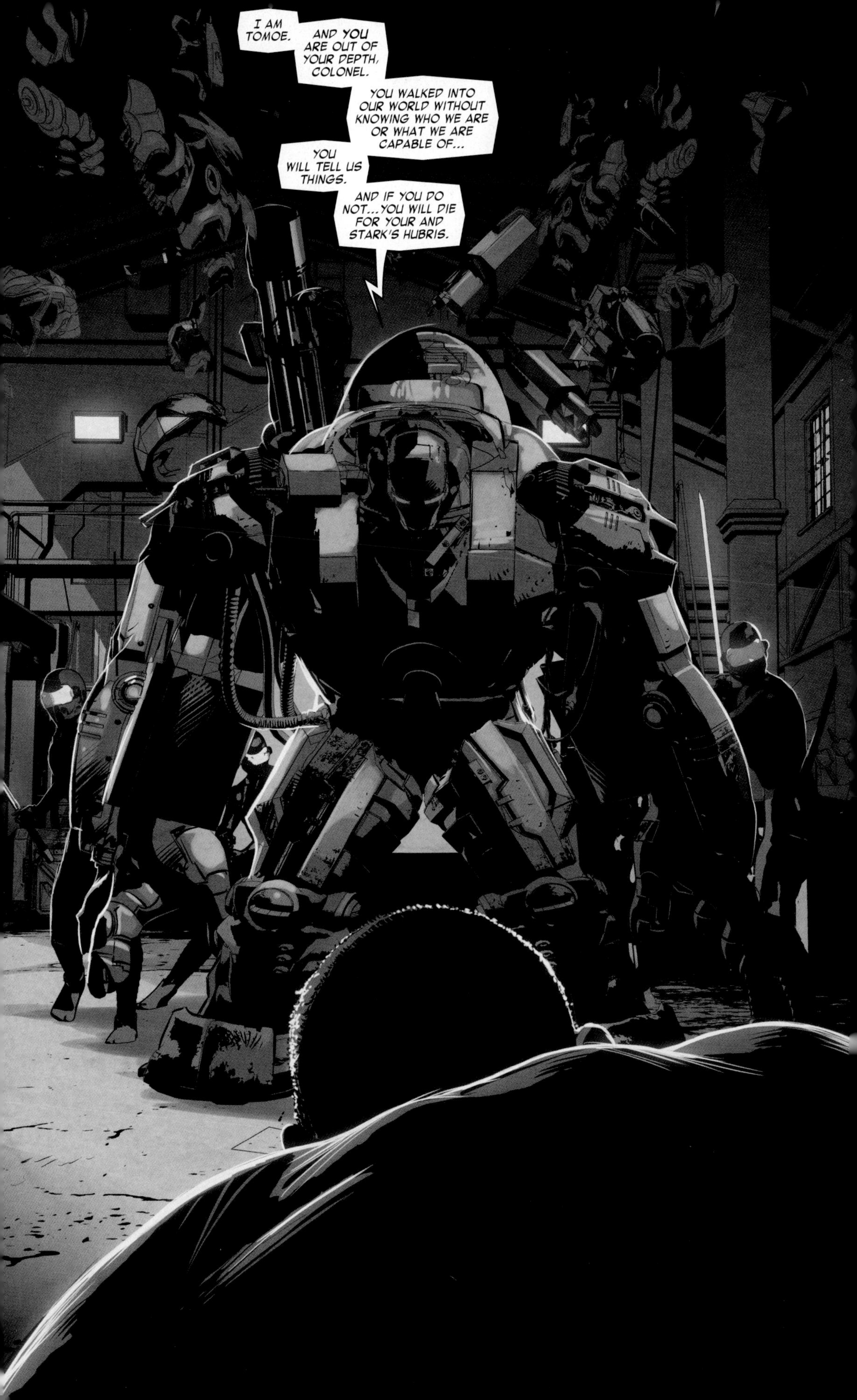
I AM TOMOE.
AND YOU ARE OUT OF YOUR DEPTH, COLONEL.
YOU WALKED INTO OUR WORLD WITHOUT KNOWING WHO WE ARE OR WHAT WE ARE CAPABLE OF...
YOU WILL TELL US THINGS.
AND IF YOU DO NOT...YOU WILL DIE FOR YOUR AND STARK'S HUBRIS.

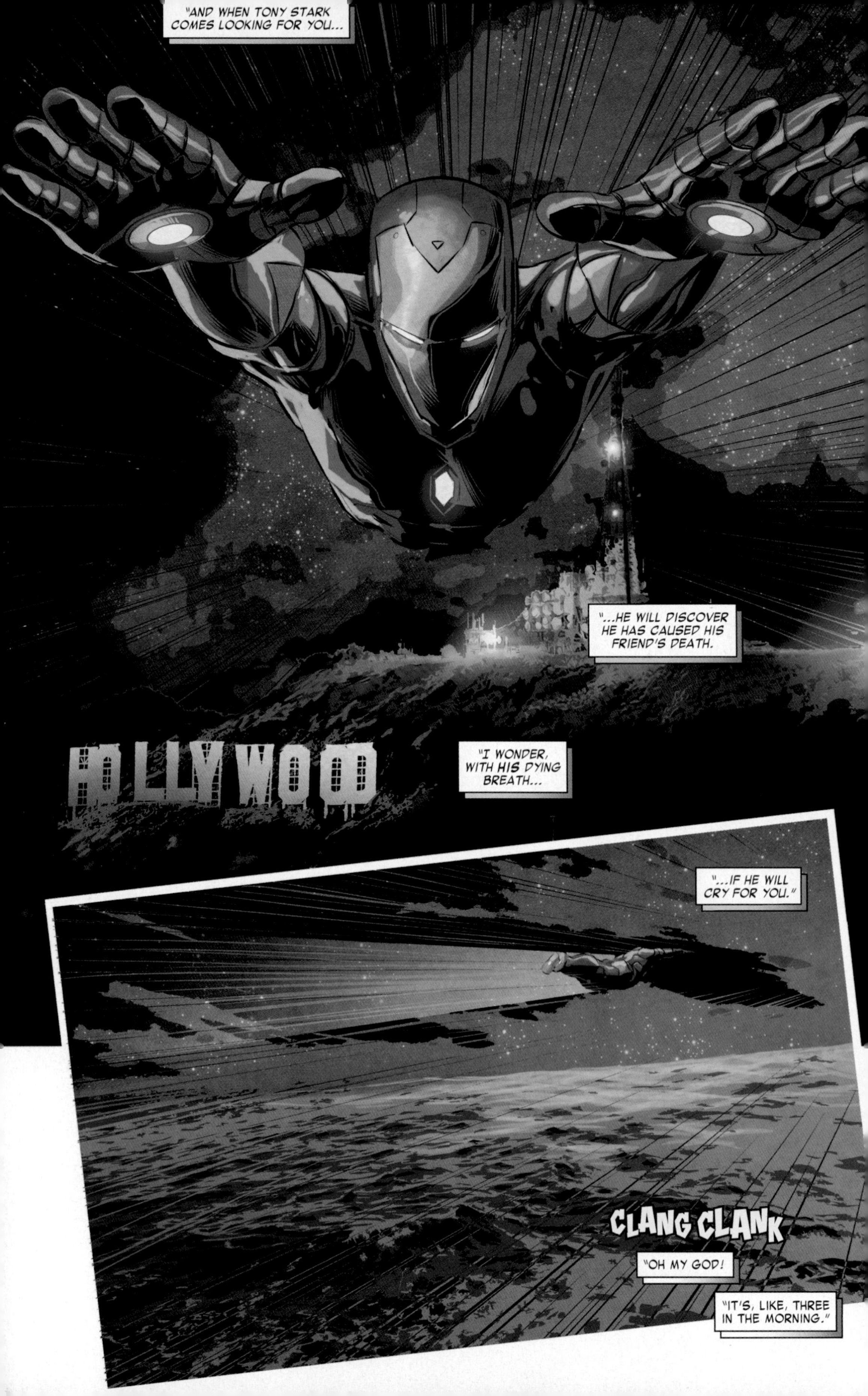

"AND WHEN TONY STARK COMES LOOKING FOR YOU...
"...HE WILL DISCOVER HE HAS CAUSED HIS FRIEND'S DEATH.
HOLLYWOOD
"I WONDER, WITH HIS DYING BREATH...
"...IF HE WILL CRY FOR YOU."
CLANG CLANK
"OH MY GOD!
"IT'S, LIKE, THREE IN THE MORNING."

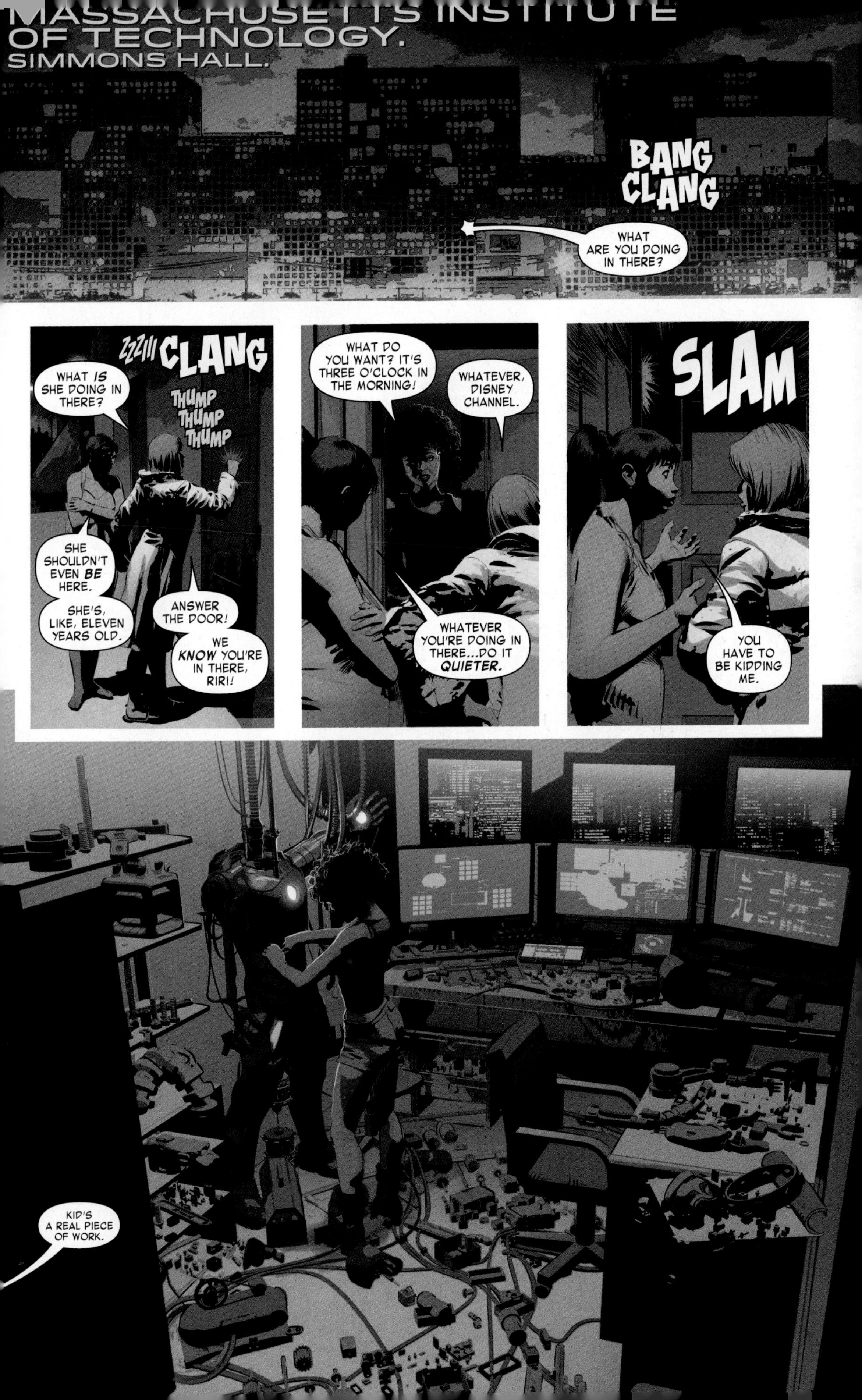

MASSACHUSETTS INSTITUTE OF TECHNOLOGY.
SIMMONS HALL.
BANG CLANG
WHAT ARE YOU DOING IN THERE?
ZZZIII CLANG
WHAT *IS* SHE DOING IN THERE?
THUMP THUMP THUMP
SHE SHOULDN'T EVEN *BE* HERE.
SHE'S, LIKE, ELEVEN YEARS OLD.
ANSWER THE DOOR!
WE *KNOW* YOU'RE IN THERE, RIRI!
WHAT DO YOU WANT? IT'S THREE O'CLOCK IN THE MORNING!
WHATEVER, DISNEY CHANNEL.
WHATEVER YOU'RE DOING IN THERE...DO IT *QUIETER.*
SLAM
YOU HAVE TO BE KIDDING ME.
KID'S A REAL PIECE OF WORK.

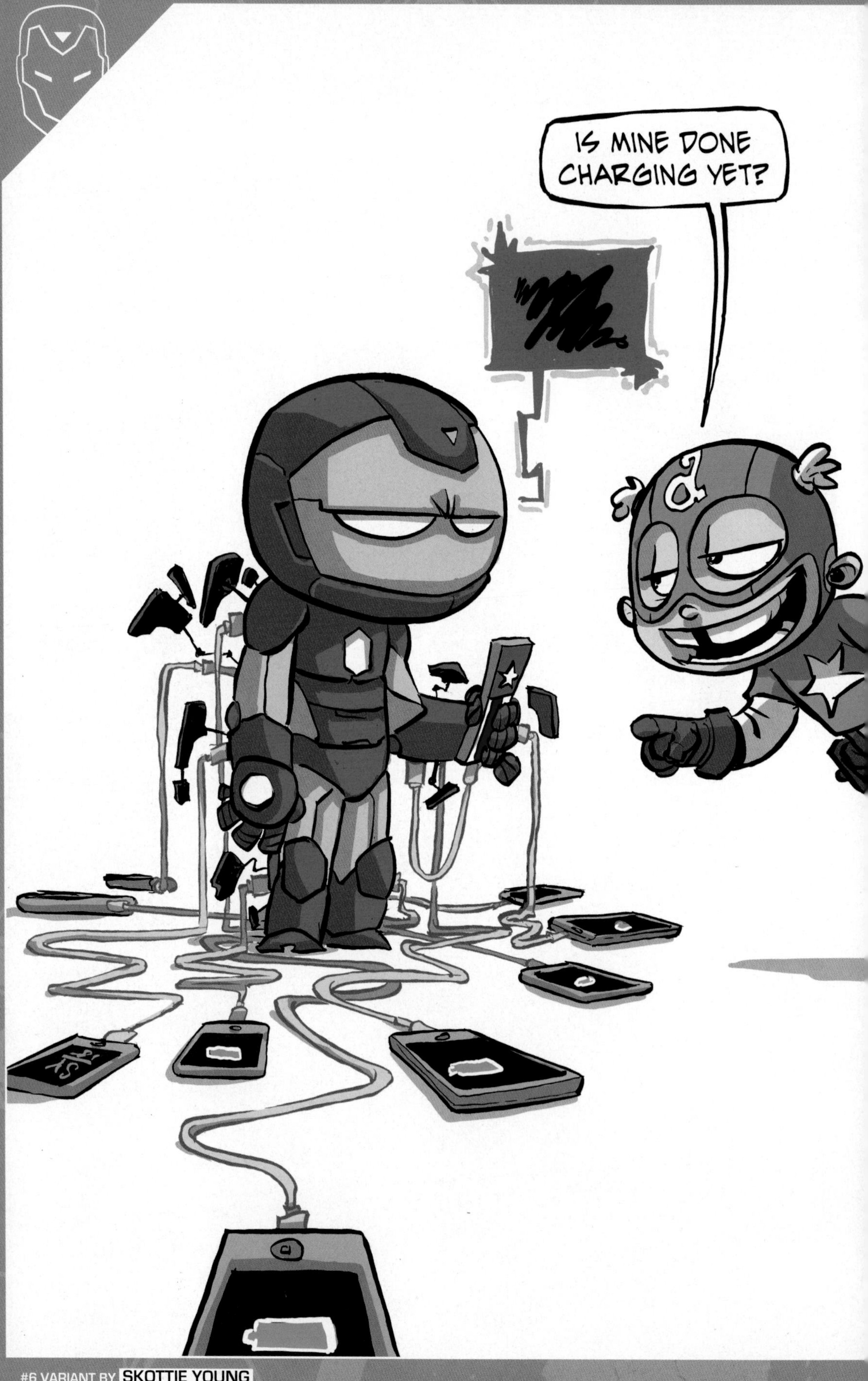
IS MINE DONE CHARGING YET?

#6 VARIANT BY SKOTTIE YOUNG

#8

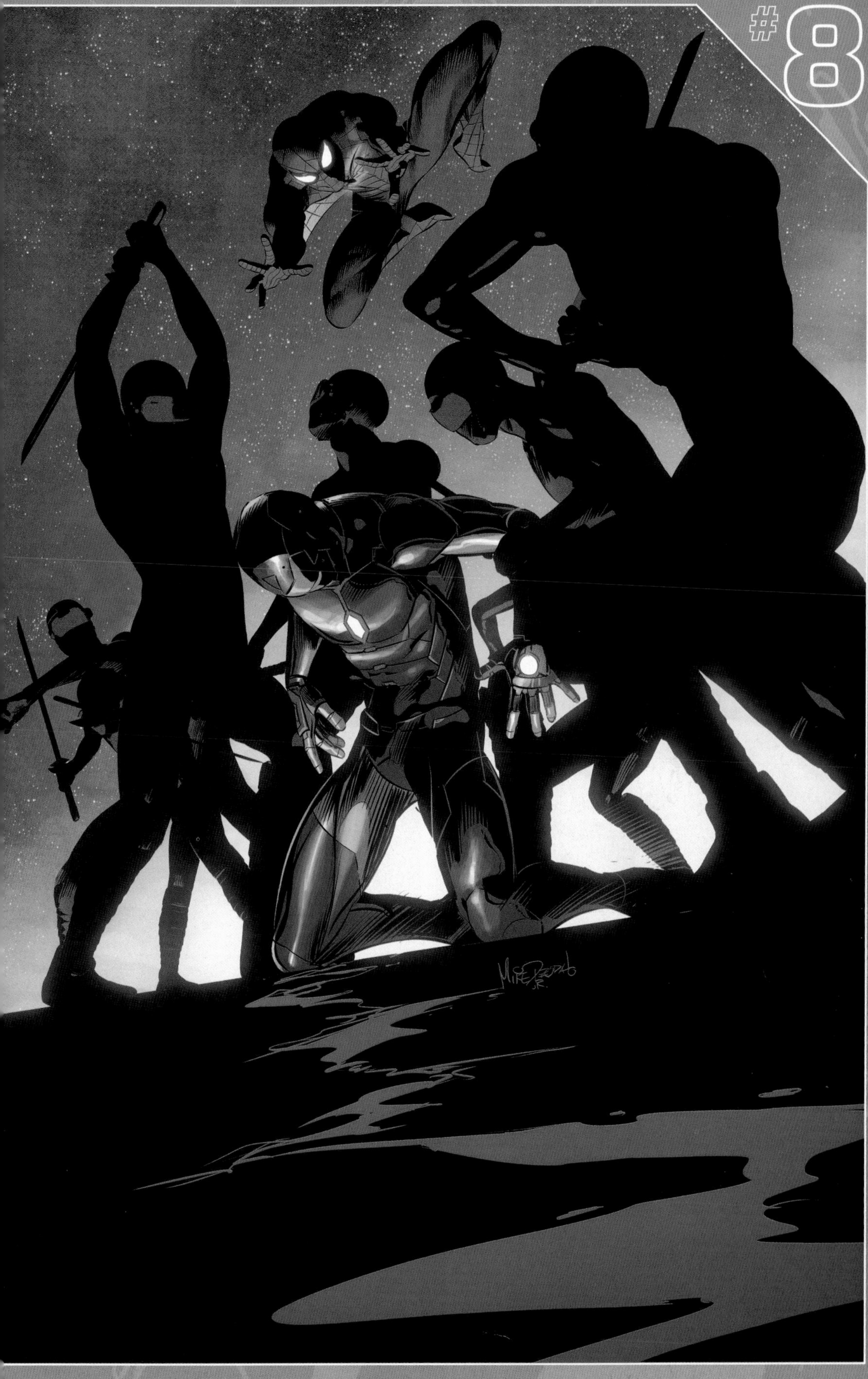

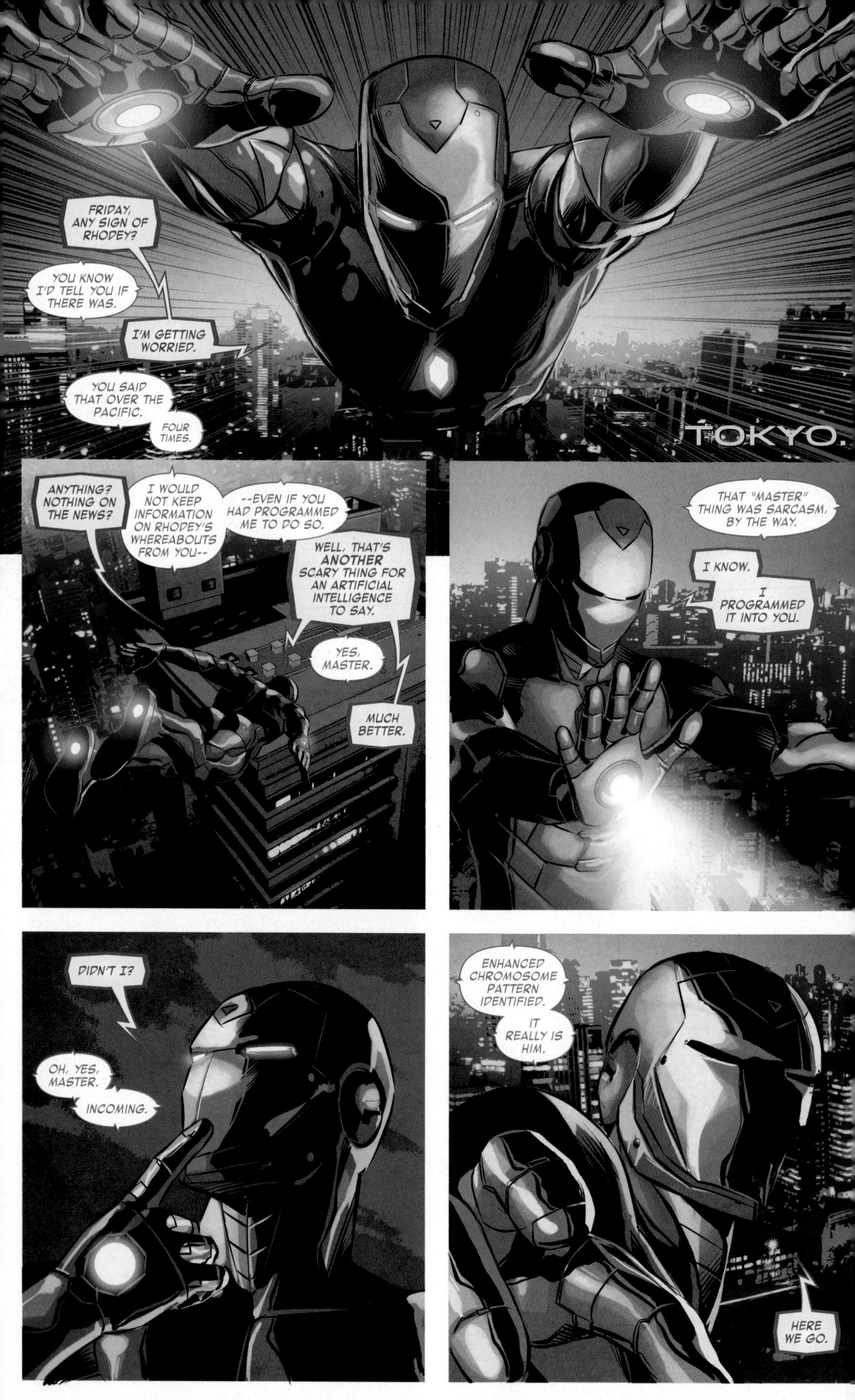
FRIDAY, ANY SIGN OF RHODEY?
YOU KNOW I'D TELL YOU IF THERE WAS.
I'M GETTING WORRIED.
YOU SAID THAT OVER THE PACIFIC.
FOUR TIMES.
TOKYO.
ANYTHING? NOTHING ON THE NEWS?
I WOULD NOT KEEP INFORMATION ON RHODEY'S WHEREABOUTS FROM YOU--
--EVEN IF YOU HAD PROGRAMMED ME TO DO SO.
WELL, THAT'S ANOTHER SCARY THING FOR AN ARTIFICIAL INTELLIGENCE TO SAY.
YES, MASTER.
MUCH BETTER.
THAT "MASTER" THING WAS SARCASM, BY THE WAY.
I KNOW.
I PROGRAMMED IT INTO YOU.
DIDN'T I?
OH, YES, MASTER.
INCOMING.
ENHANCED CHROMOSOME PATTERN IDENTIFIED.
IT REALLY IS HIM.
HERE WE GO.

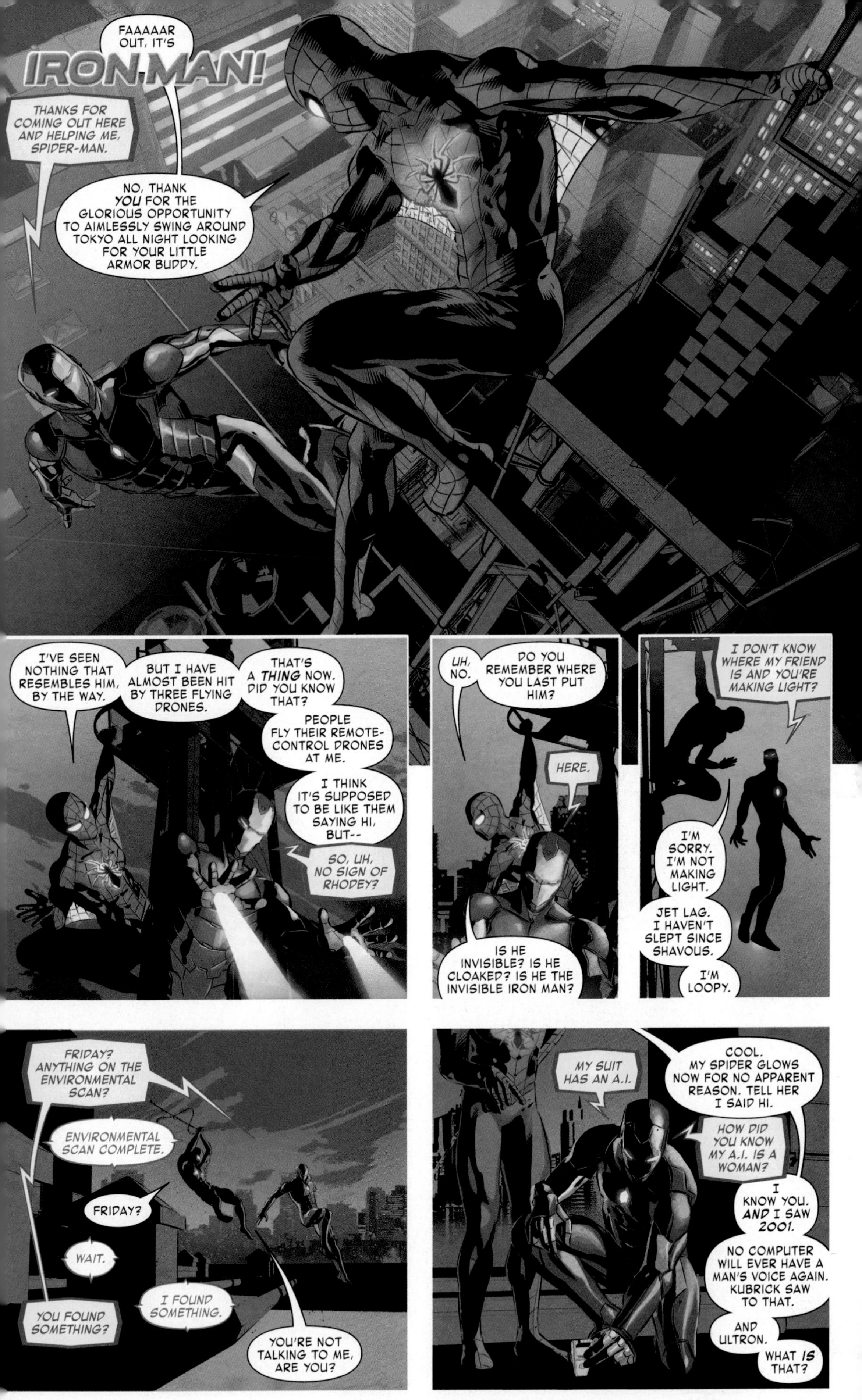

FAAAAAR OUT, IT'S
IRON MAN!
THANKS FOR COMING OUT HERE AND HELPING ME, SPIDER-MAN.
NO, THANK YOU FOR THE GLORIOUS OPPORTUNITY TO AIMLESSLY SWING AROUND TOKYO ALL NIGHT LOOKING FOR YOUR LITTLE ARMOR BUDDY.
I'VE SEEN NOTHING THAT RESEMBLES HIM, BY THE WAY.
BUT I HAVE ALMOST BEEN HIT BY THREE FLYING DRONES.
THAT'S A THING NOW. DID YOU KNOW THAT?
PEOPLE FLY THEIR REMOTE-CONTROL DRONES AT ME.
I THINK IT'S SUPPOSED TO BE LIKE THEM SAYING HI, BUT--
SO, UH, NO SIGN OF RHODEY?
UH, NO.
DO YOU REMEMBER WHERE YOU LAST PUT HIM?
HERE.
IS HE INVISIBLE? IS HE CLOAKED? IS HE THE INVISIBLE IRON MAN?
I DON'T KNOW WHERE MY FRIEND IS AND YOU'RE MAKING LIGHT?
I'M SORRY. I'M NOT MAKING LIGHT.
JET LAG. I HAVEN'T SLEPT SINCE SHAVOUS.
I'M LOOPY.
FRIDAY? ANYTHING ON THE ENVIRONMENTAL SCAN?
ENVIRONMENTAL SCAN COMPLETE.
FRIDAY?
WAIT.
YOU FOUND SOMETHING?
I FOUND SOMETHING.
YOU'RE NOT TALKING TO ME, ARE YOU?
MY SUIT HAS AN A.I.
COOL. MY SPIDER GLOWS NOW FOR NO APPARENT REASON. TELL HER I SAID HI.
HOW DID YOU KNOW MY A.I. IS A WOMAN?
I KNOW YOU. AND I SAW 2001.
NO COMPUTER WILL EVER HAVE A MAN'S VOICE AGAIN. KUBRICK SAW TO THAT.
AND ULTRON.
WHAT IS THAT?

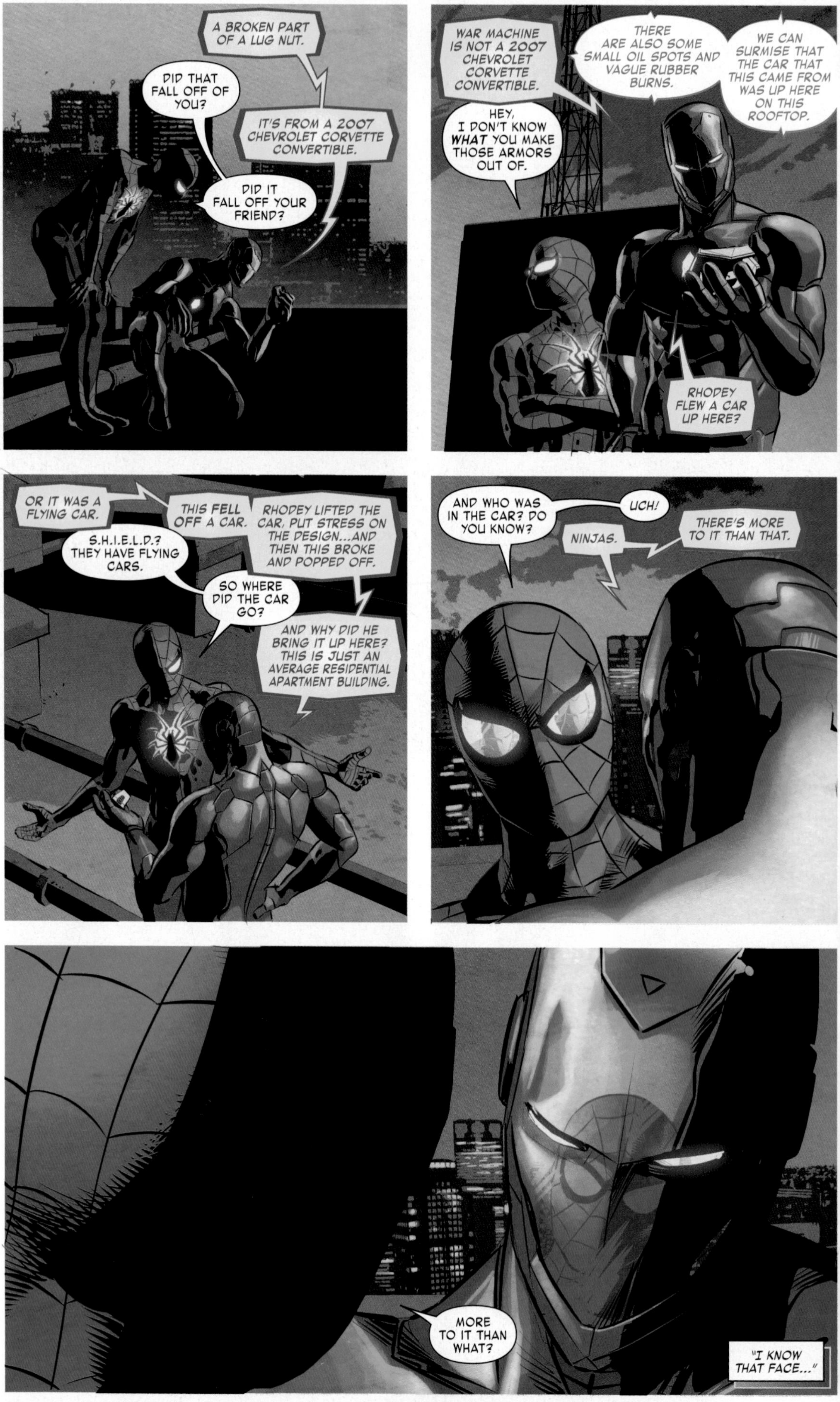
A BROKEN PART OF A LUG NUT.
DID THAT FALL OFF OF YOU?
IT'S FROM A 2007 CHEVROLET CORVETTE CONVERTIBLE.
DID IT FALL OFF YOUR FRIEND?
WAR MACHINE IS NOT A 2007 CHEVROLET CORVETTE CONVERTIBLE.
HEY, I DON'T KNOW WHAT YOU MAKE THOSE ARMORS OUT OF.
THERE ARE ALSO SOME SMALL OIL SPOTS AND VAGUE RUBBER BURNS.
WE CAN SURMISE THAT THE CAR THAT THIS CAME FROM WAS UP HERE ON THIS ROOFTOP.
RHODEY FLEW A CAR UP HERE?
OR IT WAS A FLYING CAR.
THIS FELL OFF A CAR.
RHODEY LIFTED THE CAR, PUT STRESS ON THE DESIGN...AND THEN THIS BROKE AND POPPED OFF.
S.H.I.E.L.D.? THEY HAVE FLYING CARS.
SO WHERE DID THE CAR GO?
AND WHY DID HE BRING IT UP HERE? THIS IS JUST AN AVERAGE RESIDENTIAL APARTMENT BUILDING.
AND WHO WAS IN THE CAR? DO YOU KNOW?
UCH!
NINJAS.
THERE'S MORE TO IT THAN THAT.
MORE TO IT THAN WHAT?
"I KNOW THAT FACE..."

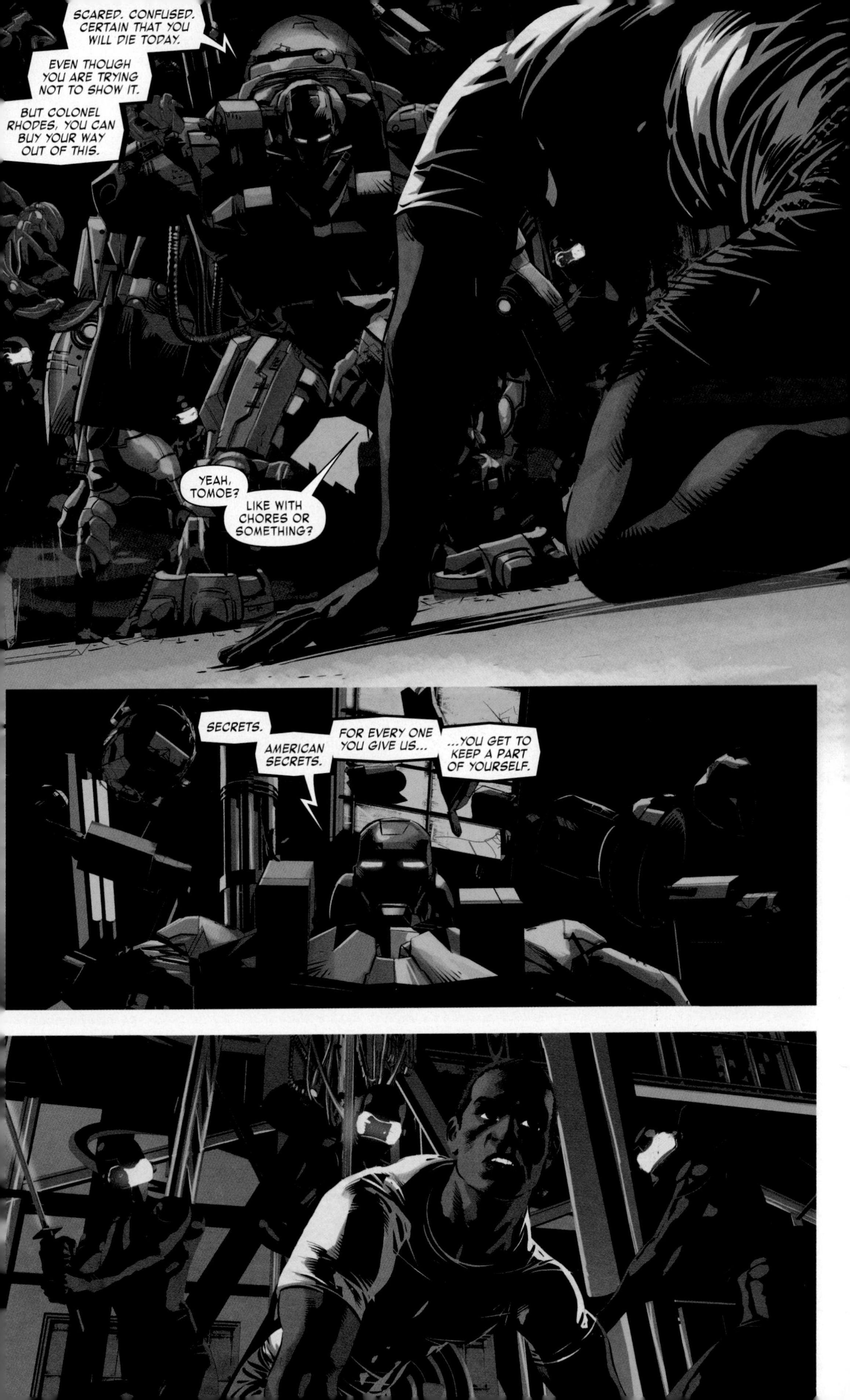
SCARED. CONFUSED. CERTAIN THAT YOU WILL DIE TODAY.
EVEN THOUGH YOU ARE TRYING NOT TO SHOW IT.
BUT COLONEL RHODES, YOU CAN BUY YOUR WAY OUT OF THIS.
YEAH, TOMOE?
LIKE WITH CHORES OR SOMETHING?
SECRETS.
AMERICAN SECRETS.
FOR EVERY ONE YOU GIVE US...
...YOU GET TO KEEP A PART OF YOURSELF.

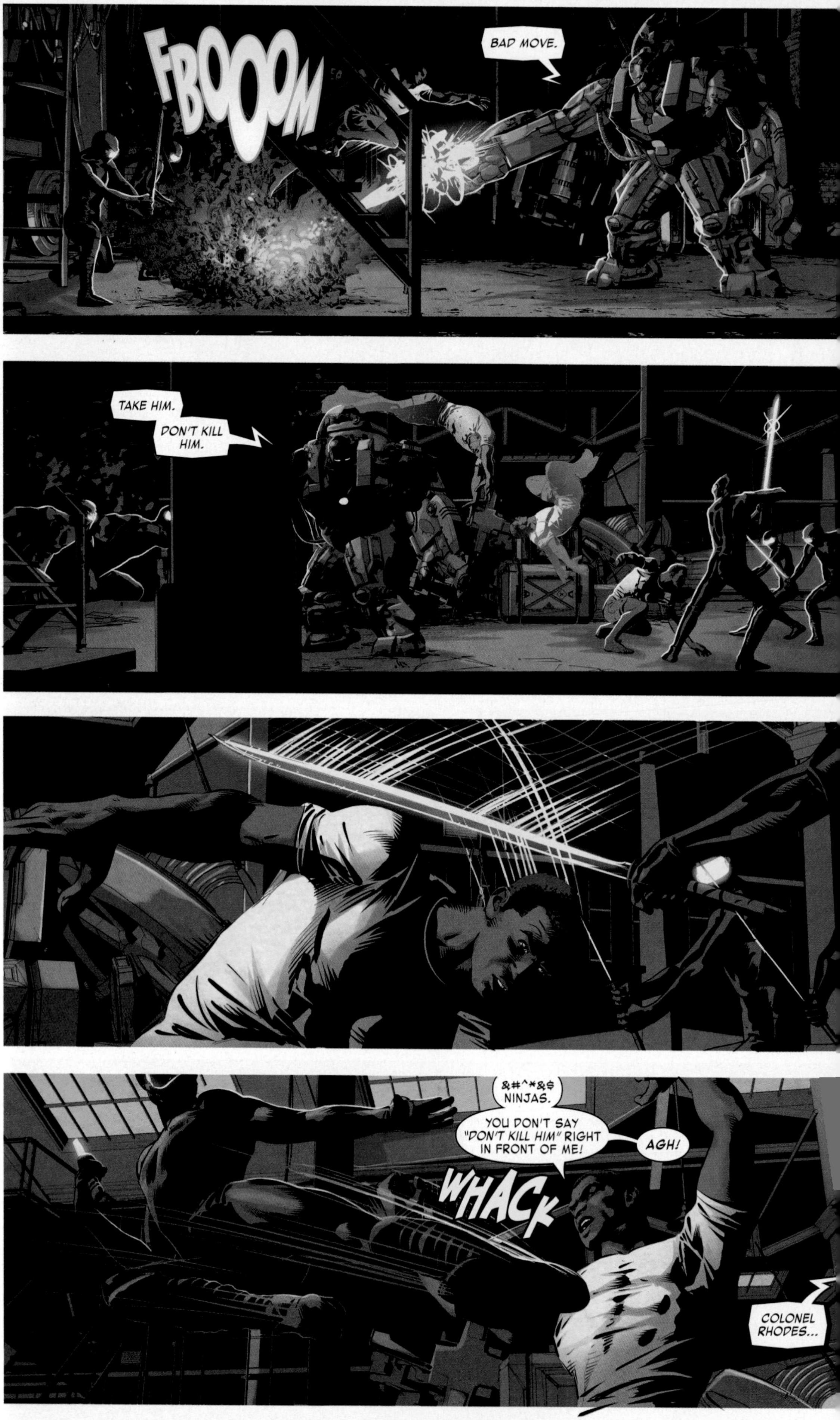
FBOOOM
BAD MOVE.
TAKE HIM.
DON'T KILL HIM.
&#^*&$ NINJAS.
YOU DON'T SAY "DON'T KILL HIM" RIGHT IN FRONT OF ME!
AGH!
WHACK
COLONEL RHODES...

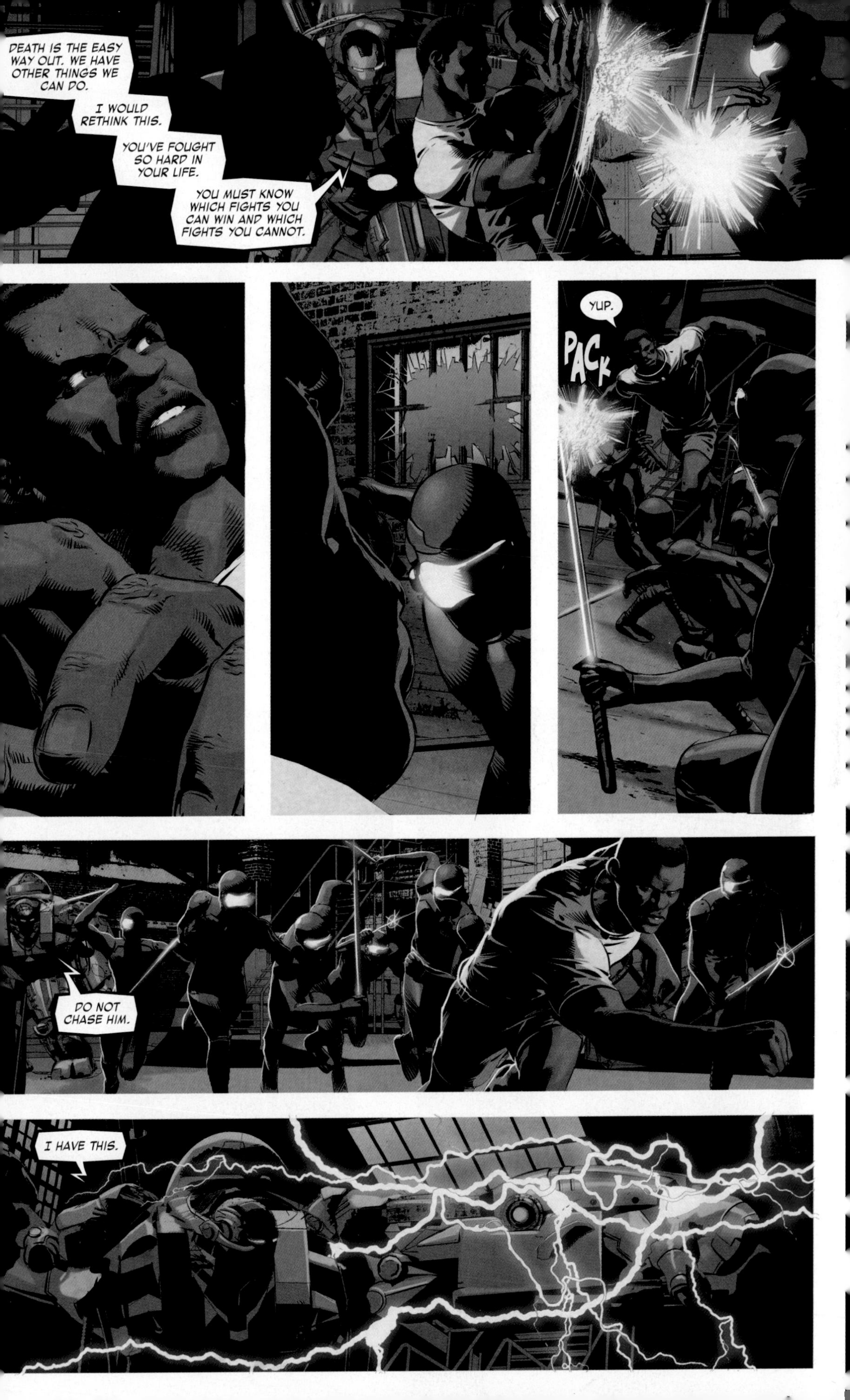
DEATH IS THE EASY WAY OUT. WE HAVE OTHER THINGS WE CAN DO.
I WOULD RETHINK THIS.
YOU'VE FOUGHT SO HARD IN YOUR LIFE.
YOU MUST KNOW WHICH FIGHTS YOU CAN WIN AND WHICH FIGHTS YOU CANNOT.
YUP.
PACK
DO NOT CHASE HIM.
I HAVE THIS.

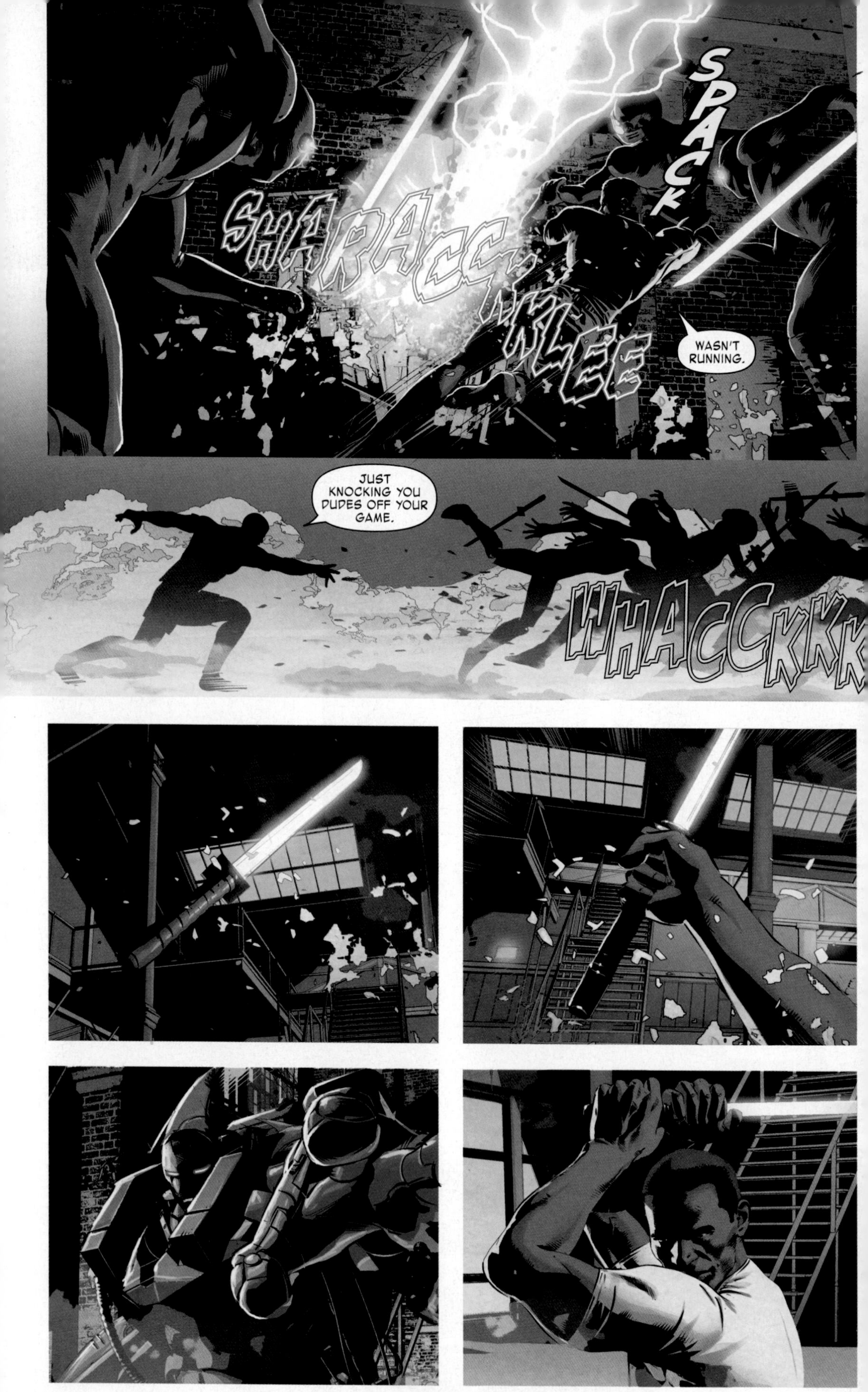
SPACK
SHRACCKLEE
WASN'T RUNNING.
JUST KNOCKING YOU DUDES OFF YOUR GAME.
WHACCKKK

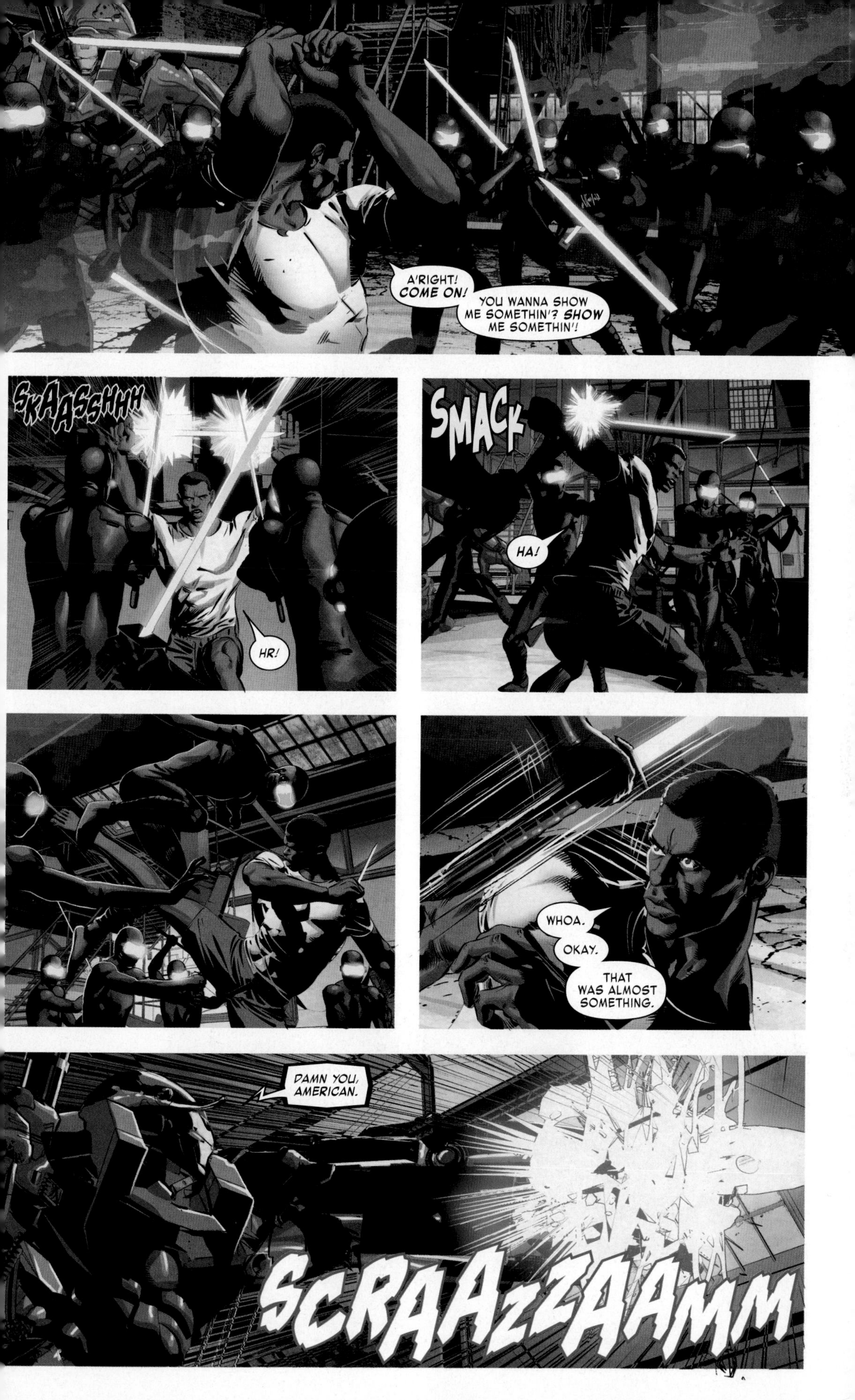
A'RIGHT! COME ON!
YOU WANNA SHOW ME SOMETHIN'? SHOW ME SOMETHIN'!
SKAASSHHH
HR!
SMACK
HA!
WHOA.
OKAY.
THAT WAS ALMOST SOMETHING.
DAMN YOU, AMERICAN.
SCRAAZZAAMM

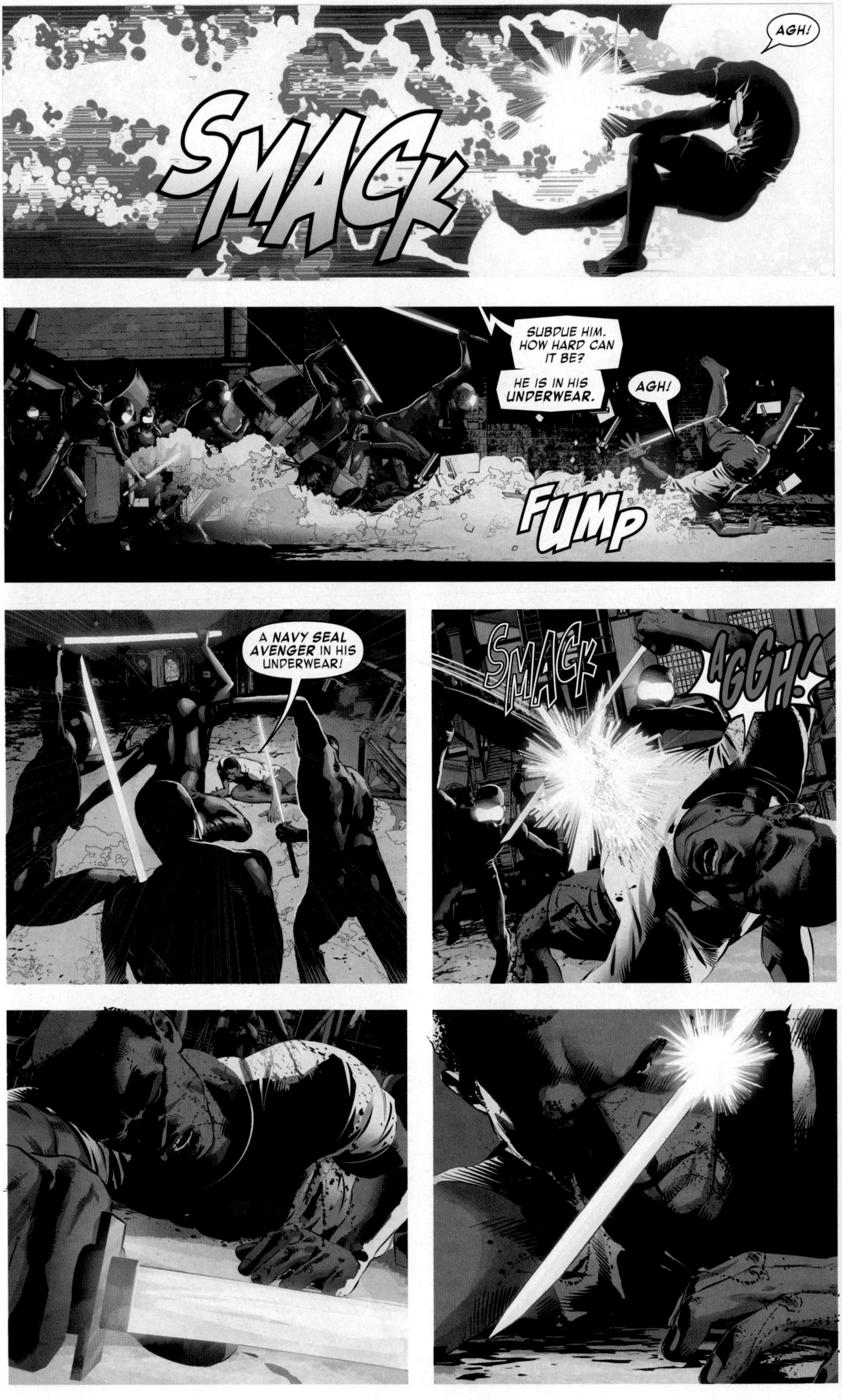
AGH!
SMACK
SUBDUE HIM. HOW HARD CAN IT BE?
HE IS IN HIS UNDERWEAR.
AGH!
FUMP
A NAVY SEAL AVENGER IN HIS UNDERWEAR!
SMACK
AGGH!

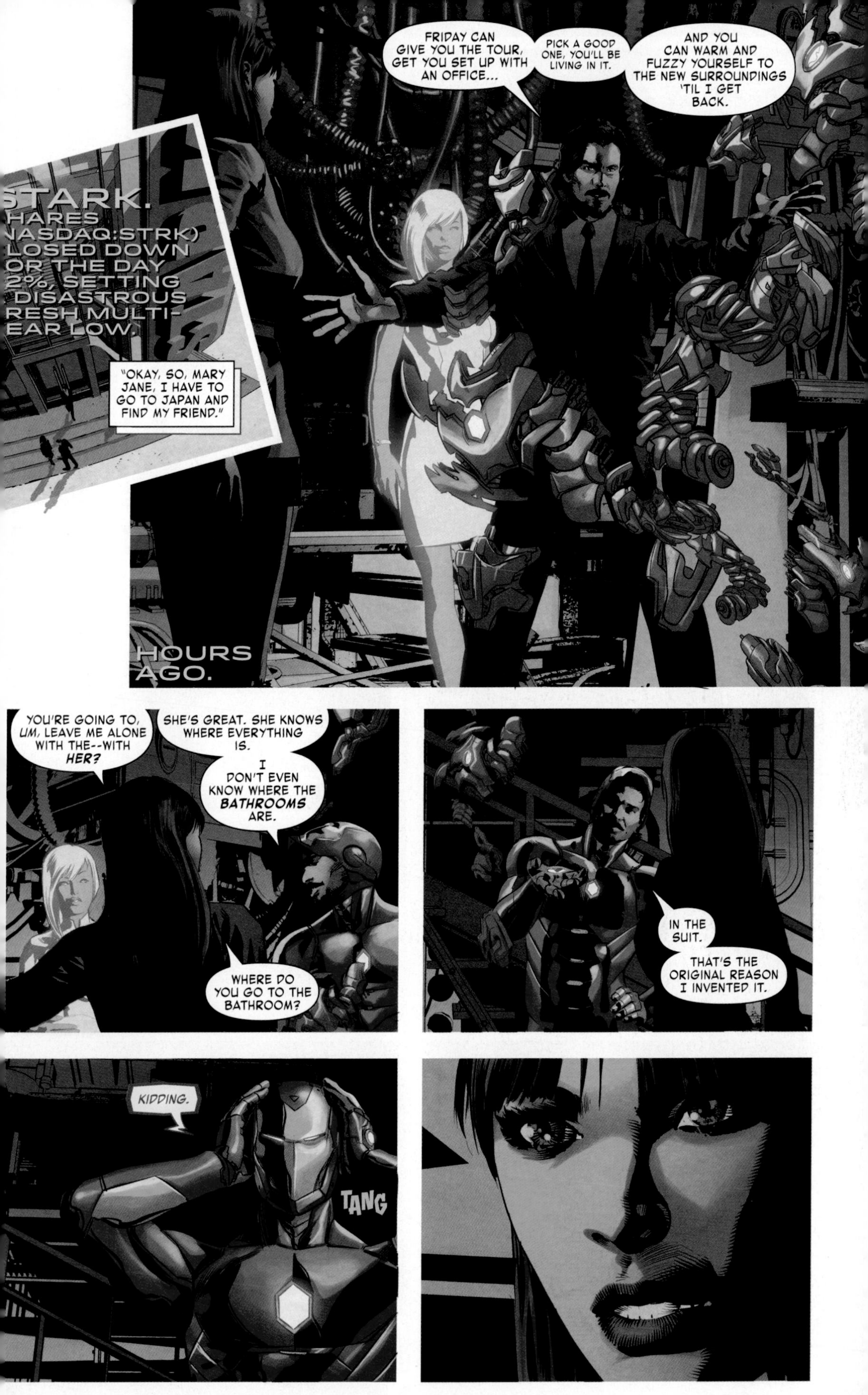
FRIDAY CAN GIVE YOU THE TOUR, GET YOU SET UP WITH AN OFFICE...
PICK A GOOD ONE, YOU'LL BE LIVING IN IT.
AND YOU CAN WARM AND FUZZY YOURSELF TO THE NEW SURROUNDINGS 'TIL I GET BACK.
STARK. HARES NASDAQ:STRK) LOSED DOWN OR THE DAY 2%, SETTING DISASTROUS RESH MULTI-EAR LOW.
"OKAY, SO, MARY JANE, I HAVE TO GO TO JAPAN AND FIND MY FRIEND."
HOURS AGO.
YOU'RE GOING TO, UM, LEAVE ME ALONE WITH THE--WITH HER?
SHE'S GREAT. SHE KNOWS WHERE EVERYTHING IS.
I DON'T EVEN KNOW WHERE THE BATHROOMS ARE.
WHERE DO YOU GO TO THE BATHROOM?
IN THE SUIT.
THAT'S THE ORIGINAL REASON I INVENTED IT.
KIDDING.
TANG

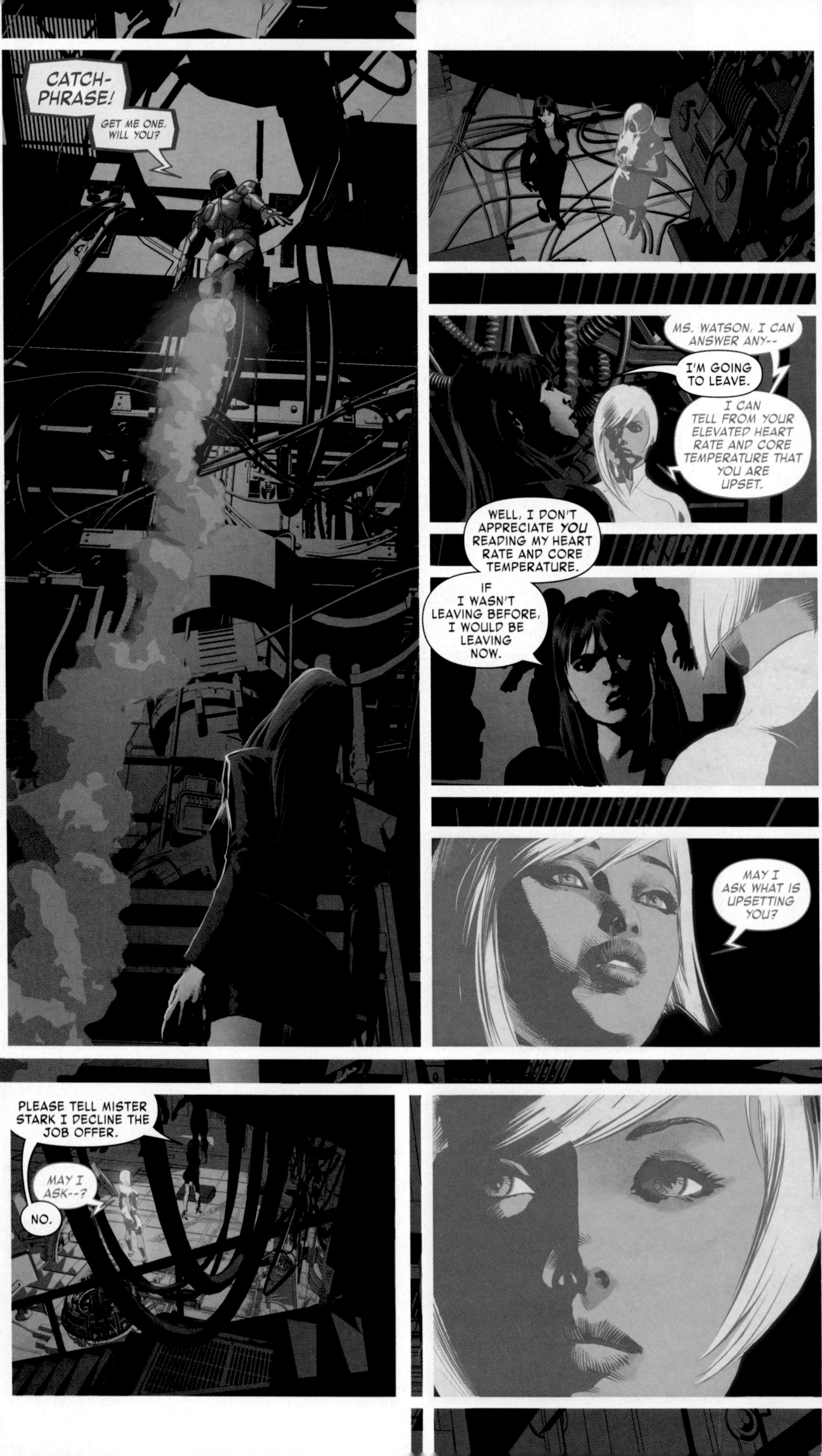
CATCH-PHRASE!
GET ME ONE, WILL YOU?
MS. WATSON, I CAN ANSWER ANY--
I'M GOING TO LEAVE.
I CAN TELL FROM YOUR ELEVATED HEART RATE AND CORE TEMPERATURE THAT YOU ARE UPSET.
WELL, I DON'T APPRECIATE YOU READING MY HEART RATE AND CORE TEMPERATURE.
IF I WASN'T LEAVING BEFORE, I WOULD BE LEAVING NOW.
MAY I ASK WHAT IS UPSETTING YOU?
PLEASE TELL MISTER STARK I DECLINE THE JOB OFFER.
MAY I ASK--?
NO.

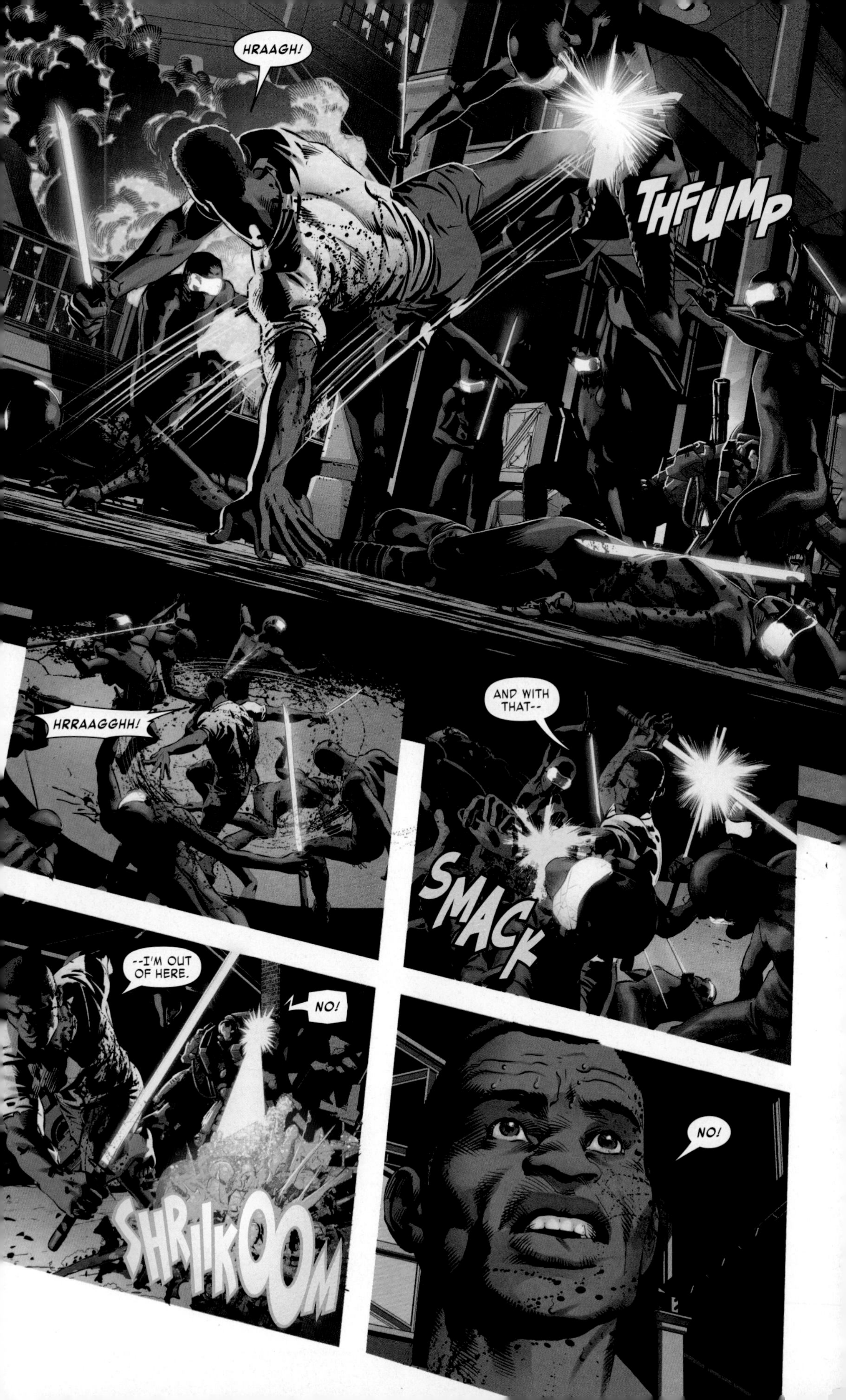
HRAAGH!
THFUMP
HRRAAGGHH!
AND WITH THAT--
SMACK
--I'M OUT OF HERE.
NO!
SHRIIKOOM
NO!

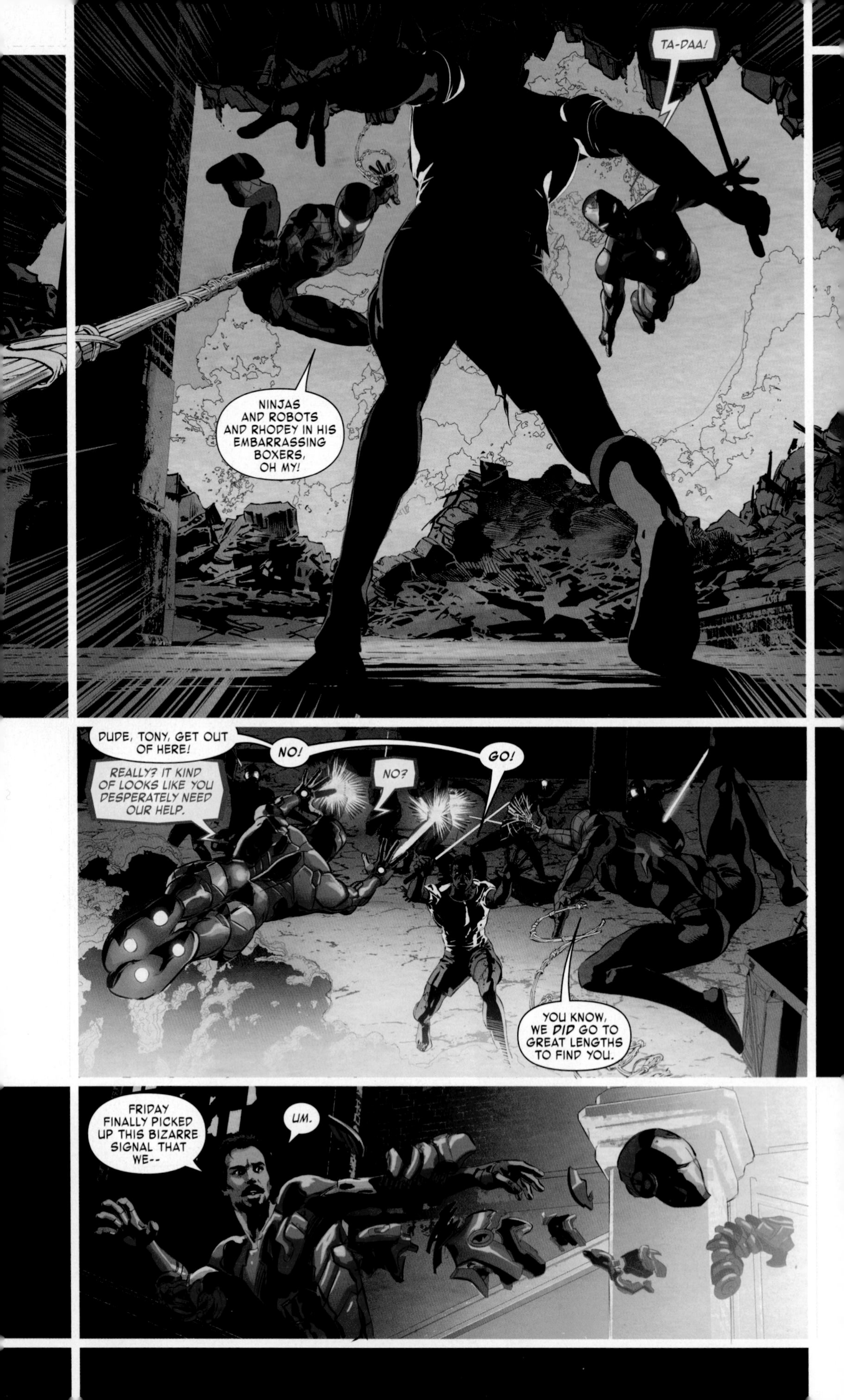
TA-DAA!
NINJAS AND ROBOTS AND RHODEY IN HIS EMBARRASSING BOXERS, OH MY!
DUDE, TONY, GET OUT OF HERE!
NO!
GO!
REALLY? IT KIND OF LOOKS LIKE YOU DESPERATELY NEED OUR HELP.
NO?
YOU KNOW, WE DID GO TO GREAT LENGTHS TO FIND YOU.
FRIDAY FINALLY PICKED UP THIS BIZARRE SIGNAL THAT WE--
UM.

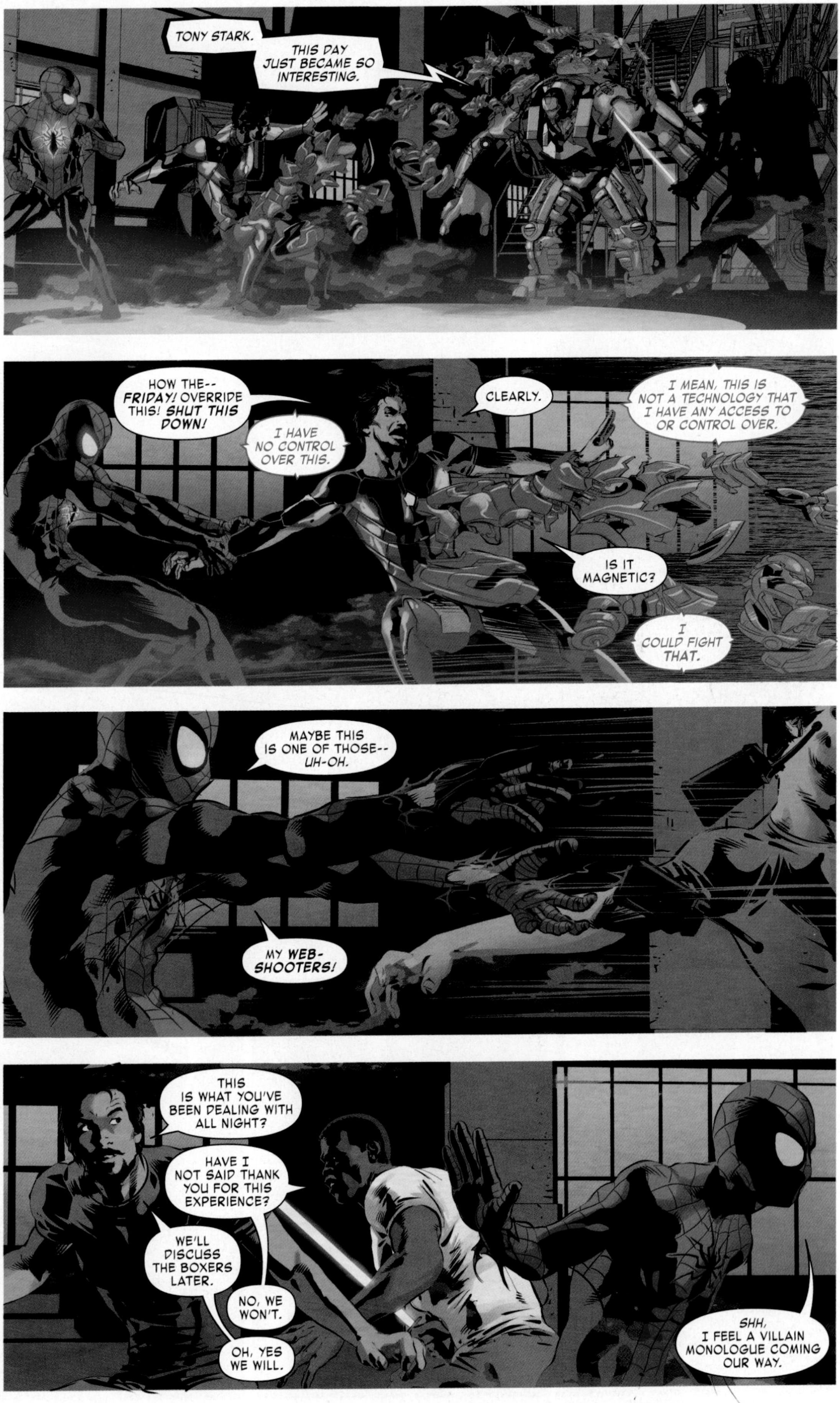
TONY STARK.
THIS DAY JUST BECAME SO INTERESTING.
HOW THE-- FRIDAY! OVERRIDE THIS! SHUT THIS DOWN!
I HAVE NO CONTROL OVER THIS.
CLEARLY.
I MEAN, THIS IS NOT A TECHNOLOGY THAT I HAVE ANY ACCESS TO OR CONTROL OVER.
IS IT MAGNETIC?
I COULD FIGHT THAT.
MAYBE THIS IS ONE OF THOSE-- UH-OH.
MY WEB-SHOOTERS!
THIS IS WHAT YOU'VE BEEN DEALING WITH ALL NIGHT?
HAVE I NOT SAID THANK YOU FOR THIS EXPERIENCE?
WE'LL DISCUSS THE BOXERS LATER.
NO, WE WON'T.
OH, YES WE WILL.
SHH, I FEEL A VILLAIN MONOLOGUE COMING OUR WAY.

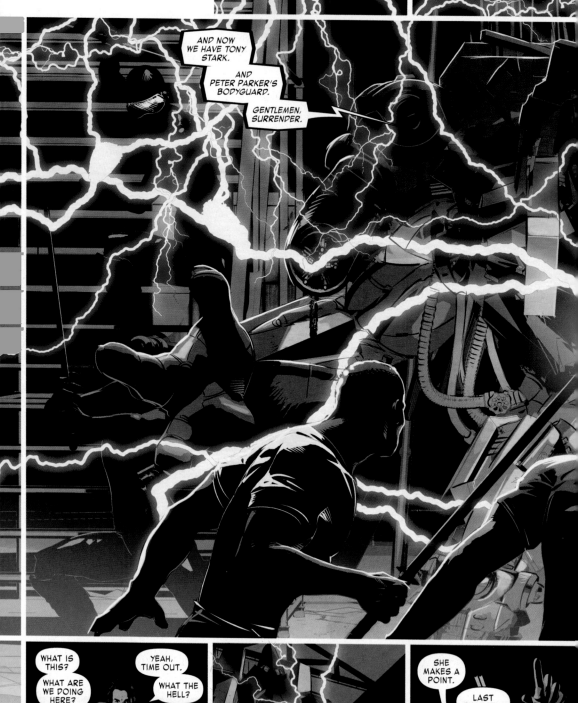

AND NOW WE HAVE TONY STARK.

AND PETER PARKER'S BODYGUARD.

GENTLEMEN, SURRENDER.

WHAT IS THIS?

WHAT ARE WE DOING HERE?

YEAH, TIME OUT.

WHAT THE HELL?

YOU ARE OVERPOWERED AND OUTMANNED.

I UNDERSTAND YOU LIKE TO LIVE YOUR LIFE AGAINST THE ODDS, BUT THIS IS THE END, TONY STARK.

SHE MAKES A POINT.

LAST CHANCE...

GIVE ME MY ARMOR BACK.

OR SUFFER THE CONSEQUENCES.

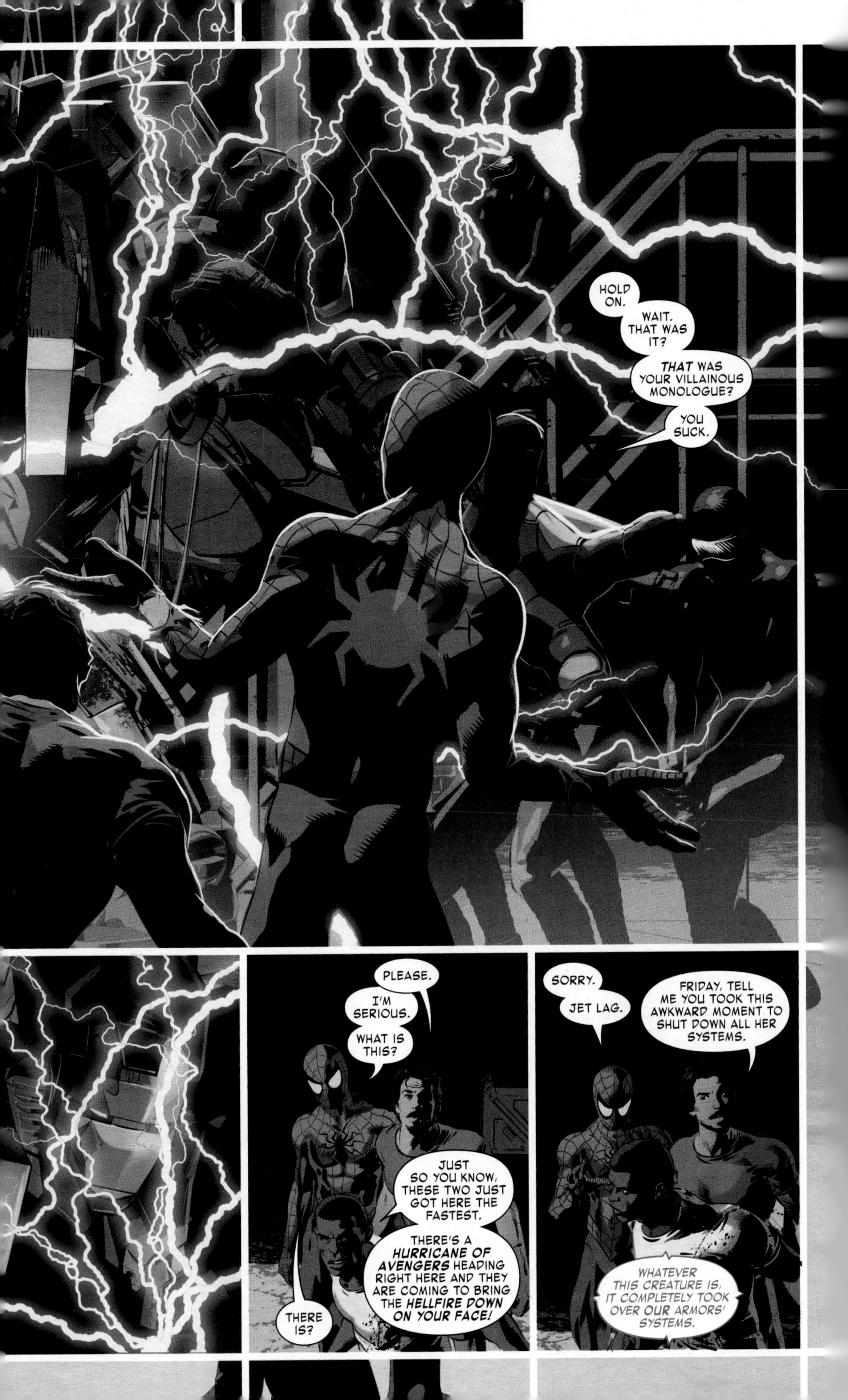
HOLD ON.
WAIT. THAT WAS IT?
THAT WAS YOUR VILLAINOUS MONOLOGUE?
YOU SUCK.
PLEASE.
I'M SERIOUS.
WHAT IS THIS?
JUST SO YOU KNOW, THESE TWO JUST GOT HERE THE FASTEST.
THERE'S A HURRICANE OF AVENGERS HEADING RIGHT HERE AND THEY ARE COMING TO BRING THE HELLFIRE DOWN ON YOUR FACE!
THERE IS?
SORRY.
JET LAG.
FRIDAY, TELL ME YOU TOOK THIS AWKWARD MOMENT TO SHUT DOWN ALL HER SYSTEMS.
WHATEVER THIS CREATURE IS, IT COMPLETELY TOOK OVER OUR ARMORS' SYSTEMS.

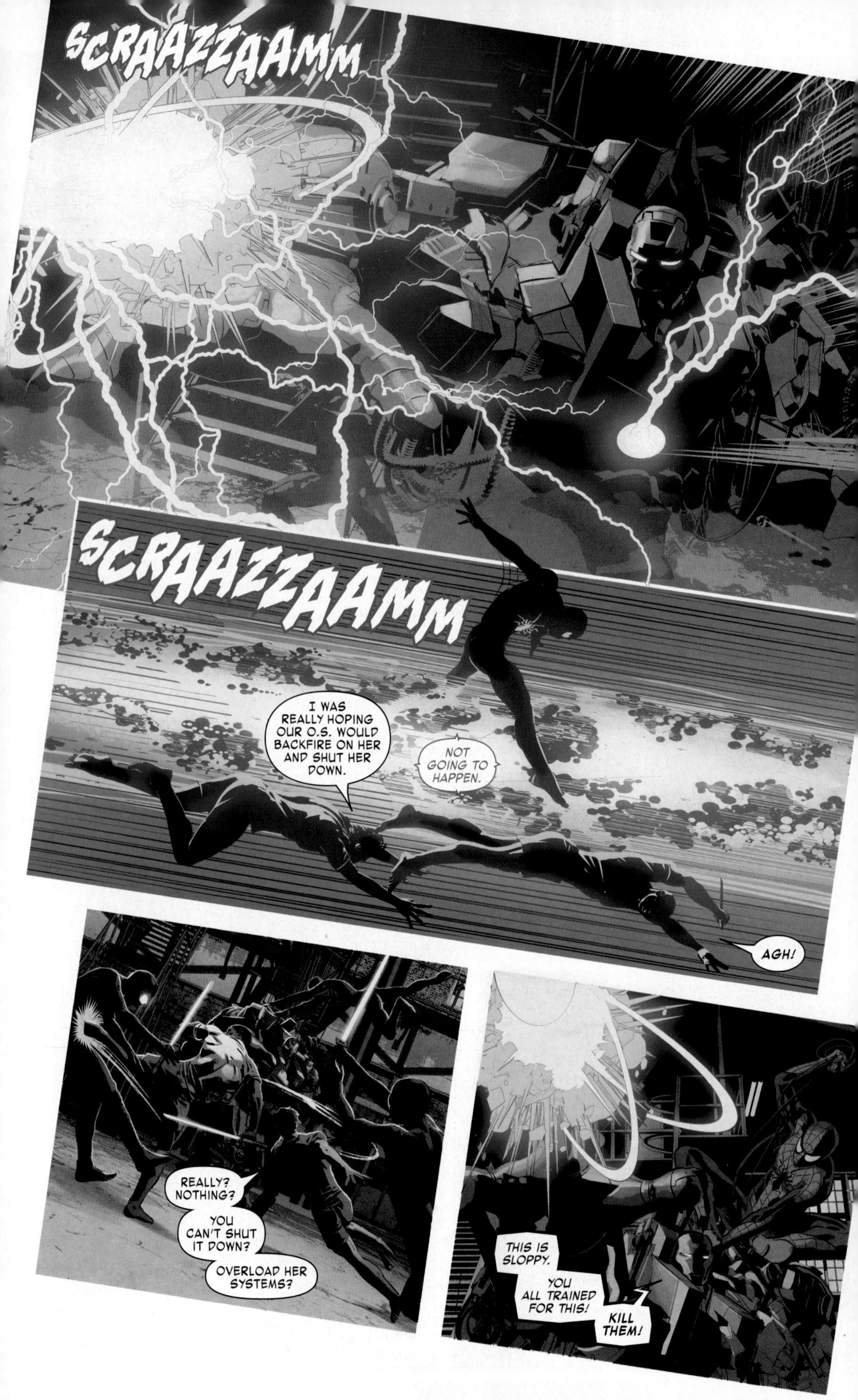
SCRAAZZAAMM
SCRAAZZAAMM
I WAS REALLY HOPING OUR O.S. WOULD BACKFIRE ON HER AND SHUT HER DOWN.
NOT GOING TO HAPPEN.
AGH!
REALLY? NOTHING?
YOU CAN'T SHUT IT DOWN?
OVERLOAD HER SYSTEMS?
THIS IS SLOPPY.
YOU ALL TRAINED FOR THIS!
KILL THEM!

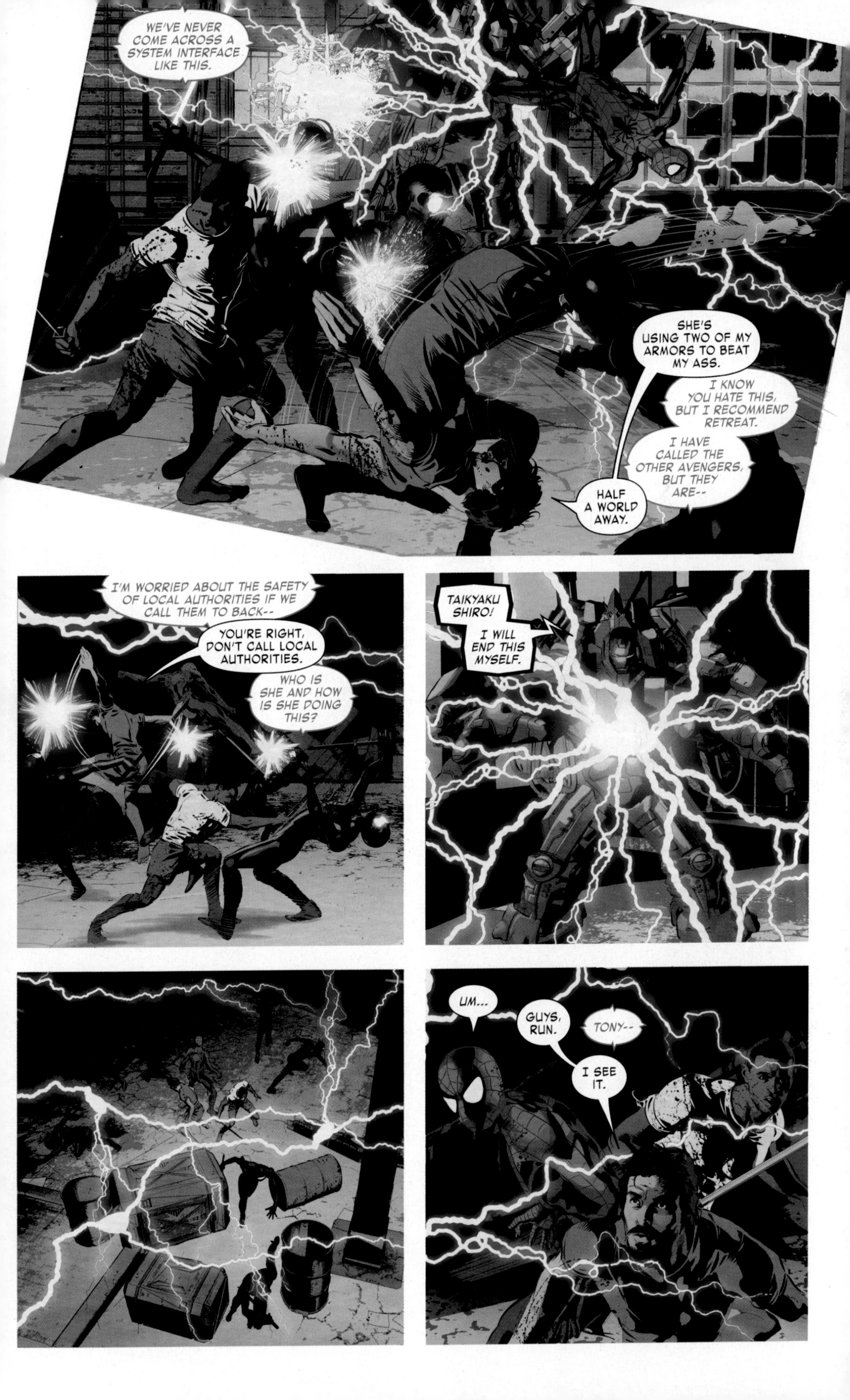
WE'VE NEVER COME ACROSS A SYSTEM INTERFACE LIKE THIS.
SHE'S USING TWO OF MY ARMORS TO BEAT MY ASS.
I KNOW YOU HATE THIS, BUT I RECOMMEND RETREAT.
I HAVE CALLED THE OTHER AVENGERS, BUT THEY ARE--
HALF A WORLD AWAY.
I'M WORRIED ABOUT THE SAFETY OF LOCAL AUTHORITIES IF WE CALL THEM TO BACK--
YOU'RE RIGHT, DON'T CALL LOCAL AUTHORITIES.
WHO IS SHE AND HOW IS SHE DOING THIS?
TAIKYAKU SHIRO!
I WILL END THIS MYSELF.
UM...
GUYS, RUN.
TONY--
I SEE IT.

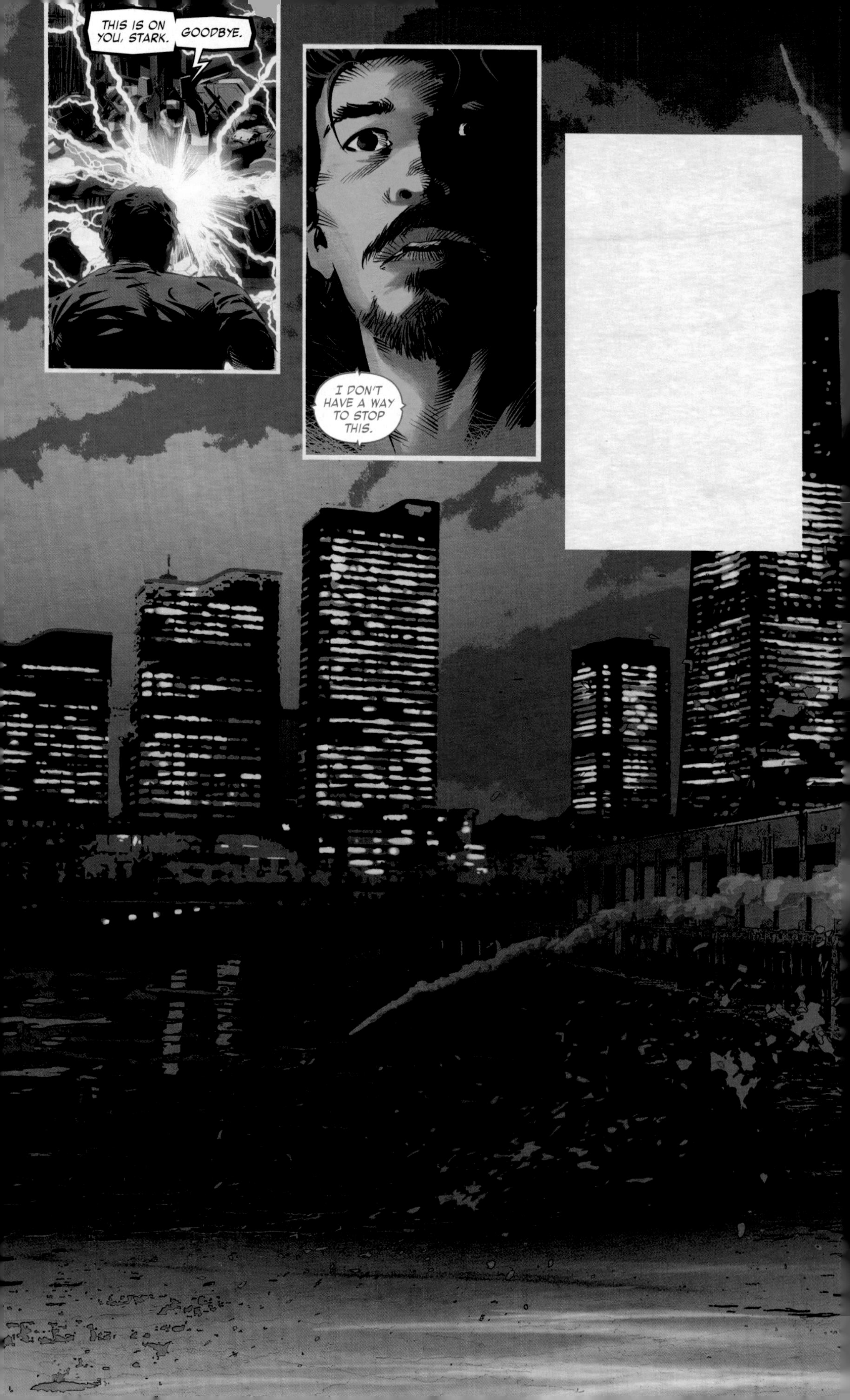
THIS IS ON YOU, STARK.
GOODBYE.
I DON'T HAVE A WAY TO STOP THIS.

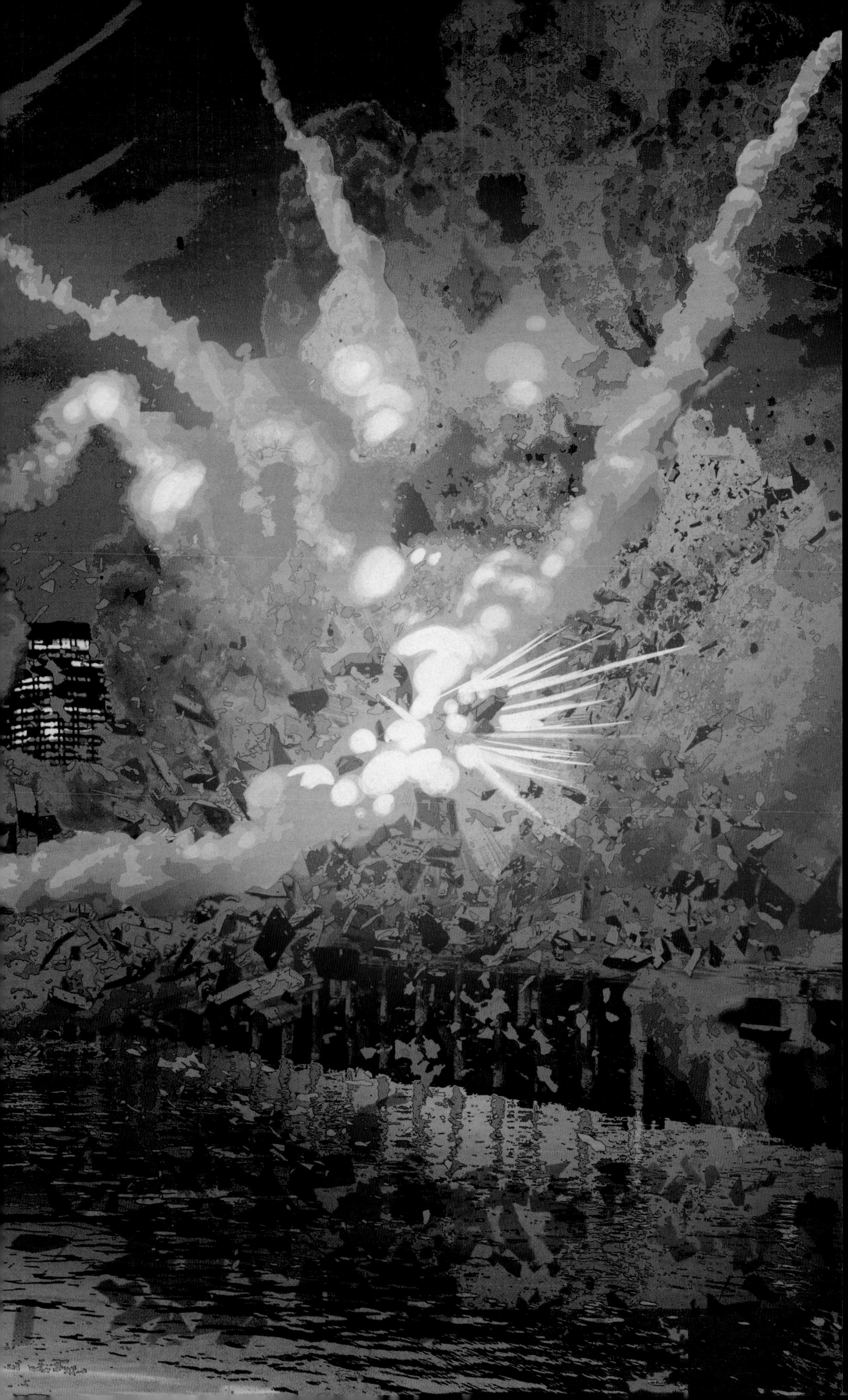

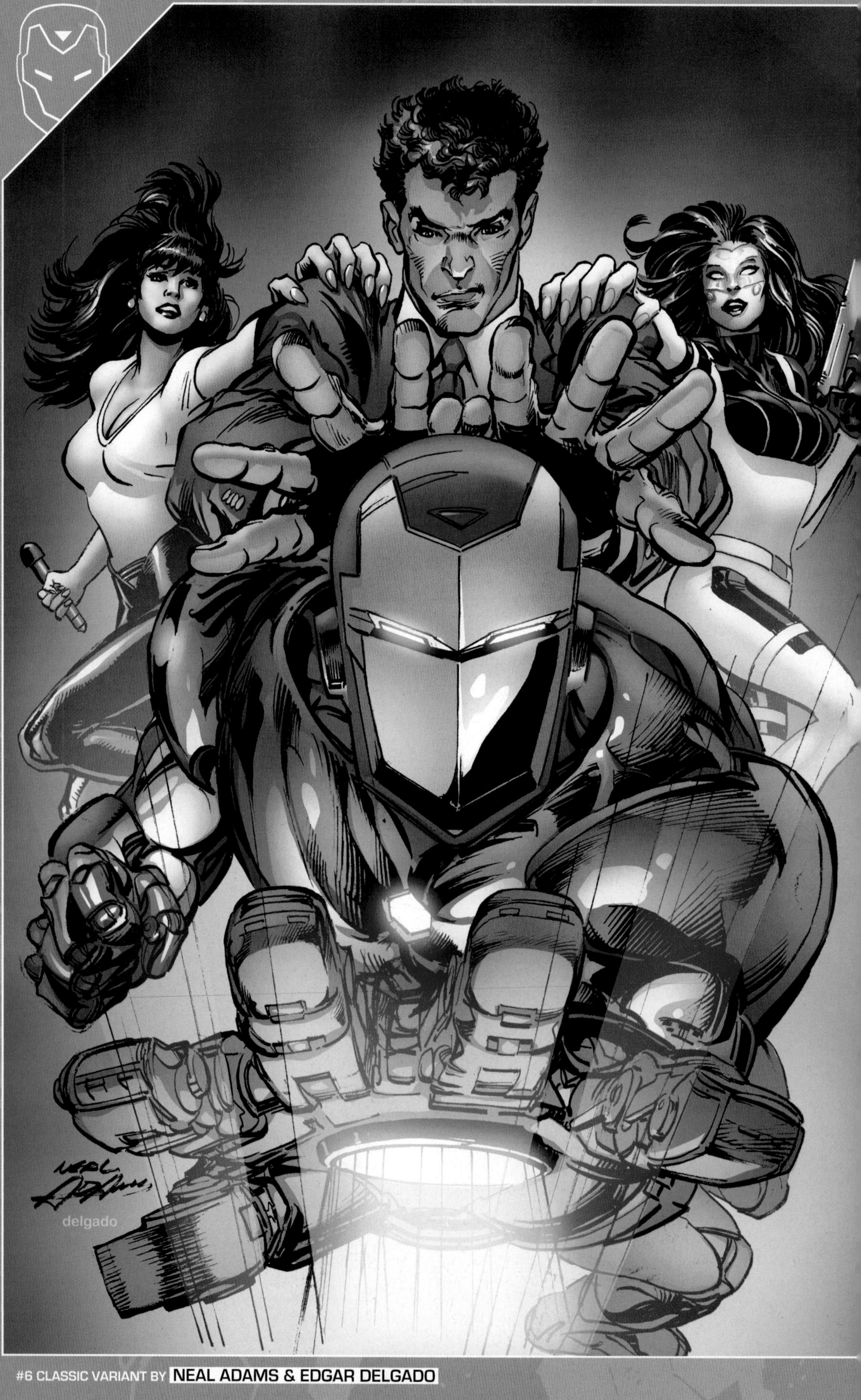
delgado

#6 CLASSIC VARIANT BY NEAL ADAMS & EDGAR DELGADO

#9

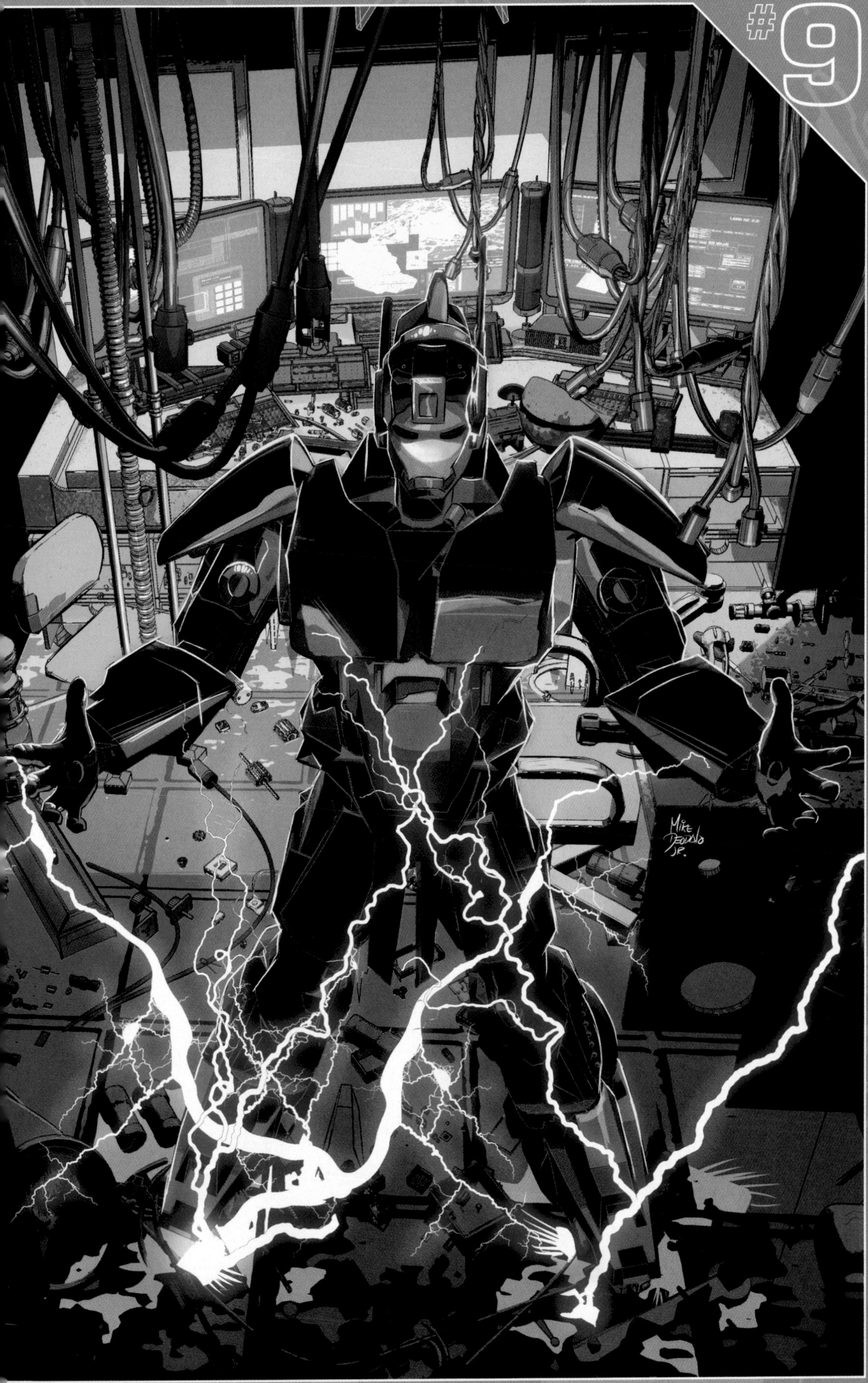
MIKE DEODATO JR.

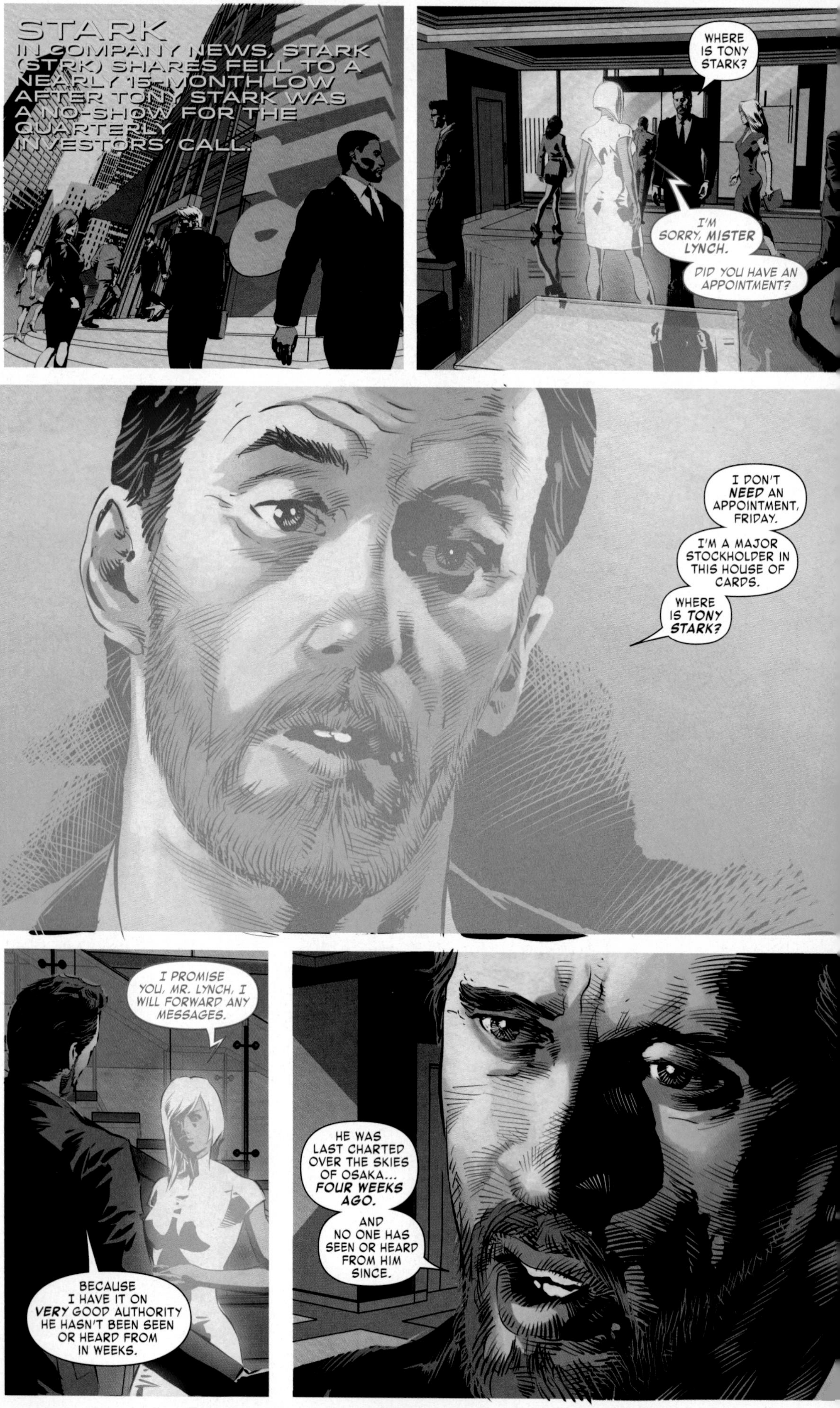
STARK
IN COMPANY NEWS, STARK (STRK) SHARES FELL TO A NEARLY 15-MONTH LOW AFTER TONY STARK WAS A NO-SHOW FOR THE QUARTERLY INVESTORS' CALL.
WHERE IS TONY STARK?
I'M SORRY, MISTER LYNCH.
DID YOU HAVE AN APPOINTMENT?
I DON'T NEED AN APPOINTMENT, FRIDAY.
I'M A MAJOR STOCKHOLDER IN THIS HOUSE OF CARDS.
WHERE IS TONY STARK?
I PROMISE YOU, MR. LYNCH, I WILL FORWARD ANY MESSAGES.
BECAUSE I HAVE IT ON VERY GOOD AUTHORITY HE HASN'T BEEN SEEN OR HEARD FROM IN WEEKS.
HE WAS LAST CHARTED OVER THE SKIES OF OSAKA... FOUR WEEKS AGO.
AND NO ONE HAS SEEN OR HEARD FROM HIM SINCE.

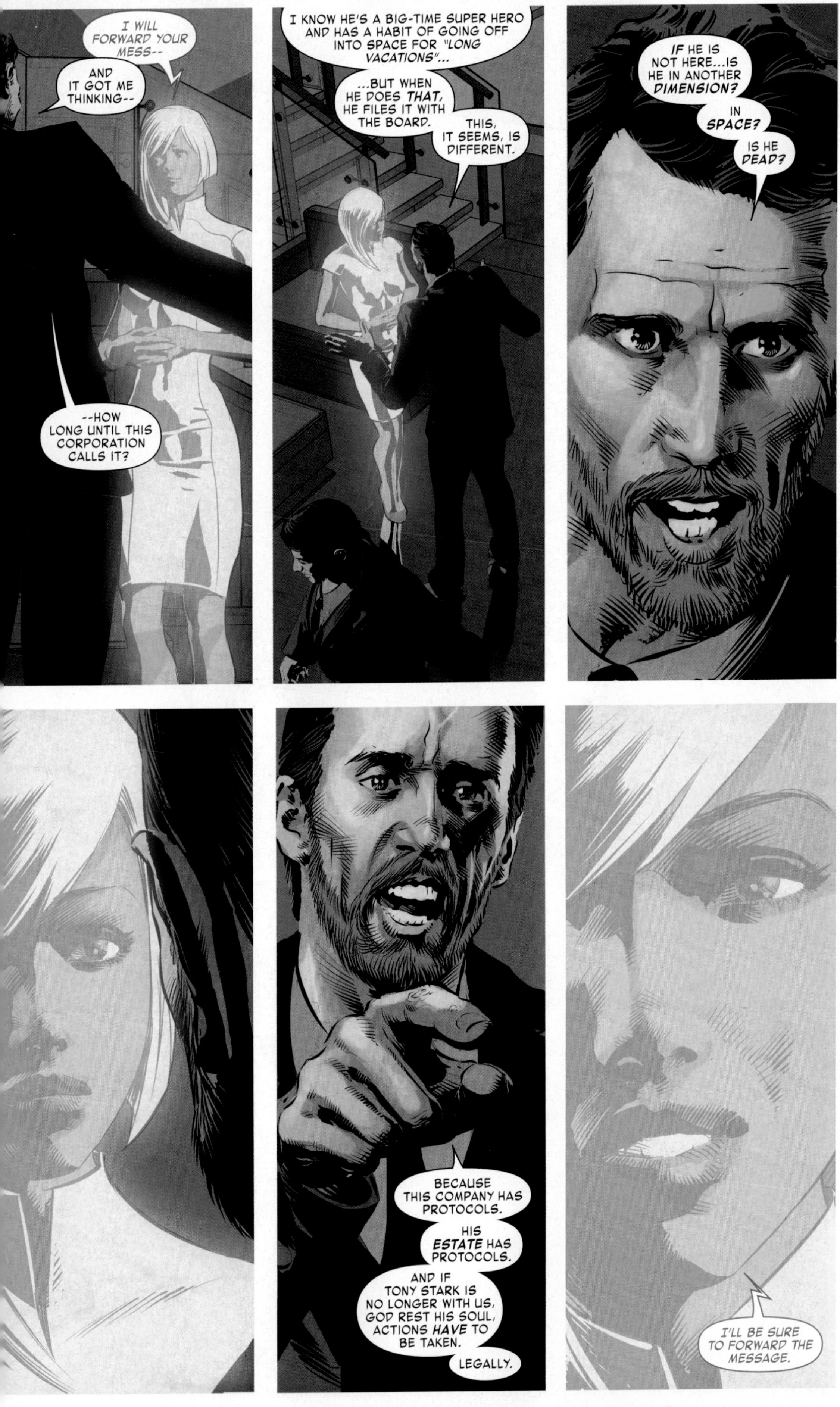
I WILL FORWARD YOUR MESS--
AND IT GOT ME THINKING--
--HOW LONG UNTIL THIS CORPORATION CALLS IT?
I KNOW HE'S A BIG-TIME SUPER HERO AND HAS A HABIT OF GOING OFF INTO SPACE FOR "LONG VACATIONS"...
...BUT WHEN HE DOES THAT, HE FILES IT WITH THE BOARD.
THIS, IT SEEMS, IS DIFFERENT.
IF HE IS NOT HERE...IS HE IN ANOTHER DIMENSION?
IN SPACE?
IS HE DEAD?
BECAUSE THIS COMPANY HAS PROTOCOLS.
HIS ESTATE HAS PROTOCOLS.
AND IF TONY STARK IS NO LONGER WITH US, GOD REST HIS SOUL, ACTIONS HAVE TO BE TAKEN.
LEGALLY.
I'LL BE SURE TO FORWARD THE MESSAGE.

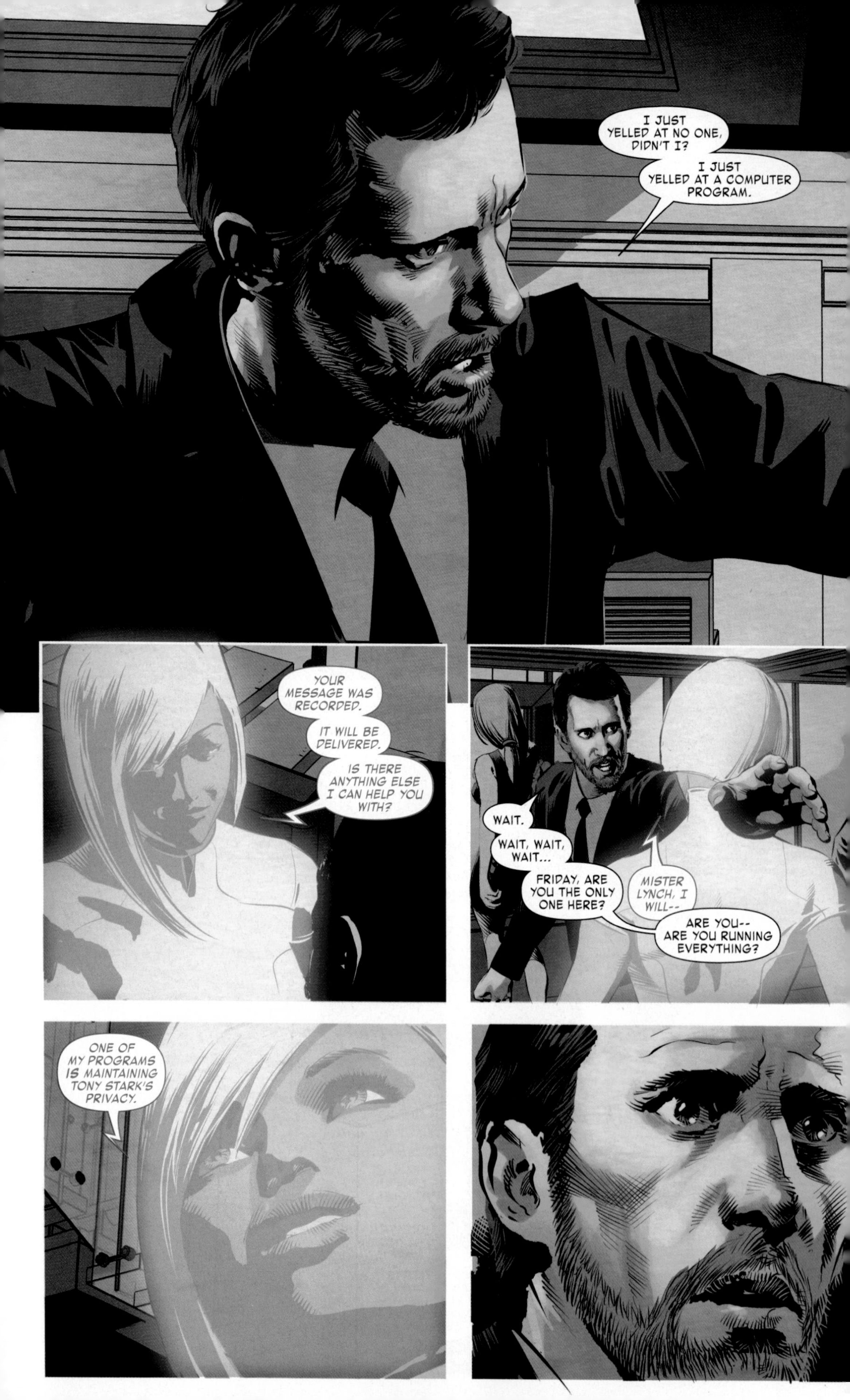
I JUST YELLED AT NO ONE, DIDN'T I?
I JUST YELLED AT A COMPUTER PROGRAM.
YOUR MESSAGE WAS RECORDED.
IT WILL BE DELIVERED.
IS THERE ANYTHING ELSE I CAN HELP YOU WITH?
WAIT.
WAIT, WAIT, WAIT...
FRIDAY, ARE YOU THE ONLY ONE HERE?
MISTER LYNCH, I WILL--
ARE YOU-- ARE YOU RUNNING EVERYTHING?
ONE OF MY PROGRAMS IS MAINTAINING TONY STARK'S PRIVACY.

HAVE YOU BEEN RUNNING *STARK* ALL BY YOURSELF?

IS AN ARTIFICIAL INTELLIGENCE RUNNING THIS COMPANY UNATTENDED?

I ASSURE YOU...

...MY PROGRAMMING IS FULLY FUNCTIONAL.

MY PROGRAMMING IS FULLY FUNCTIONAL.

BUT AS FAR AS YOUR CONCERNS ABOUT MISTER STARK, I HOPE YOU'LL TAKE NO INSULT FROM THIS AND APPRECIATE MY DISCRETION.

%¢&*!

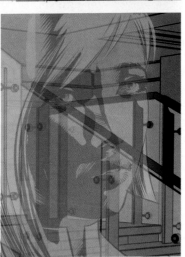

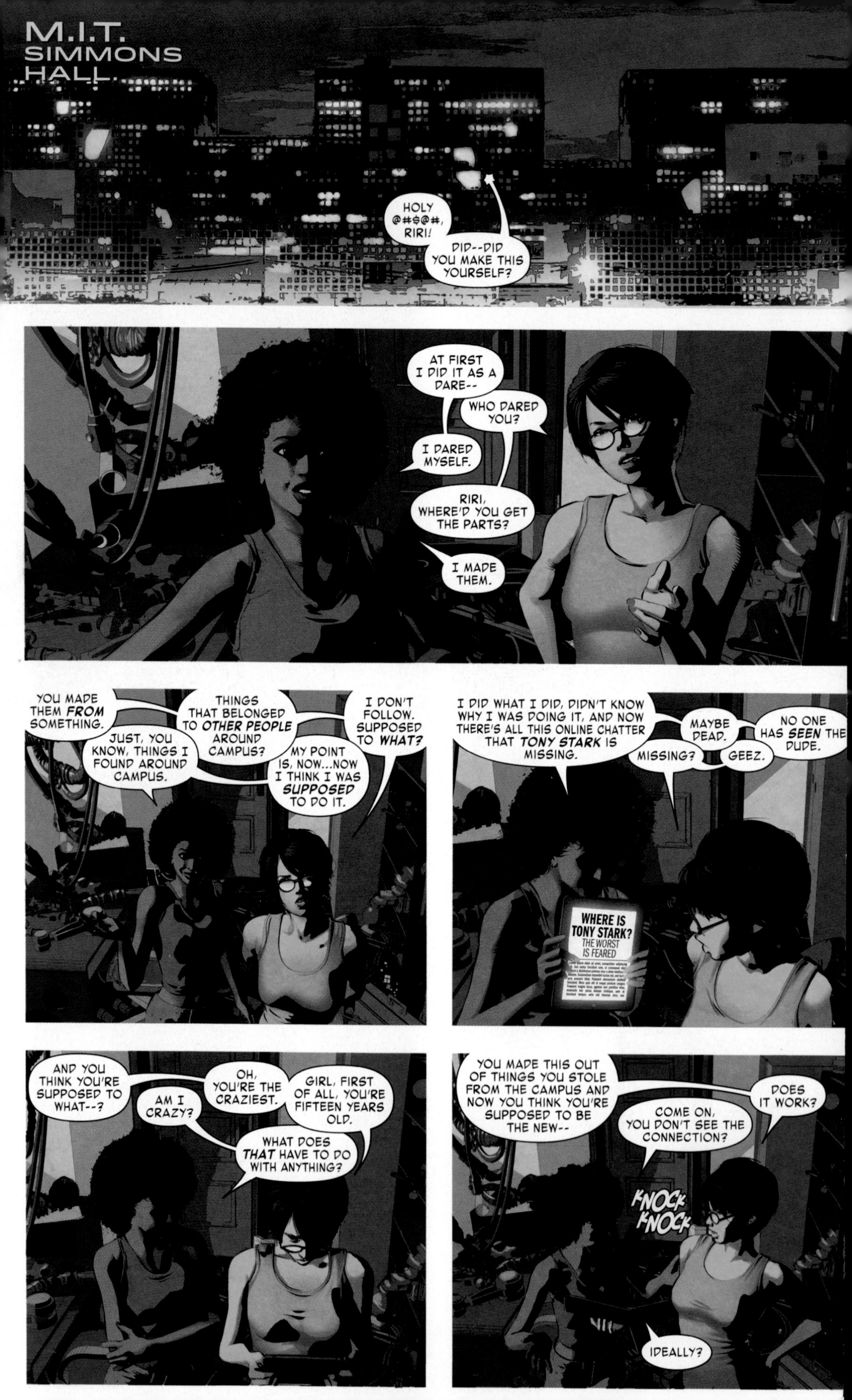
M.I.T. SIMMONS HALL.
HOLY @#$@#, RIRI!
DID--DID YOU MAKE THIS YOURSELF?
AT FIRST I DID IT AS A DARE--
WHO DARED YOU?
I DARED MYSELF.
RIRI, WHERE'D YOU GET THE PARTS?
I MADE THEM.
YOU MADE THEM **FROM** SOMETHING.
JUST, YOU KNOW, THINGS I FOUND AROUND CAMPUS.
THINGS THAT BELONGED TO **OTHER PEOPLE** AROUND CAMPUS?
MY POINT IS, NOW...NOW I THINK I WAS **SUPPOSED** TO DO IT.
I DON'T FOLLOW. SUPPOSED TO **WHAT?**
I DID WHAT I DID, DIDN'T KNOW WHY I WAS DOING IT, AND NOW THERE'S ALL THIS ONLINE CHATTER THAT **TONY STARK** IS MISSING.
MISSING?
MAYBE DEAD.
GEEZ.
NO ONE HAS **SEEN** THE DUDE.
WHERE IS TONY STARK? THE WORST IS FEARED
AND YOU THINK YOU'RE SUPPOSED TO WHAT--?
AM I CRAZY?
OH, YOU'RE THE CRAZIEST.
GIRL, FIRST OF ALL, YOU'RE FIFTEEN YEARS OLD.
WHAT DOES **THAT** HAVE TO DO WITH ANYTHING?
YOU MADE THIS OUT OF THINGS YOU STOLE FROM THE CAMPUS AND NOW YOU THINK YOU'RE SUPPOSED TO BE THE NEW--
COME ON, YOU DON'T SEE THE CONNECTION?
DOES IT WORK?
KNOCK KNOCK
IDEALLY?

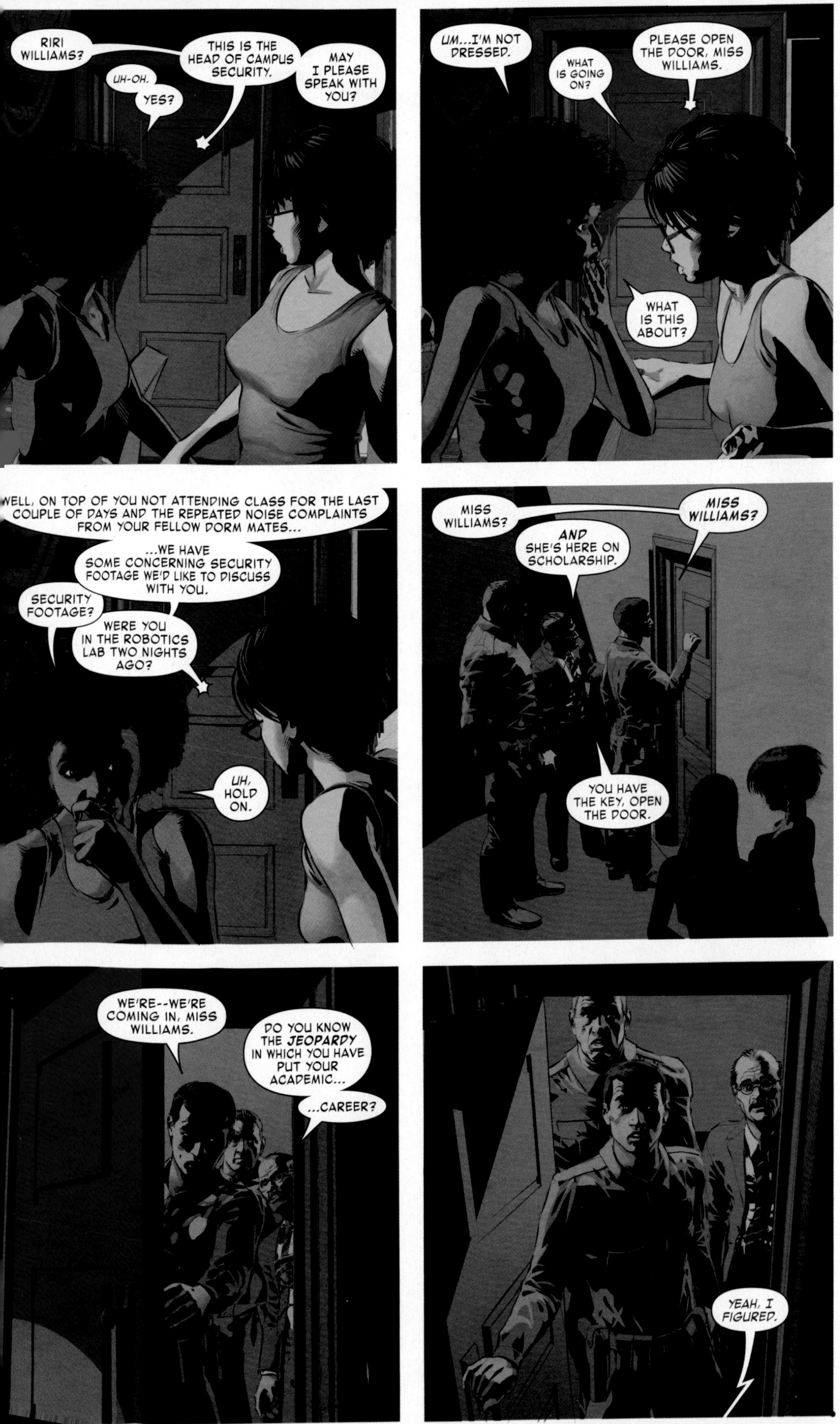
RIRI WILLIAMS?
THIS IS THE HEAD OF CAMPUS SECURITY.
UH-OH.
YES?
MAY I PLEASE SPEAK WITH YOU?
UM...I'M NOT DRESSED.
WHAT IS GOING ON?
PLEASE OPEN THE DOOR, MISS WILLIAMS.
WHAT IS THIS ABOUT?
WELL, ON TOP OF YOU NOT ATTENDING CLASS FOR THE LAST COUPLE OF DAYS AND THE REPEATED NOISE COMPLAINTS FROM YOUR FELLOW DORM MATES...
...WE HAVE SOME CONCERNING SECURITY FOOTAGE WE'D LIKE TO DISCUSS WITH YOU.
SECURITY FOOTAGE?
WERE YOU IN THE ROBOTICS LAB TWO NIGHTS AGO?
UH, HOLD ON.
MISS WILLIAMS?
MISS WILLIAMS?
AND SHE'S HERE ON SCHOLARSHIP.
YOU HAVE THE KEY, OPEN THE DOOR.
WE'RE--WE'RE COMING IN, MISS WILLIAMS.
DO YOU KNOW THE JEOPARDY IN WHICH YOU HAVE PUT YOUR ACADEMIC...
...CAREER?
YEAH, I FIGURED.

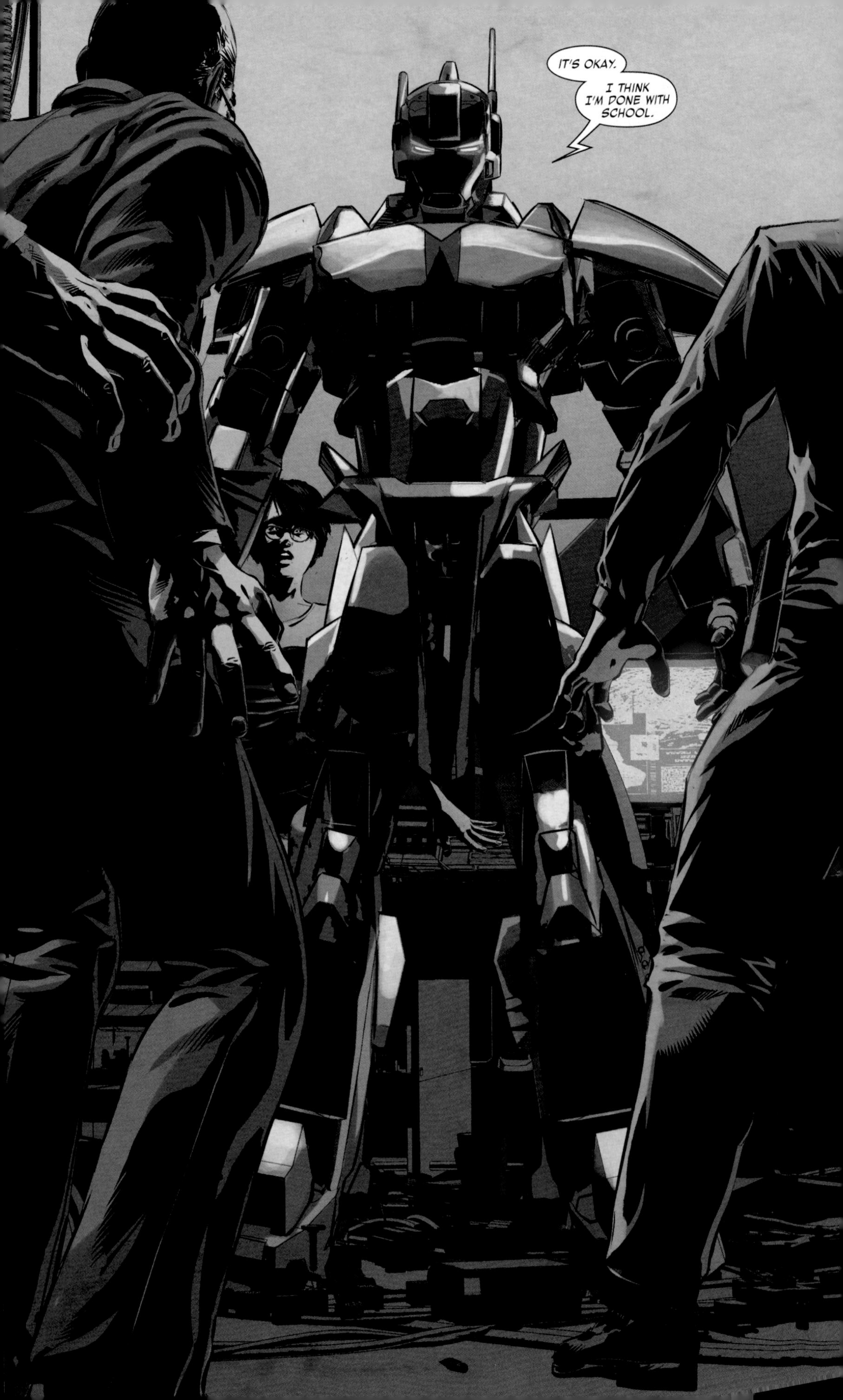
IT'S OKAY.
I THINK I'M DONE WITH SCHOOL.

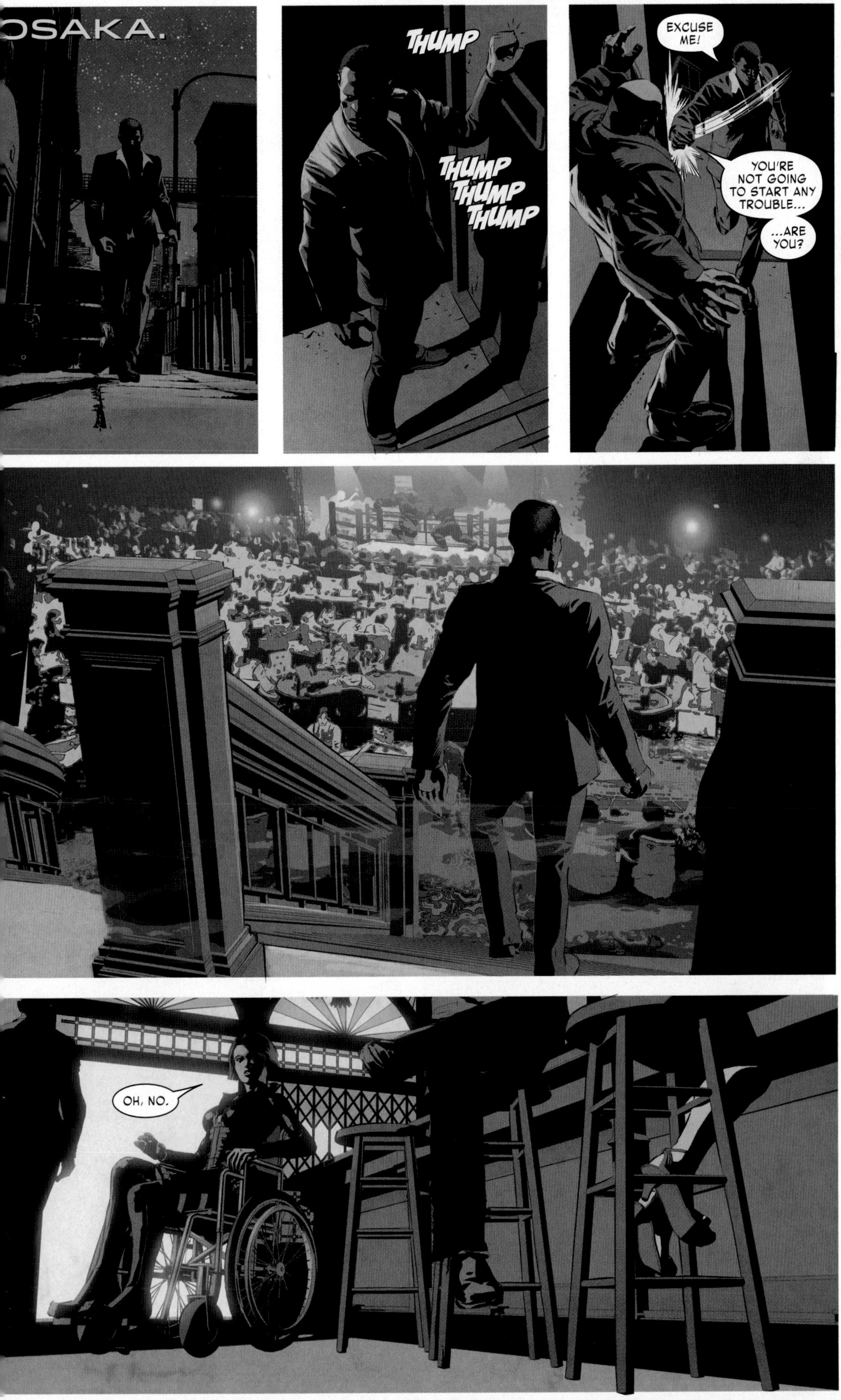
OSAKA.
THUMP
THUMP
THUMP
THUMP
EXCUSE ME!
YOU'RE NOT GOING TO START ANY TROUBLE...
...ARE YOU?
OH, NO.

YUKIO, LAST CHANCE.

WHERE IS HE?

COLONEL RHODES, THIS ISN'T FAIR.

I DO NOT KNOW WHERE TONY STARK IS. NO ONE KNOWS--

SEE, YUKIO, THE WAY I SEE IT IS WE HELP EACH OTHER.

YOU GET TO DO WHATEVER YOU DO HERE, AN' EVERY ONCE IN A WHILE YOU HELP ME.

YOU *STOP* HELPING ME? I START LOSING INTEREST IN HELPING YOU.

I PROMISE YOU...I--I HAVE MY EAR TO THE GROUND.

WHERE IS HE?

I THINK-- HONESTLY, I THINK HE'S DEAD.

I'M SORRY.

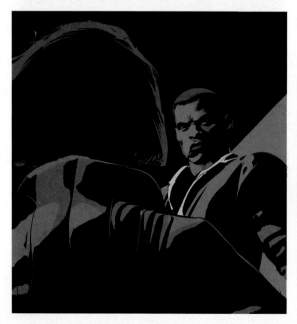

THIS IS RHODES.

THE WORD IS GIVEN.

SHUT IT DOWN.

NO.

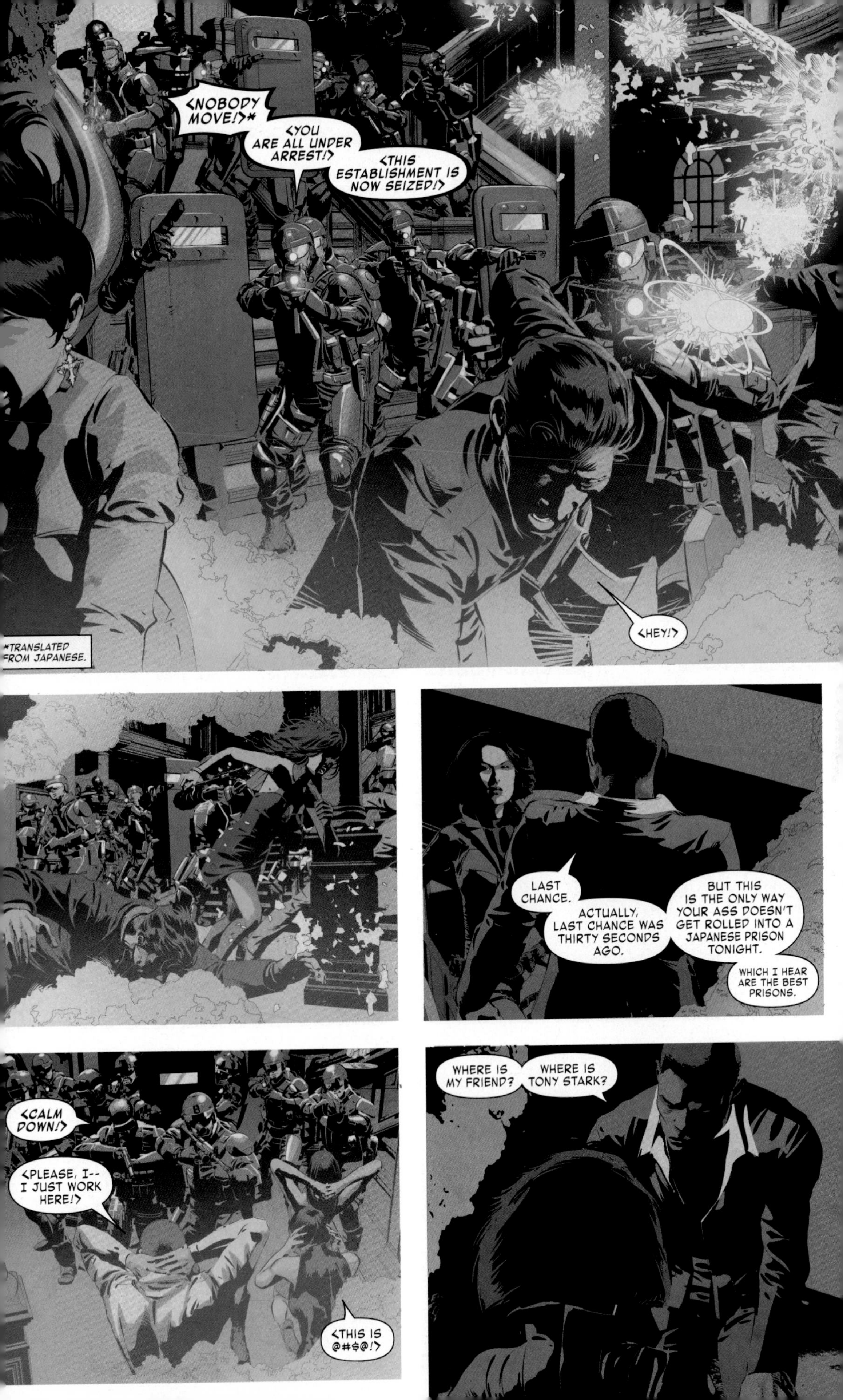
<NOBODY MOVE!>*
<YOU ARE ALL UNDER ARREST!>
<THIS ESTABLISHMENT IS NOW SEIZED!>
<HEY!>
*TRANSLATED FROM JAPANESE.
LAST CHANCE.
ACTUALLY, LAST CHANCE WAS THIRTY SECONDS AGO.
BUT THIS IS THE ONLY WAY YOUR ASS DOESN'T GET ROLLED INTO A JAPANESE PRISON TONIGHT.
WHICH I HEAR ARE THE BEST PRISONS.
<CALM DOWN!>
<PLEASE, I-- I JUST WORK HERE!>
<THIS IS @#$@!>
WHERE IS MY FRIEND?
WHERE IS TONY STARK?

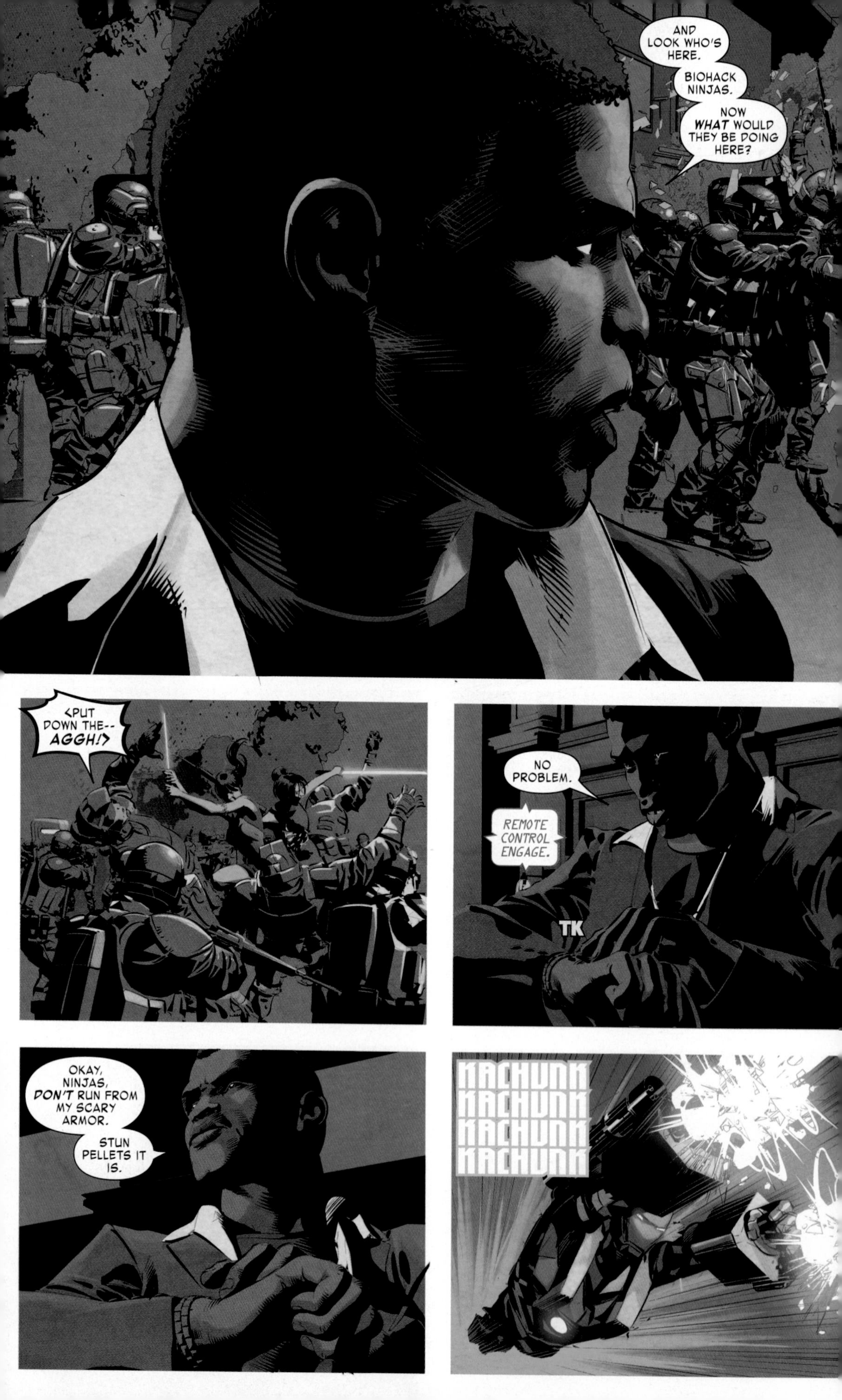
AND LOOK WHO'S HERE.
BIOHACK NINJAS.
NOW *WHAT* WOULD THEY BE DOING HERE?
<PUT DOWN THE-- *AGGH!*>
NO PROBLEM.
REMOTE CONTROL ENGAGE.
TK
OKAY, NINJAS, *DON'T* RUN FROM MY SCARY ARMOR.
STUN PELLETS IT IS.
KACHUNK KACHUNK KACHUNK KACHUNK

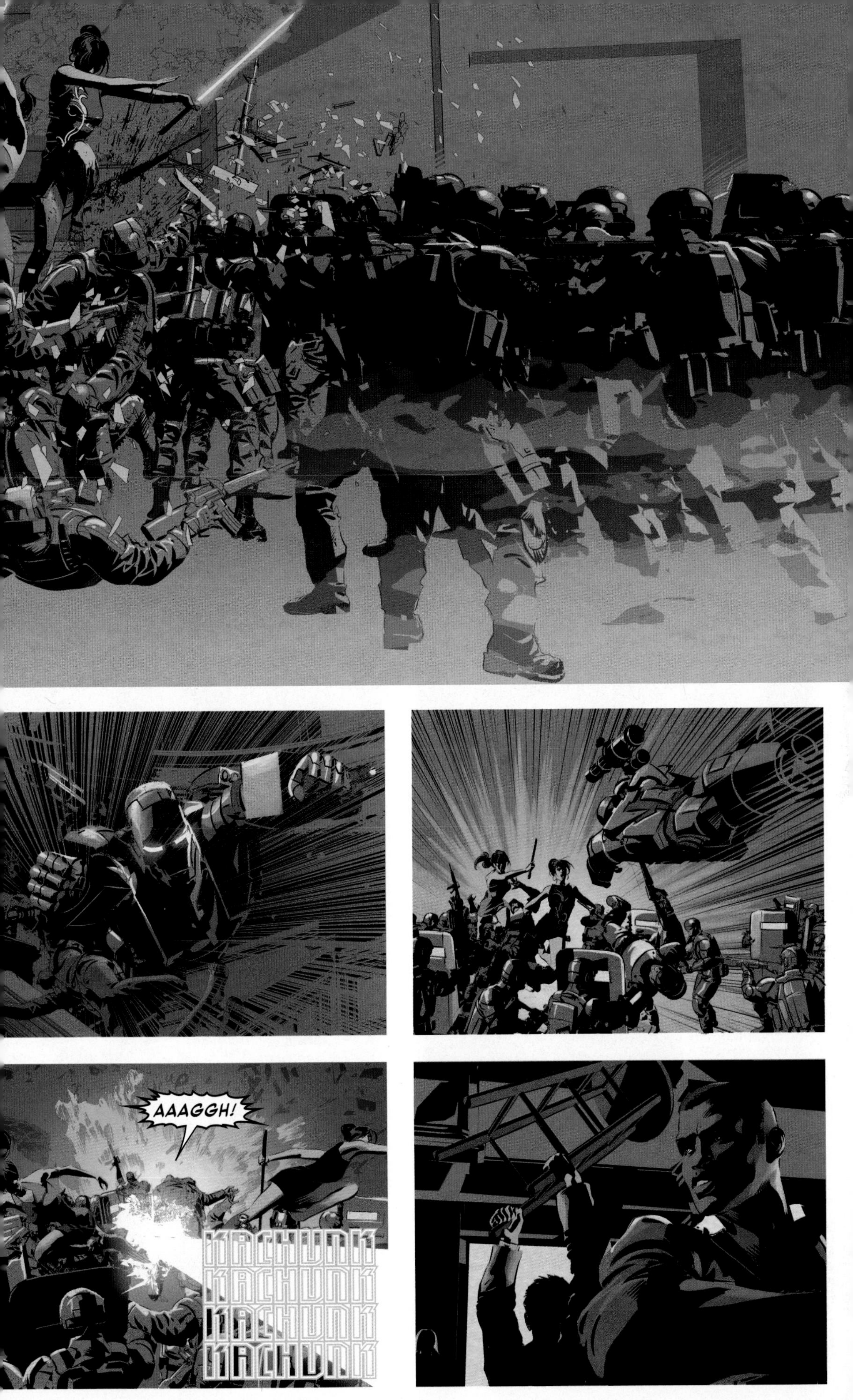
AAAGGH!
KACHUNK
KACHUNK
KACHUNK
KACHUNK

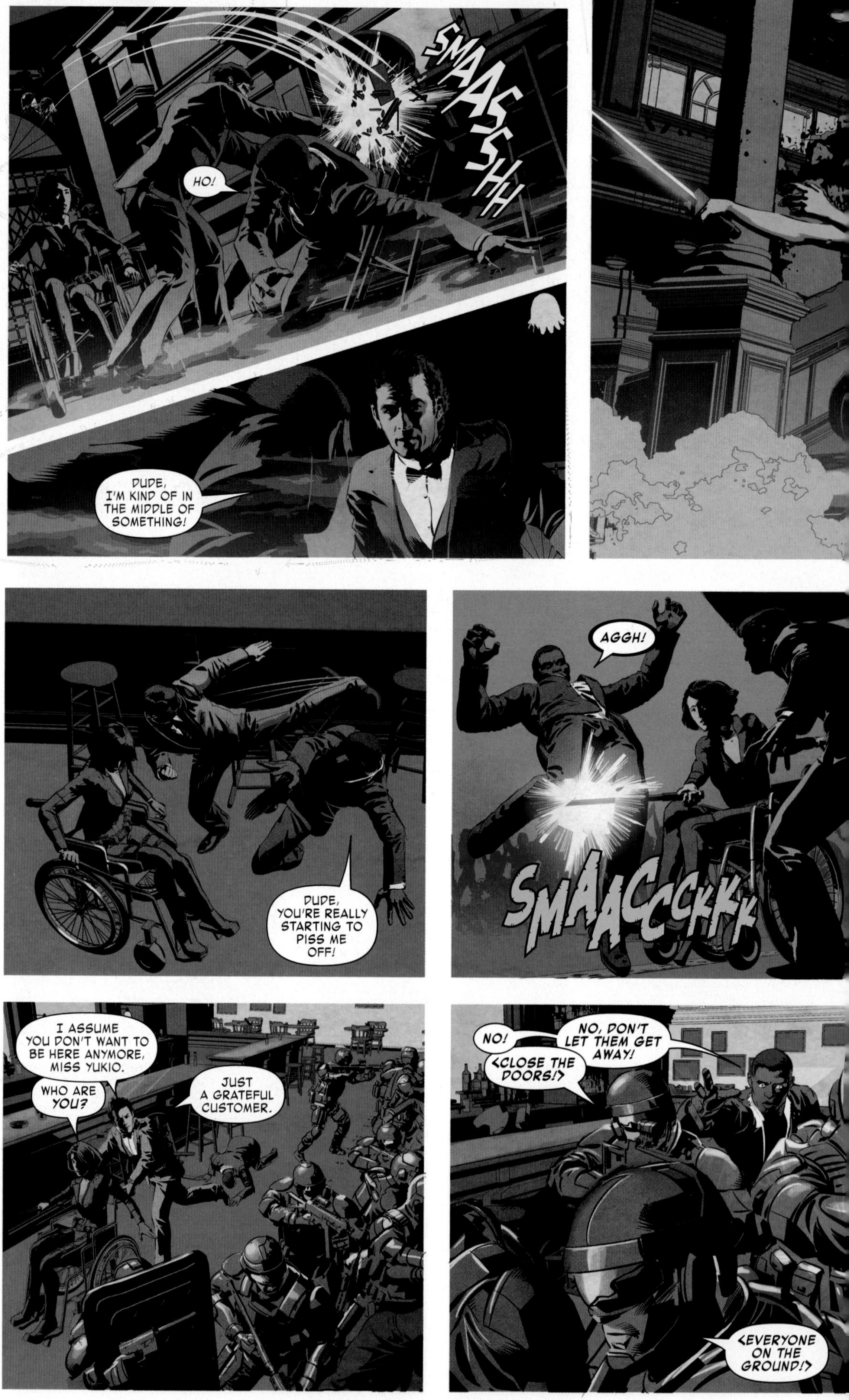
SMAASSHH
HO!
DUDE, I'M KIND OF IN THE MIDDLE OF SOMETHING!
DUDE, YOU'RE REALLY STARTING TO PISS ME OFF!
AGGH!
SMAACCCKKK
I ASSUME YOU DON'T WANT TO BE HERE ANYMORE, MISS YUKIO.
WHO ARE YOU?
JUST A GRATEFUL CUSTOMER.
NO!
NO, DON'T LET THEM GET AWAY!
<CLOSE THE DOORS!>
<EVERYONE ON THE GROUND!>

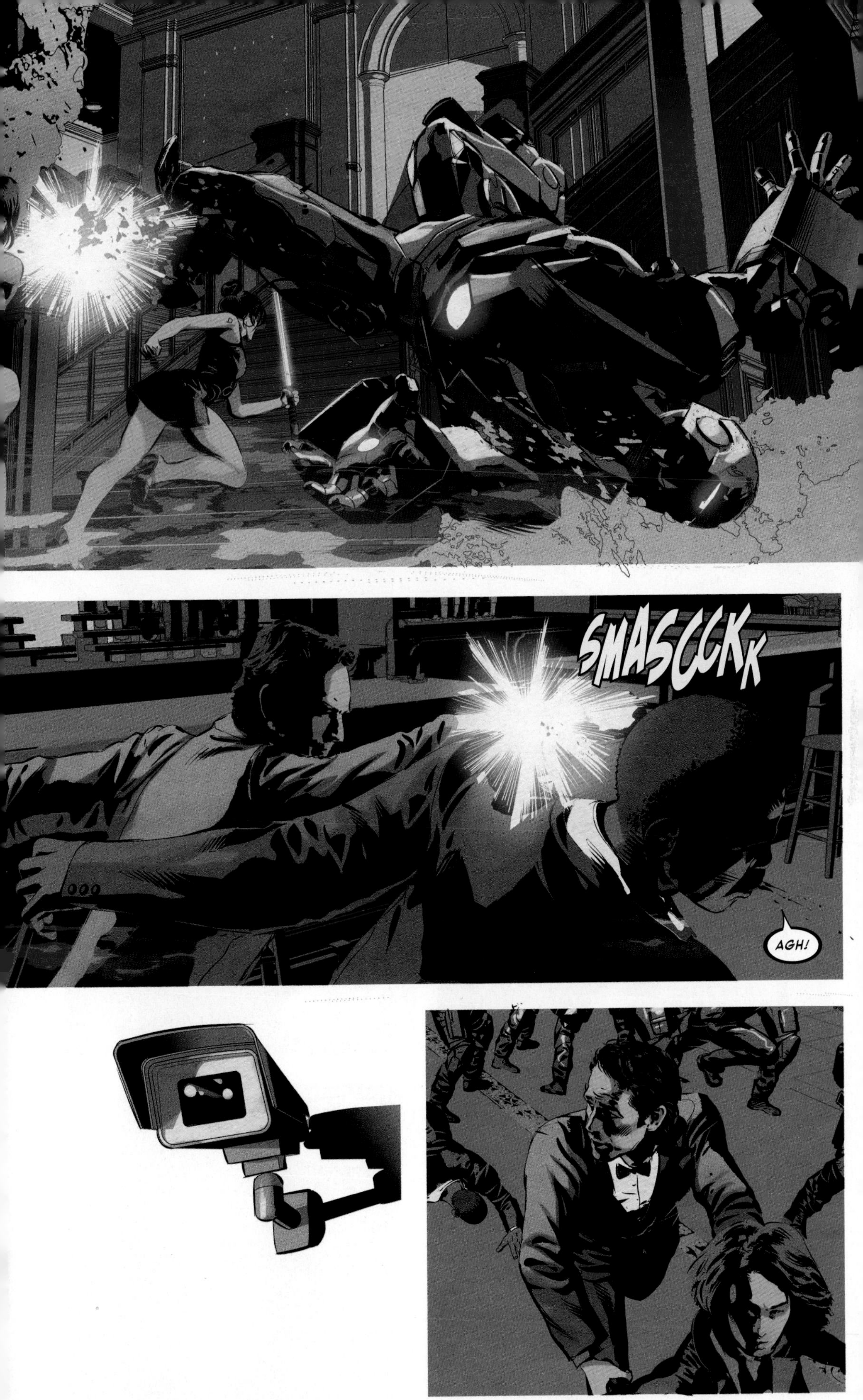
SMASCCKK
AGH!

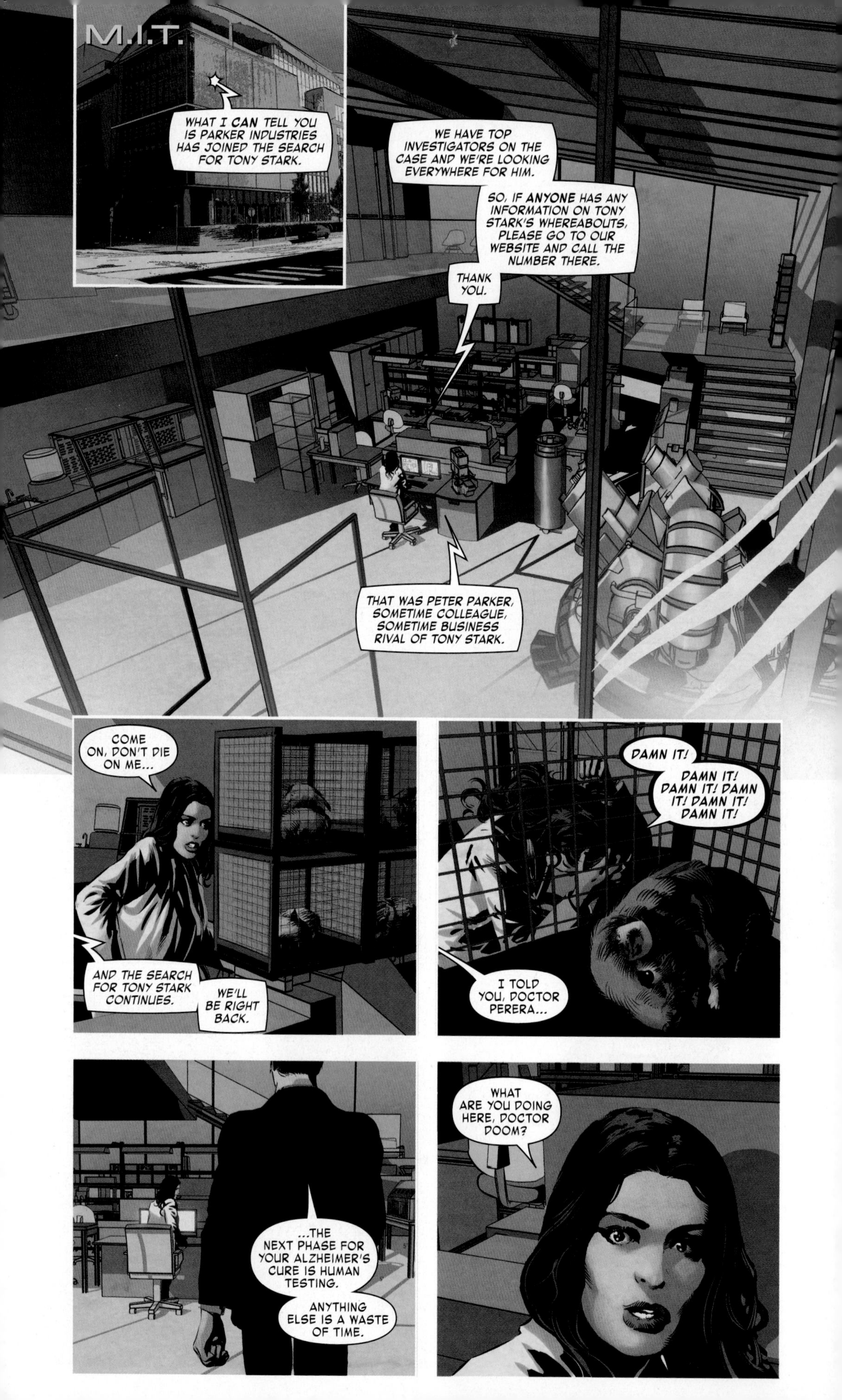
M.I.T.
WHAT I CAN TELL YOU IS PARKER INDUSTRIES HAS JOINED THE SEARCH FOR TONY STARK.
WE HAVE TOP INVESTIGATORS ON THE CASE AND WE'RE LOOKING EVERYWHERE FOR HIM.
SO, IF ANYONE HAS ANY INFORMATION ON TONY STARK'S WHEREABOUTS, PLEASE GO TO OUR WEBSITE AND CALL THE NUMBER THERE.
THANK YOU.
THAT WAS PETER PARKER, SOMETIME COLLEAGUE, SOMETIME BUSINESS RIVAL OF TONY STARK.
COME ON, DON'T DIE ON ME...
AND THE SEARCH FOR TONY STARK CONTINUES.
WE'LL BE RIGHT BACK.
DAMN IT!
DAMN IT! DAMN IT! DAMN IT! DAMN IT! DAMN IT!
I TOLD YOU, DOCTOR PERERA...
...THE NEXT PHASE FOR YOUR ALZHEIMER'S CURE IS HUMAN TESTING.
ANYTHING ELSE IS A WASTE OF TIME.
WHAT ARE YOU DOING HERE, DOCTOR DOOM?

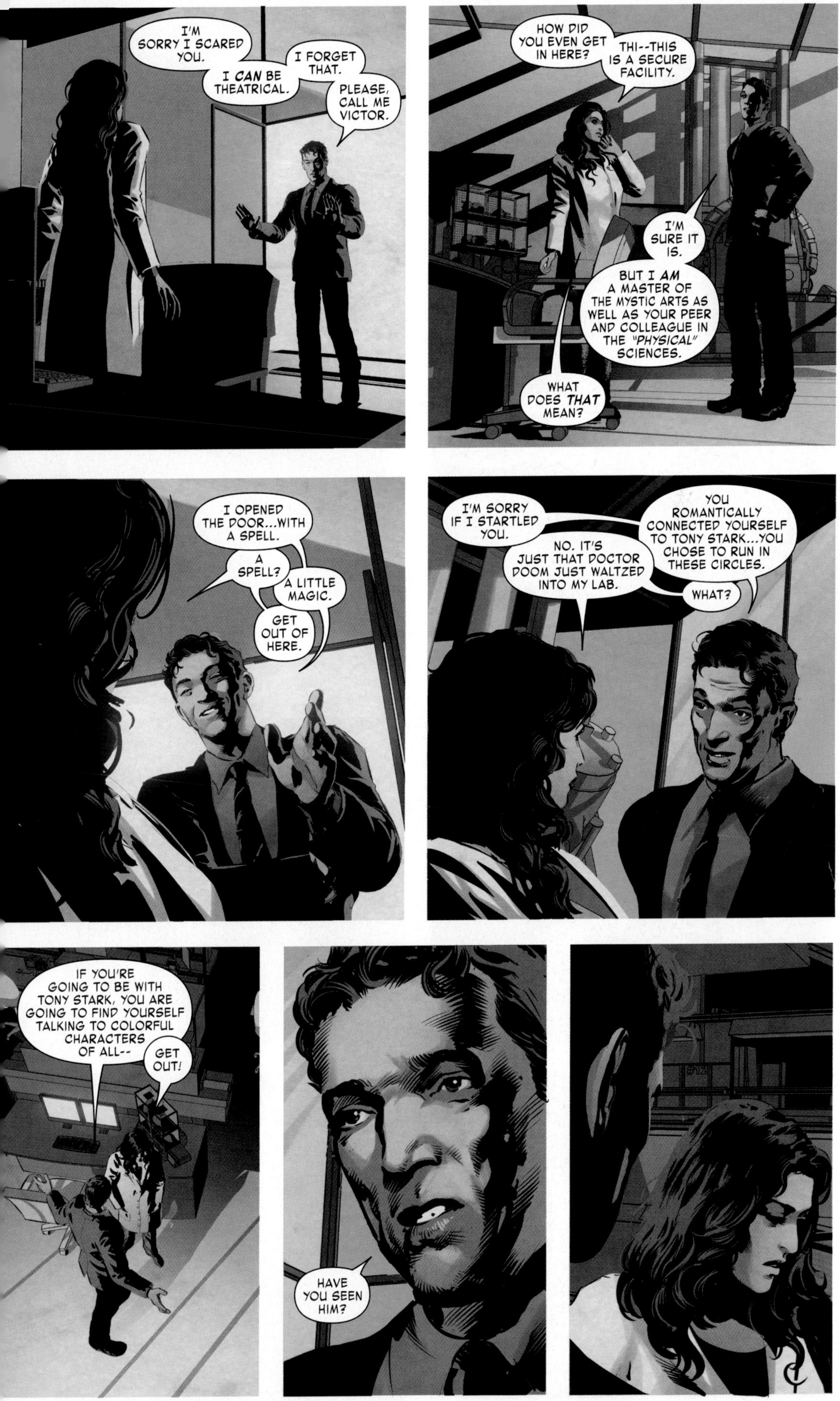
I'M SORRY I SCARED YOU.
I CAN BE THEATRICAL.
I FORGET THAT.
PLEASE, CALL ME VICTOR.
HOW DID YOU EVEN GET IN HERE?
THI--THIS IS A SECURE FACILITY.
I'M SURE IT IS.
BUT I AM A MASTER OF THE MYSTIC ARTS AS WELL AS YOUR PEER AND COLLEAGUE IN THE "PHYSICAL" SCIENCES.
WHAT DOES THAT MEAN?
I OPENED THE DOOR...WITH A SPELL.
A SPELL?
A LITTLE MAGIC.
GET OUT OF HERE.
I'M SORRY IF I STARTLED YOU.
NO. IT'S JUST THAT DOCTOR DOOM JUST WALTZED INTO MY LAB.
YOU ROMANTICALLY CONNECTED YOURSELF TO TONY STARK...YOU CHOSE TO RUN IN THESE CIRCLES.
WHAT?
IF YOU'RE GOING TO BE WITH TONY STARK, YOU ARE GOING TO FIND YOURSELF TALKING TO COLORFUL CHARACTERS OF ALL--
GET OUT!
HAVE YOU SEEN HIM?

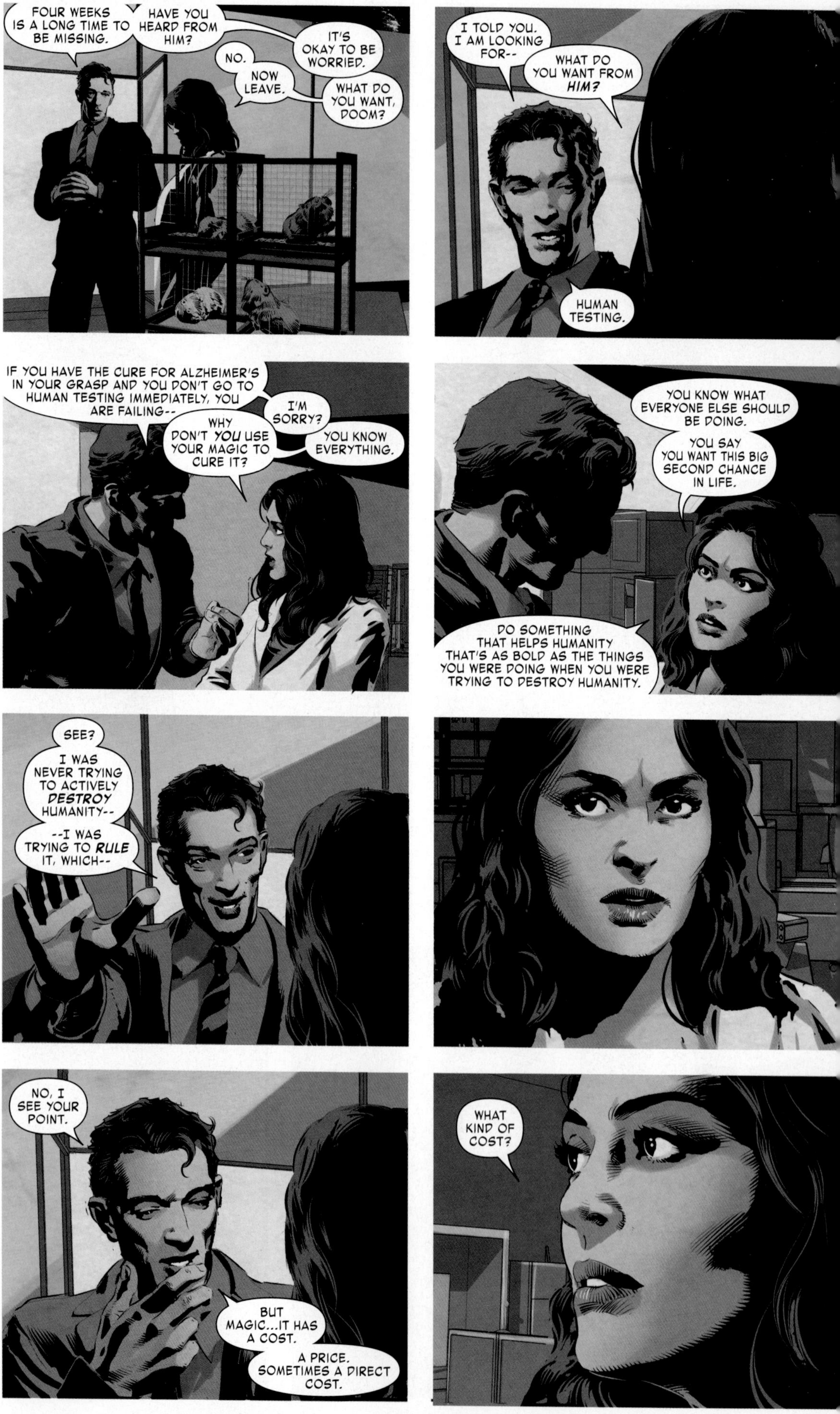

FOUR WEEKS IS A LONG TIME TO BE MISSING.
HAVE YOU HEARD FROM HIM?
IT'S OKAY TO BE WORRIED.
NO.
NOW LEAVE.
WHAT DO YOU WANT, DOOM?
I TOLD YOU. I AM LOOKING FOR--
WHAT DO YOU WANT FROM HIM?
HUMAN TESTING.
IF YOU HAVE THE CURE FOR ALZHEIMER'S IN YOUR GRASP AND YOU DON'T GO TO HUMAN TESTING IMMEDIATELY, YOU ARE FAILING--
I'M SORRY?
WHY DON'T YOU USE YOUR MAGIC TO CURE IT?
YOU KNOW EVERYTHING.
YOU KNOW WHAT EVERYONE ELSE SHOULD BE DOING.
YOU SAY YOU WANT THIS BIG SECOND CHANCE IN LIFE.
DO SOMETHING THAT HELPS HUMANITY THAT'S AS BOLD AS THE THINGS YOU WERE DOING WHEN YOU WERE TRYING TO DESTROY HUMANITY.
SEE?
I WAS NEVER TRYING TO ACTIVELY DESTROY HUMANITY--
--I WAS TRYING TO RULE IT, WHICH--
NO, I SEE YOUR POINT.
BUT MAGIC...IT HAS A COST.
A PRICE. SOMETIMES A DIRECT COST.
WHAT KIND OF COST?

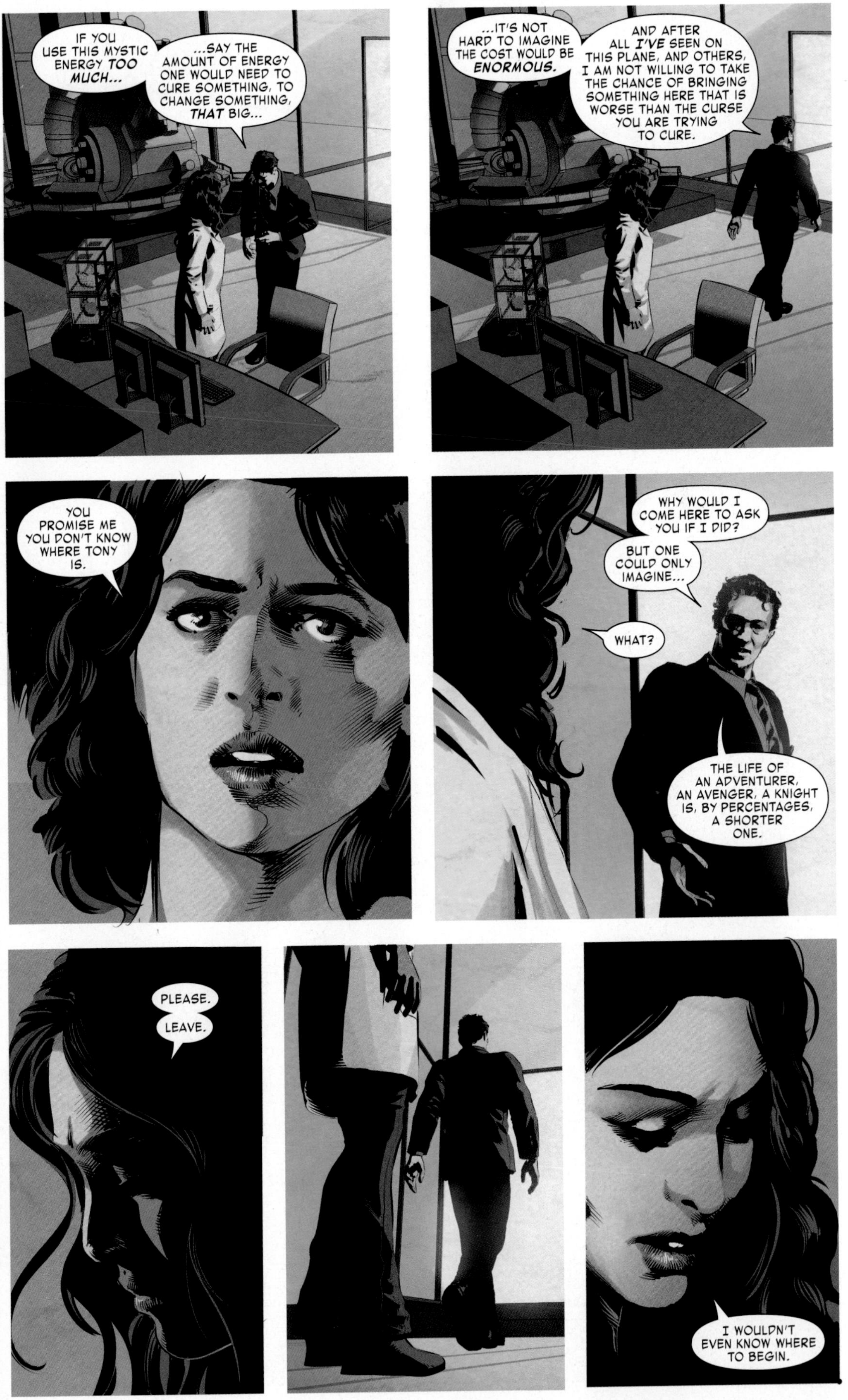
IF YOU USE THIS MYSTIC ENERGY *TOO MUCH...*
...SAY THE AMOUNT OF ENERGY ONE WOULD NEED TO CURE SOMETHING, TO CHANGE SOMETHING, *THAT* BIG...
...IT'S NOT HARD TO IMAGINE THE COST WOULD BE *ENORMOUS.*
AND AFTER ALL *I'VE* SEEN ON THIS PLANE, AND OTHERS, I AM NOT WILLING TO TAKE THE CHANCE OF BRINGING SOMETHING HERE THAT IS WORSE THAN THE CURSE YOU ARE TRYING TO CURE.
YOU PROMISE ME YOU DON'T KNOW WHERE TONY IS.
WHY WOULD I COME HERE TO ASK YOU IF I DID?
BUT ONE COULD ONLY IMAGINE...
WHAT?
THE LIFE OF AN ADVENTURER, AN AVENGER, A KNIGHT IS, BY PERCENTAGES, A SHORTER ONE.
PLEASE.
LEAVE.
I WOULDN'T EVEN KNOW WHERE TO BEGIN.

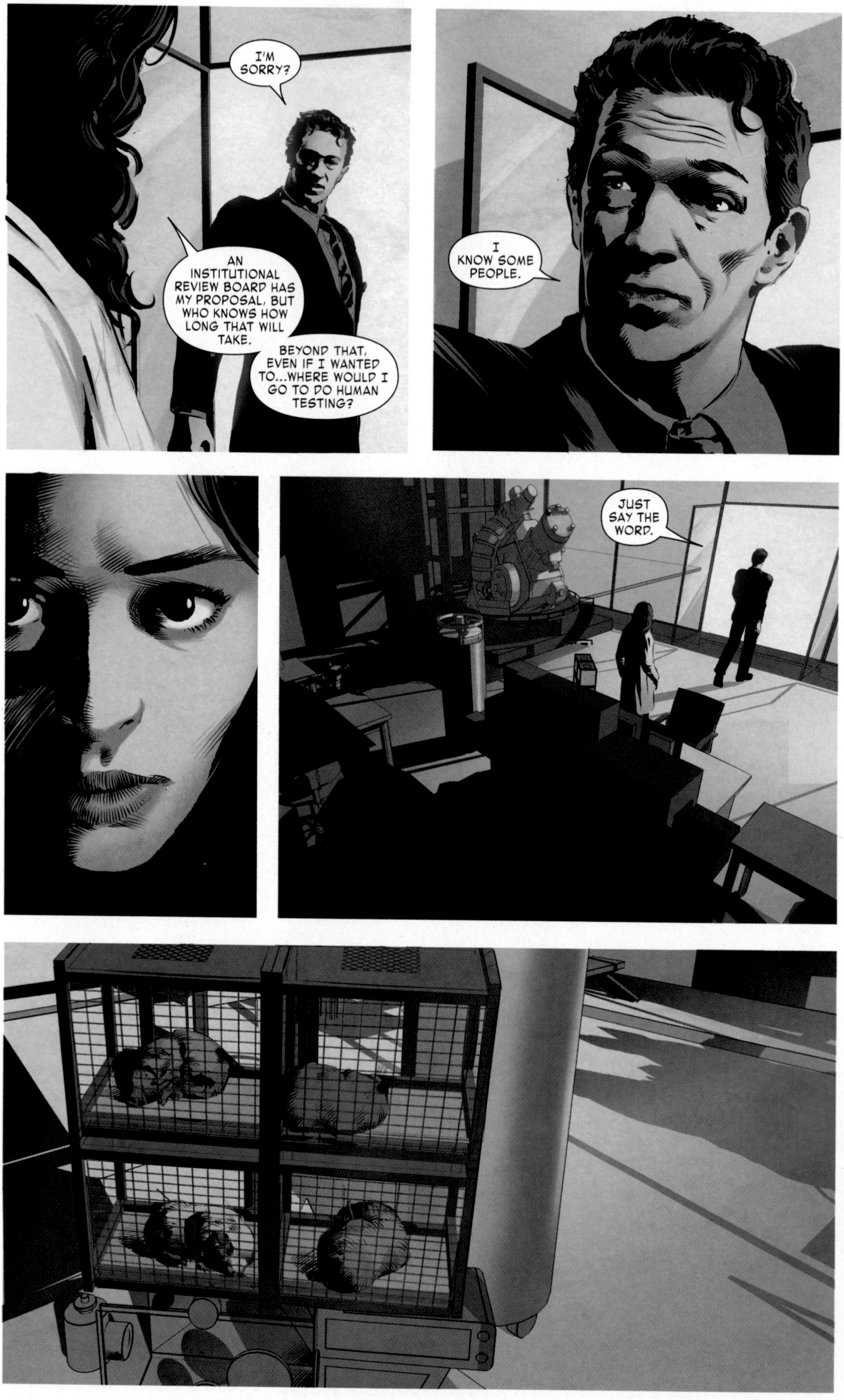
I'M SORRY?
AN INSTITUTIONAL REVIEW BOARD HAS MY PROPOSAL, BUT WHO KNOWS HOW LONG THAT WILL TAKE.
BEYOND THAT, EVEN IF I WANTED TO...WHERE WOULD I GO TO DO HUMAN TESTING?
I KNOW SOME PEOPLE.
JUST SAY THE WORD.

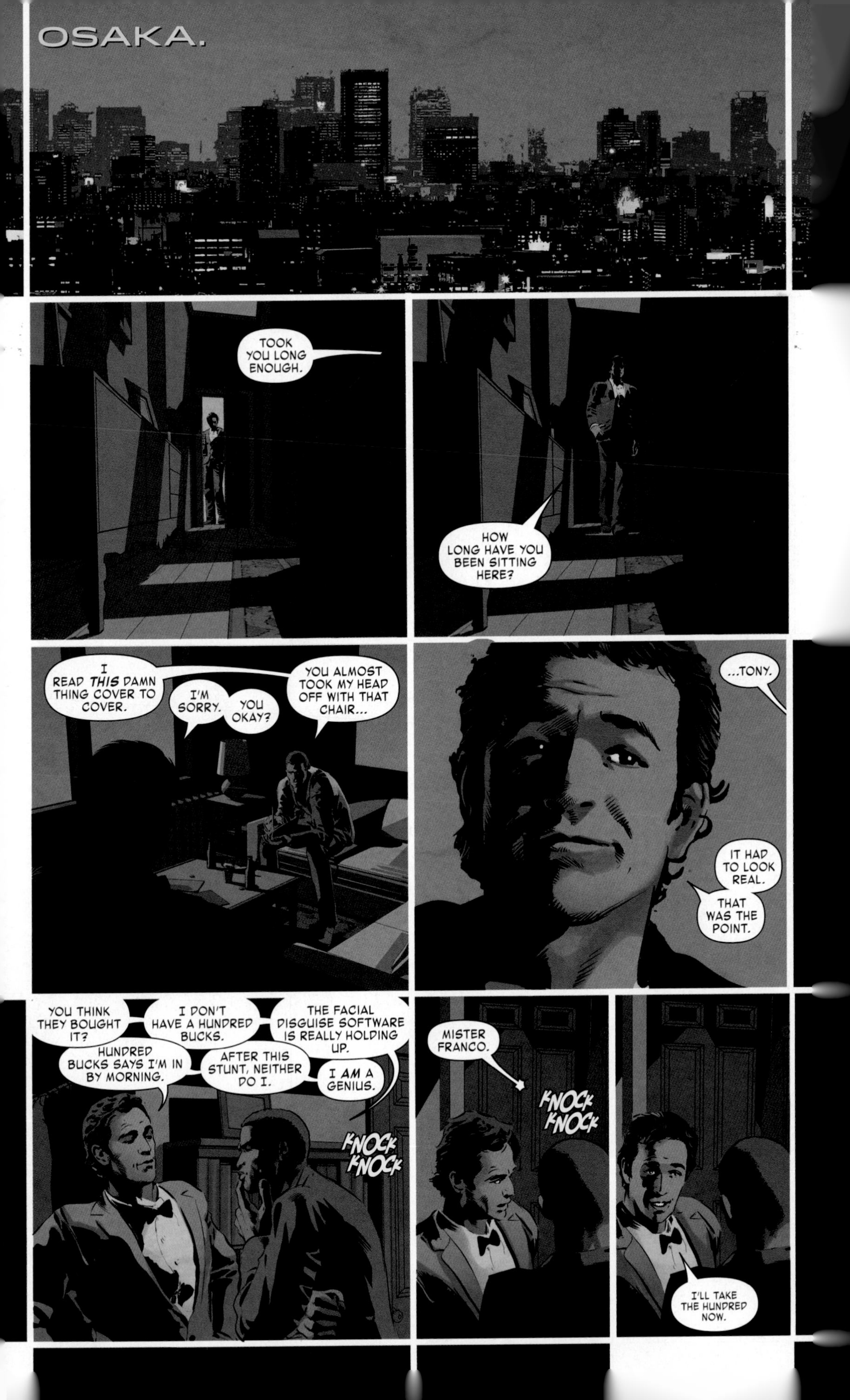
OSAKA.
TOOK YOU LONG ENOUGH.
HOW LONG HAVE YOU BEEN SITTING HERE?
I READ THIS DAMN THING COVER TO COVER.
I'M SORRY.
YOU OKAY?
YOU ALMOST TOOK MY HEAD OFF WITH THAT CHAIR...
...TONY.
IT HAD TO LOOK REAL.
THAT WAS THE POINT.
YOU THINK THEY BOUGHT IT?
I DON'T HAVE A HUNDRED BUCKS.
THE FACIAL DISGUISE SOFTWARE IS REALLY HOLDING UP.
HUNDRED BUCKS SAYS I'M IN BY MORNING.
AFTER THIS STUNT, NEITHER DO I.
I AM A GENIUS.
KNOCK KNOCK
MISTER FRANCO.
KNOCK KNOCK
I'LL TAKE THE HUNDRED NOW.

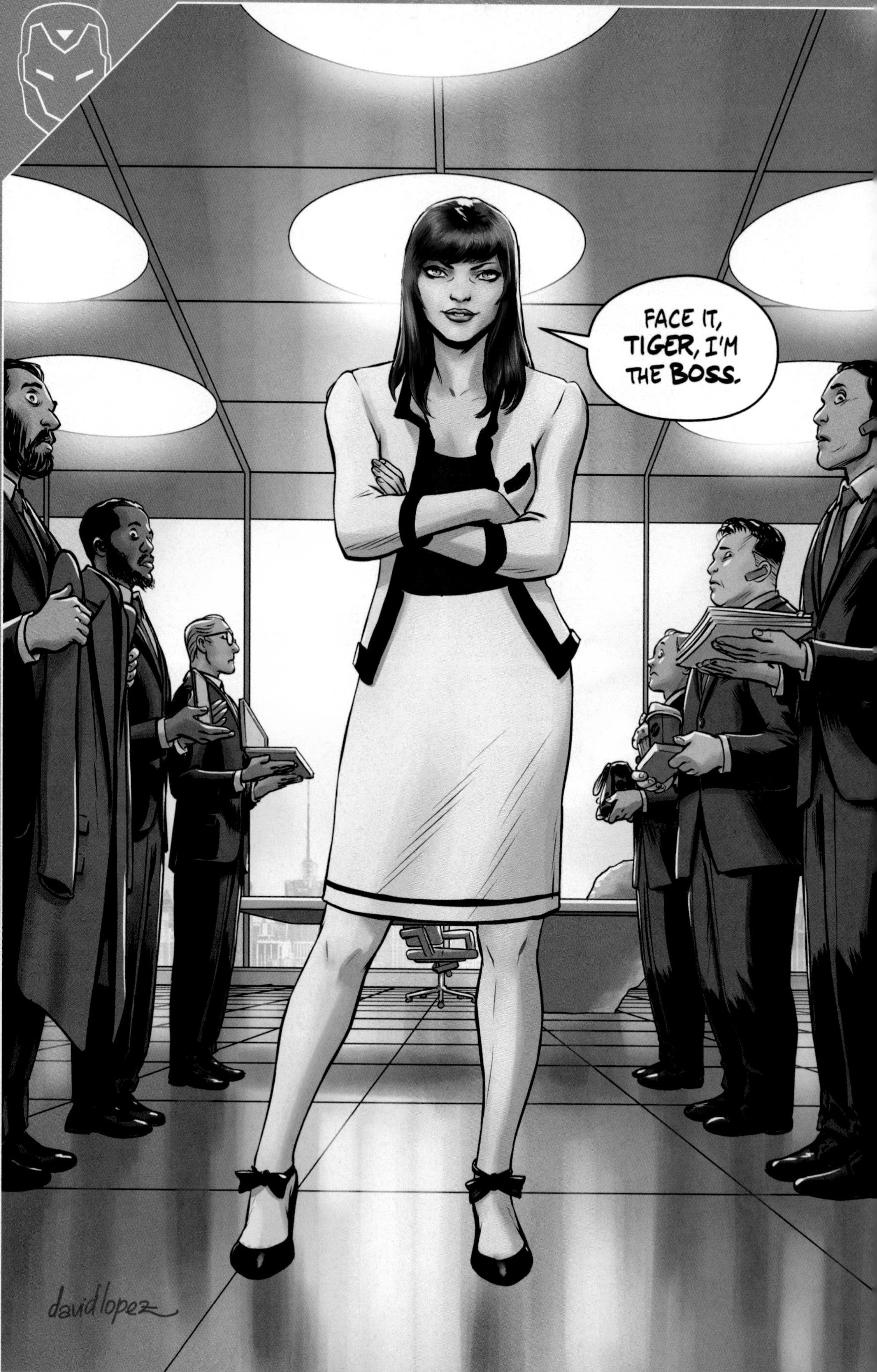
FACE IT, TIGER, I'M THE BOSS.
david lopez

#7 WOMEN OF POWER VARIANT BY DAVID LOPEZ

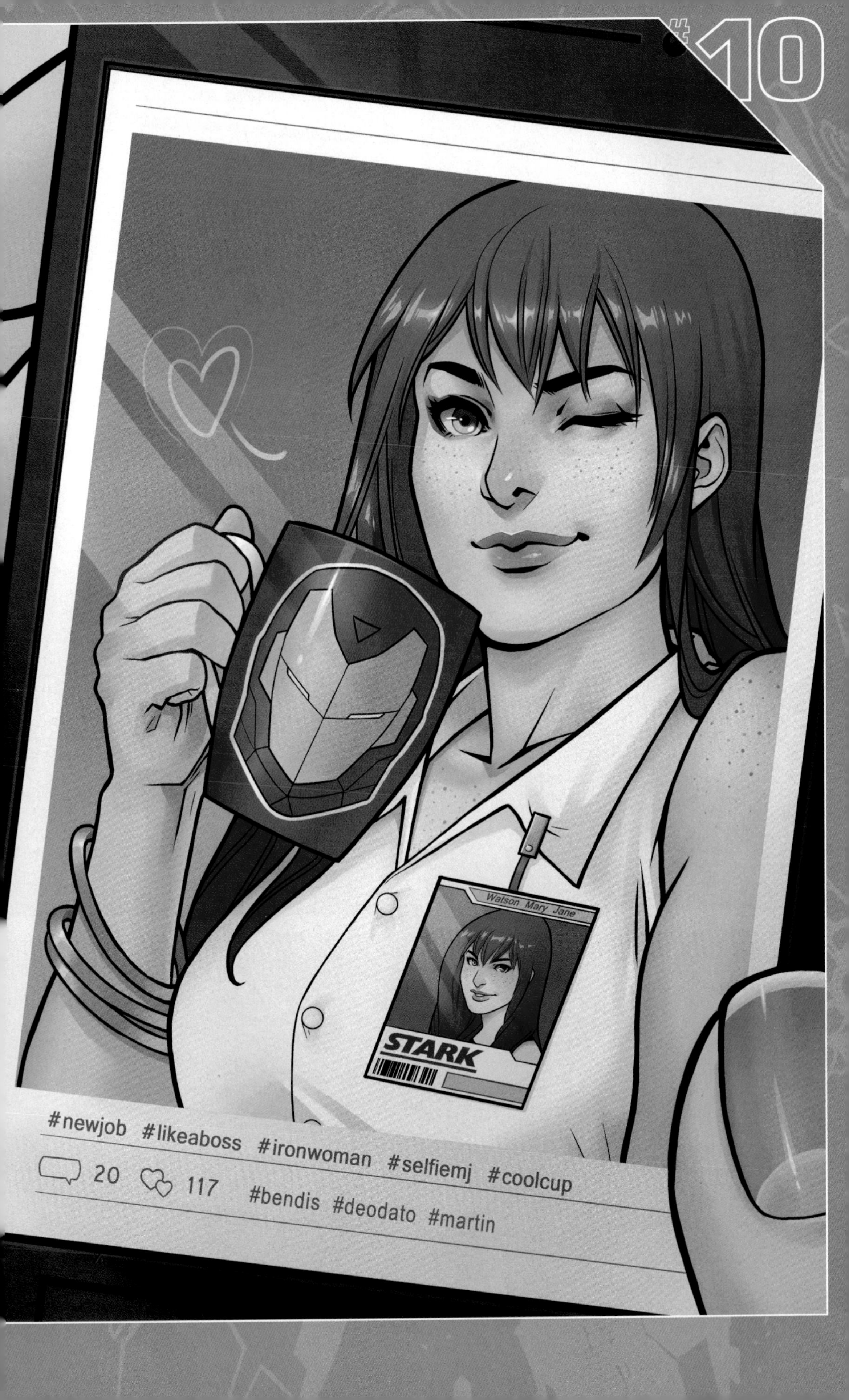
#10
Watson Mary Jane
STARK
#newjob #likeaboss #ironwoman #selfiemj #coolcup
20 117 #bendis #deodato #martin

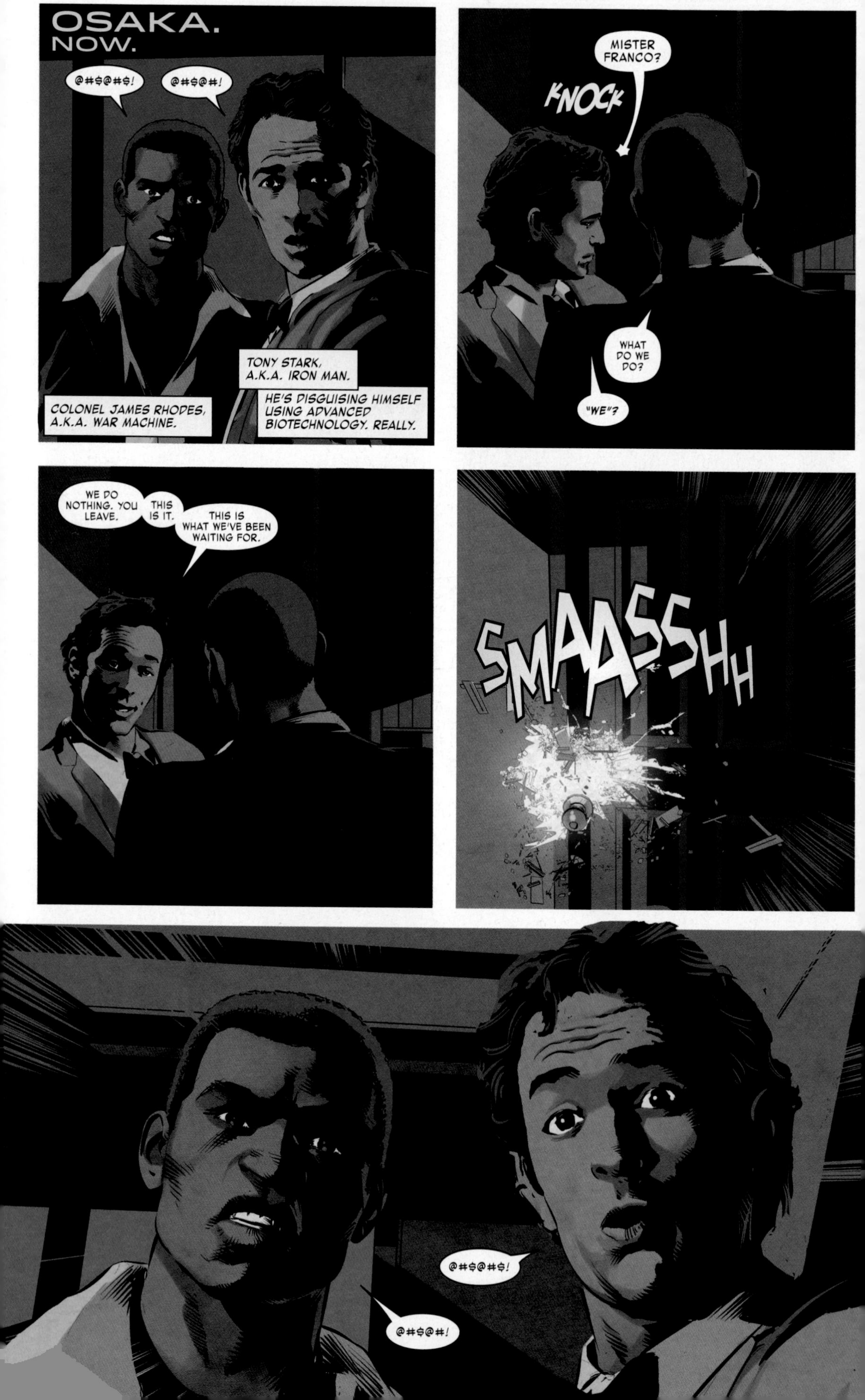
OSAKA.
NOW.
@#$@#$!
@#$@#!
COLONEL JAMES RHODES, A.K.A. WAR MACHINE.
TONY STARK, A.K.A. IRON MAN.
HE'S DISGUISING HIMSELF USING ADVANCED BIOTECHNOLOGY. REALLY.
MISTER FRANCO?
KNOCK
WHAT DO WE DO?
"WE"?
WE DO NOTHING. YOU LEAVE.
THIS IS IT.
THIS IS WHAT WE'VE BEEN WAITING FOR.
SMAASSHH
@#$@#$!
@#$@#!

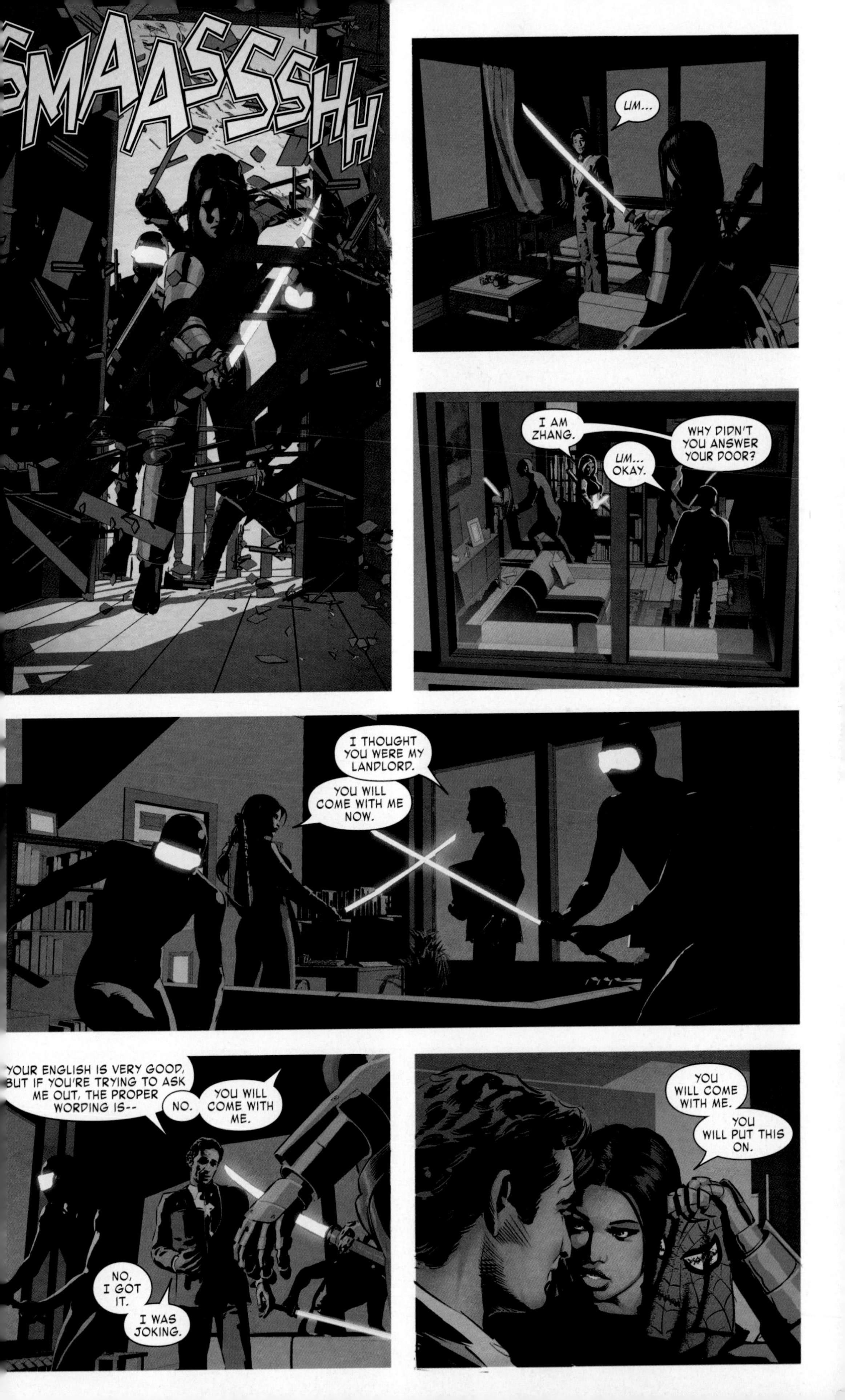
SMAASSSHH
UM...
I AM ZHANG.
WHY DIDN'T YOU ANSWER YOUR DOOR?
UM... OKAY.
I THOUGHT YOU WERE MY LANDLORD.
YOU WILL COME WITH ME NOW.
YOUR ENGLISH IS VERY GOOD, BUT IF YOU'RE TRYING TO ASK ME OUT, THE PROPER WORDING IS--
NO.
YOU WILL COME WITH ME.
NO, I GOT IT.
I WAS JOKING.
YOU WILL COME WITH ME.
YOU WILL PUT THIS ON.

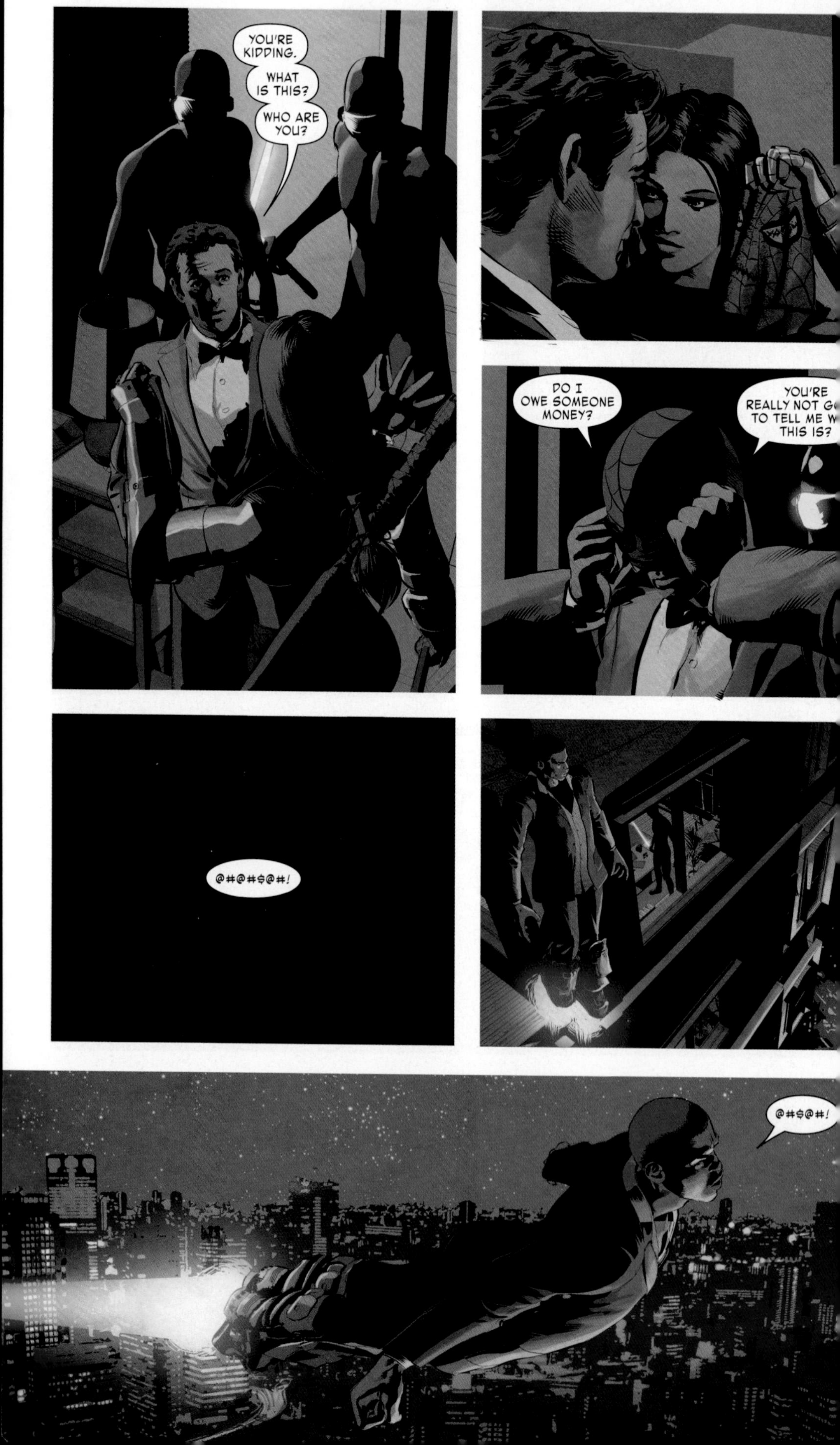
YOU'RE KIDDING.
WHAT IS THIS?
WHO ARE YOU?
DO I OWE SOMEONE MONEY?
YOU'RE REALLY NOT G
TO TELL ME W
THIS IS?
@#@#$@#!
@#$@#!

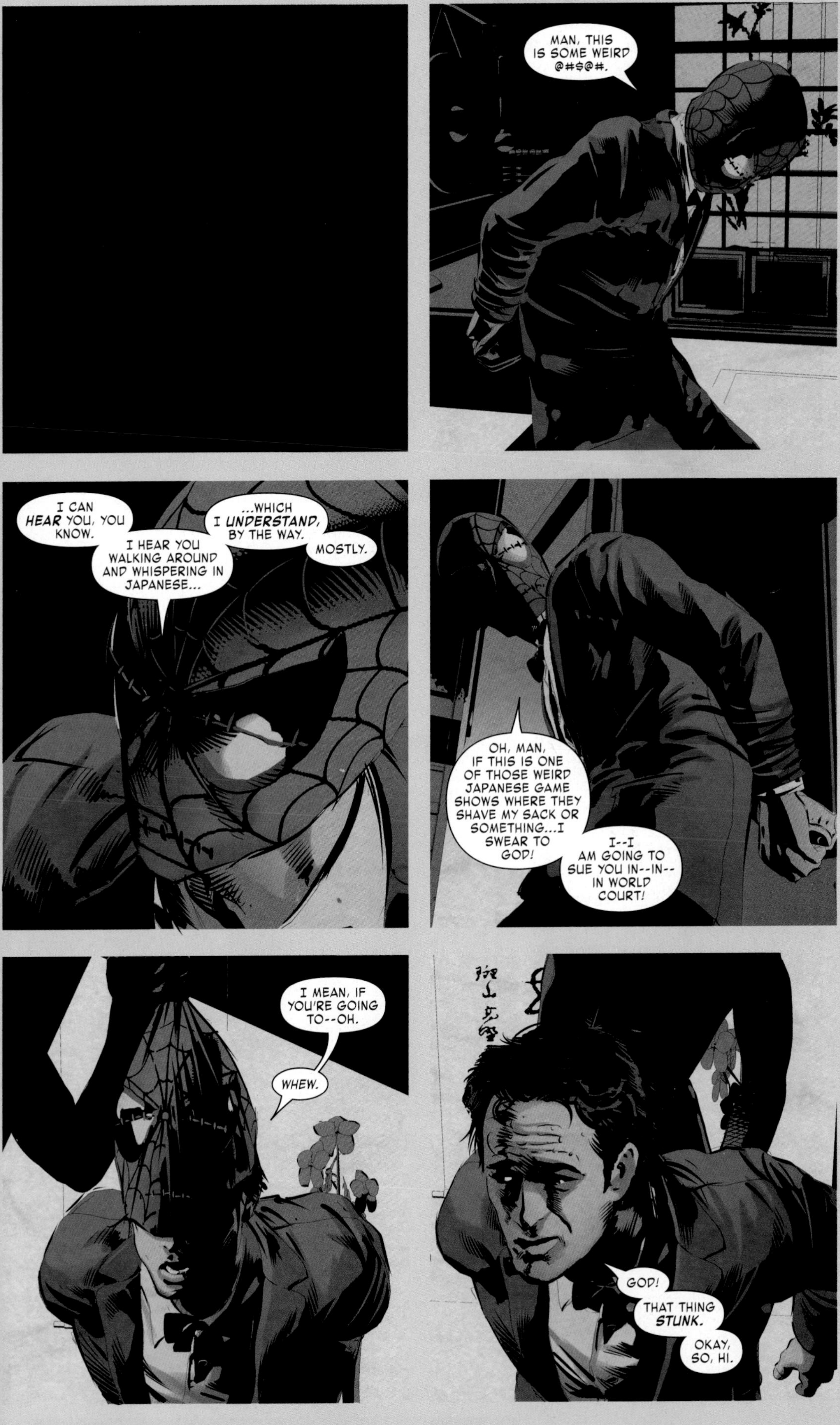
MAN, THIS IS SOME WEIRD @#$@#.
I CAN *HEAR* YOU, YOU KNOW.
I HEAR YOU WALKING AROUND AND WHISPERING IN JAPANESE...
...WHICH I *UNDERSTAND,* BY THE WAY.
MOSTLY.
OH, MAN, IF THIS IS ONE OF THOSE WEIRD JAPANESE GAME SHOWS WHERE THEY SHAVE MY SACK OR SOMETHING...I SWEAR TO GOD!
I--I AM GOING TO SUE YOU IN--IN--IN WORLD COURT!
I MEAN, IF YOU'RE GOING TO--OH.
WHEW.
GOD!
THAT THING *STUNK.*
OKAY, SO, HI.

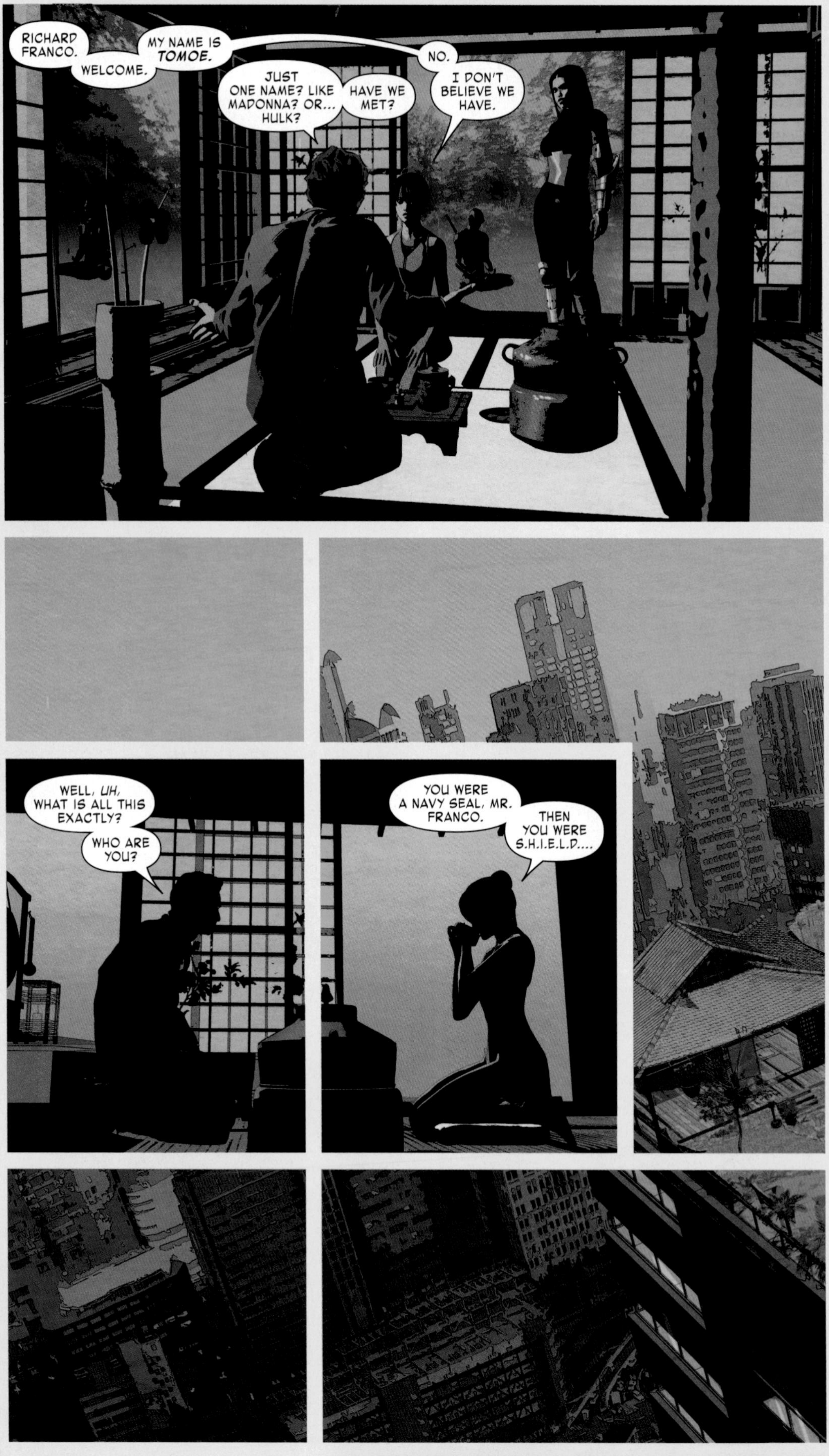
RICHARD FRANCO.
WELCOME.
MY NAME IS *TOMOE.*
NO.
JUST ONE NAME? LIKE MADONNA? OR... HULK?
HAVE WE MET?
I DON'T BELIEVE WE HAVE.
WELL, *UH,* WHAT IS ALL THIS EXACTLY?
WHO ARE YOU?
YOU WERE A NAVY SEAL, MR. FRANCO.
THEN YOU WERE S.H.I.E.L.D....

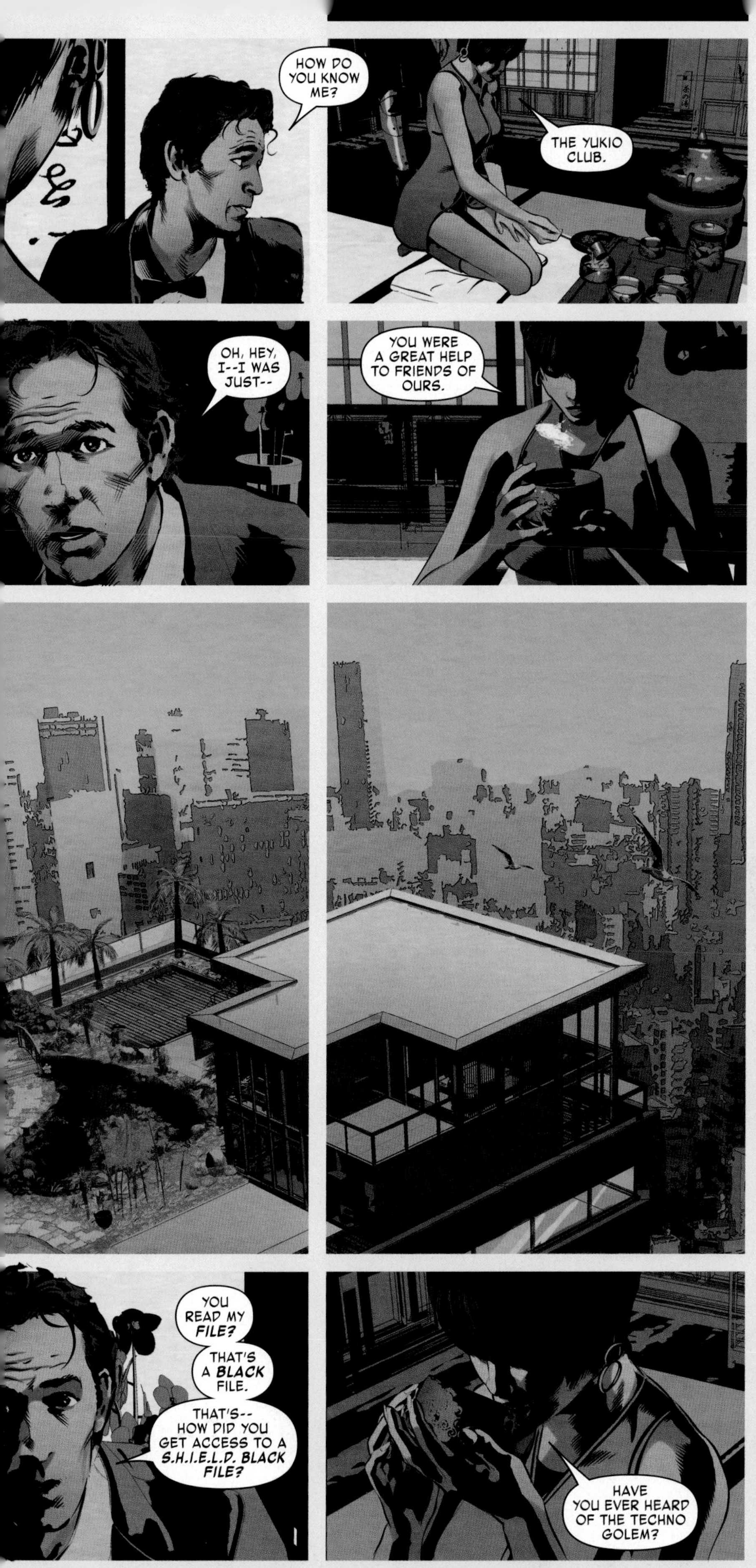
HOW DO YOU KNOW ME?
THE YUKIO CLUB.
OH, HEY, I--I WAS JUST--
YOU WERE A GREAT HELP TO FRIENDS OF OURS.
YOU READ MY FILE?
THAT'S A BLACK FILE.
THAT'S-- HOW DID YOU GET ACCESS TO A S.H.I.E.L.D. BLACK FILE?
HAVE YOU EVER HEARD OF THE TECHNO GOLEM?

NEW YORK CITY.

THIS IS MARY JANE WATSON CALLING.

OH, REALLY? HE'S *STILL* OUT?

OKAY, FINE. YES, HE KNOWS THE NUMBER.

HE *USED* TO BE MY AGENT.

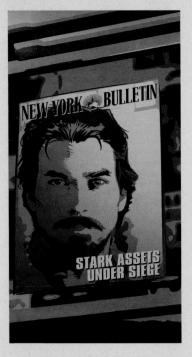

NEW YORK BULLETIN

STARK ASSETS UNDER SIEGE

HEYYO!

THERE HE GOES!

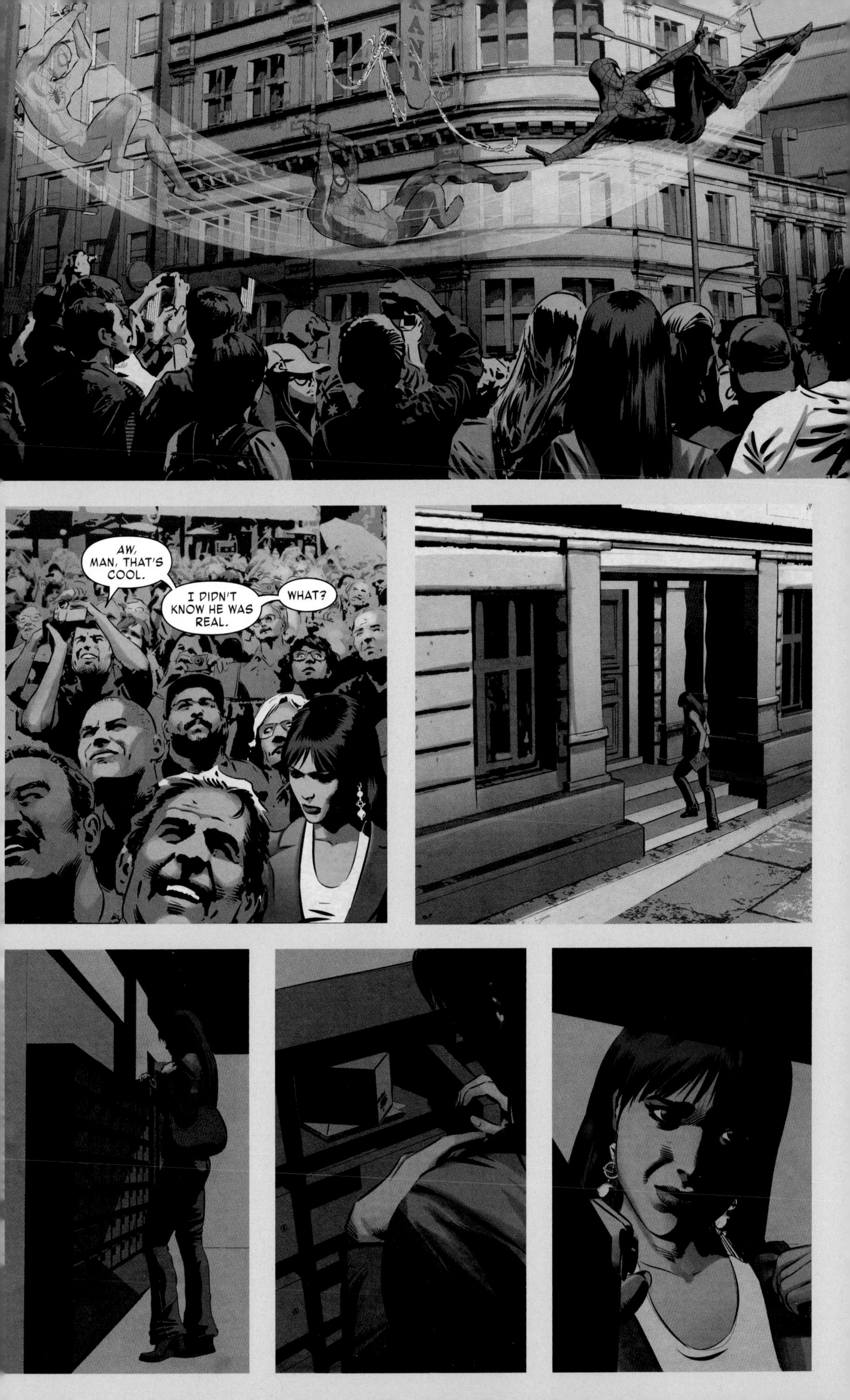
AW, MAN, THAT'S COOL.
I DIDN'T KNOW HE WAS REAL.
WHAT?

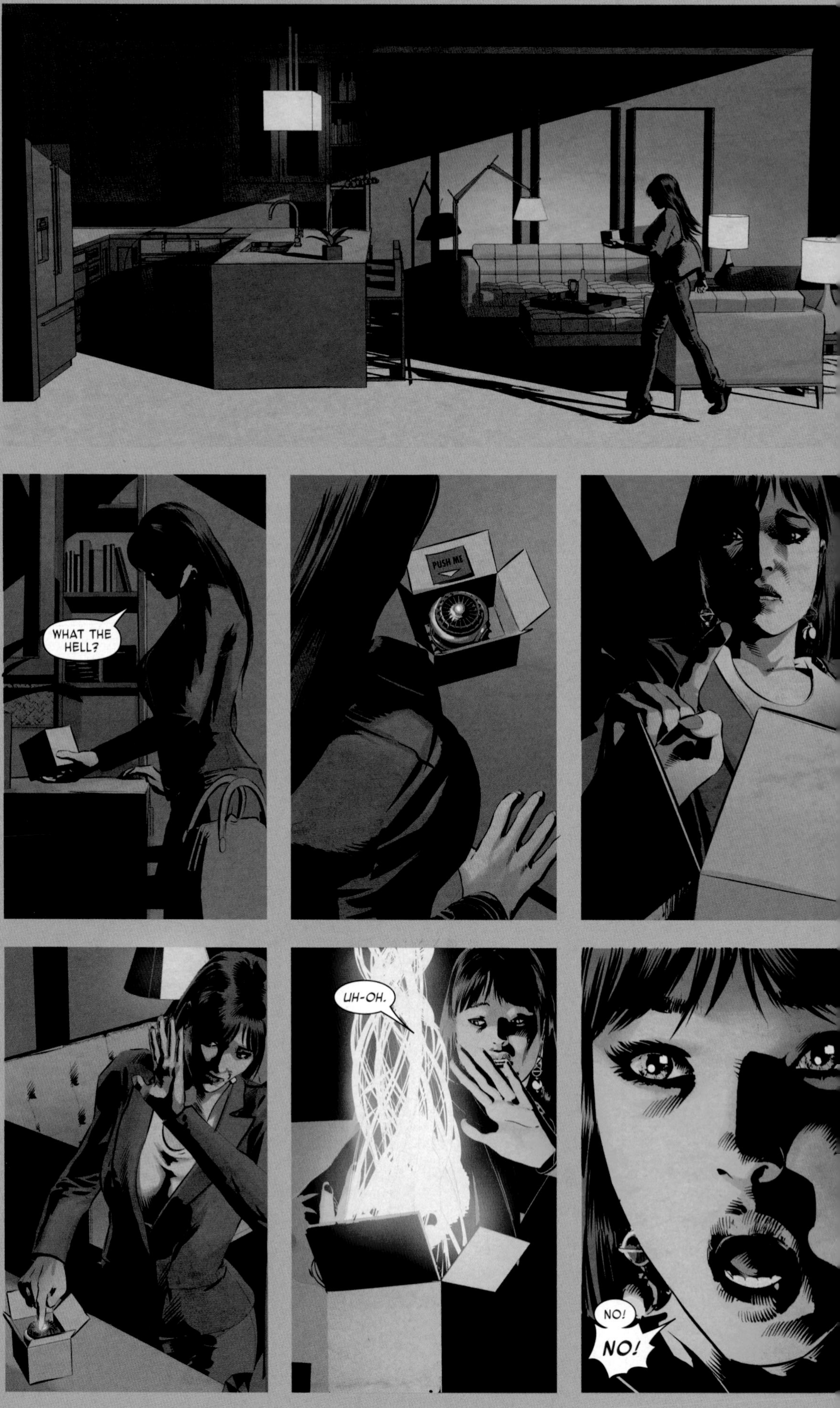
WHAT THE HELL?
PUSH ME
UH-OH.
NO!
NO!

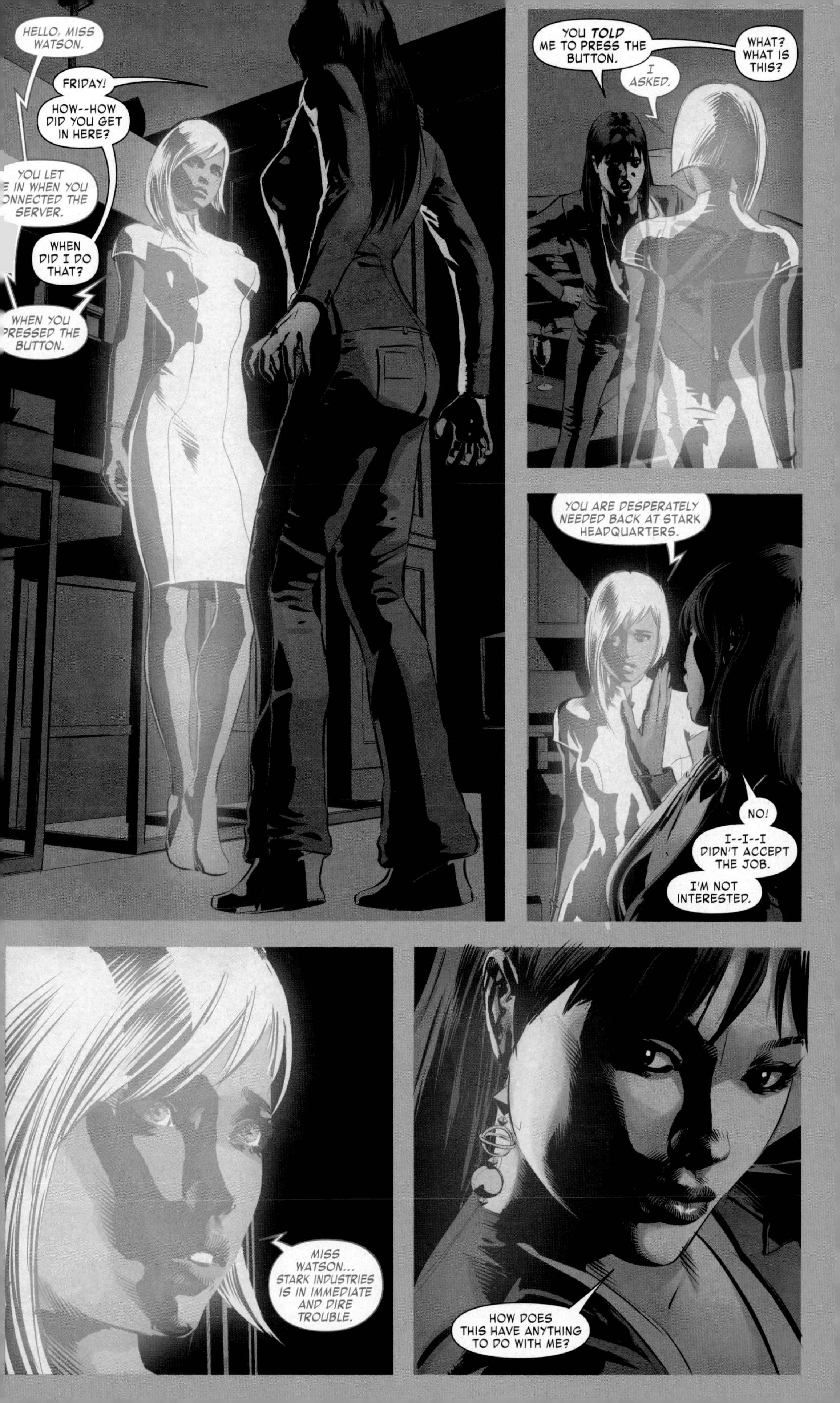
HELLO, MISS WATSON.
FRIDAY!
HOW--HOW DID YOU GET IN HERE?
YOU LET E IN WHEN YOU ONNECTED THE SERVER.
WHEN DID I DO THAT?
WHEN YOU PRESSED THE BUTTON.
YOU TOLD ME TO PRESS THE BUTTON.
I ASKED.
WHAT? WHAT IS THIS?
YOU ARE DESPERATELY NEEDED BACK AT STARK HEADQUARTERS.
NO!
I--I--I DIDN'T ACCEPT THE JOB.
I'M NOT INTERESTED.
MISS WATSON... STARK INDUSTRIES IS IN IMMEDIATE AND DIRE TROUBLE.
HOW DOES THIS HAVE ANYTHING TO DO WITH ME?

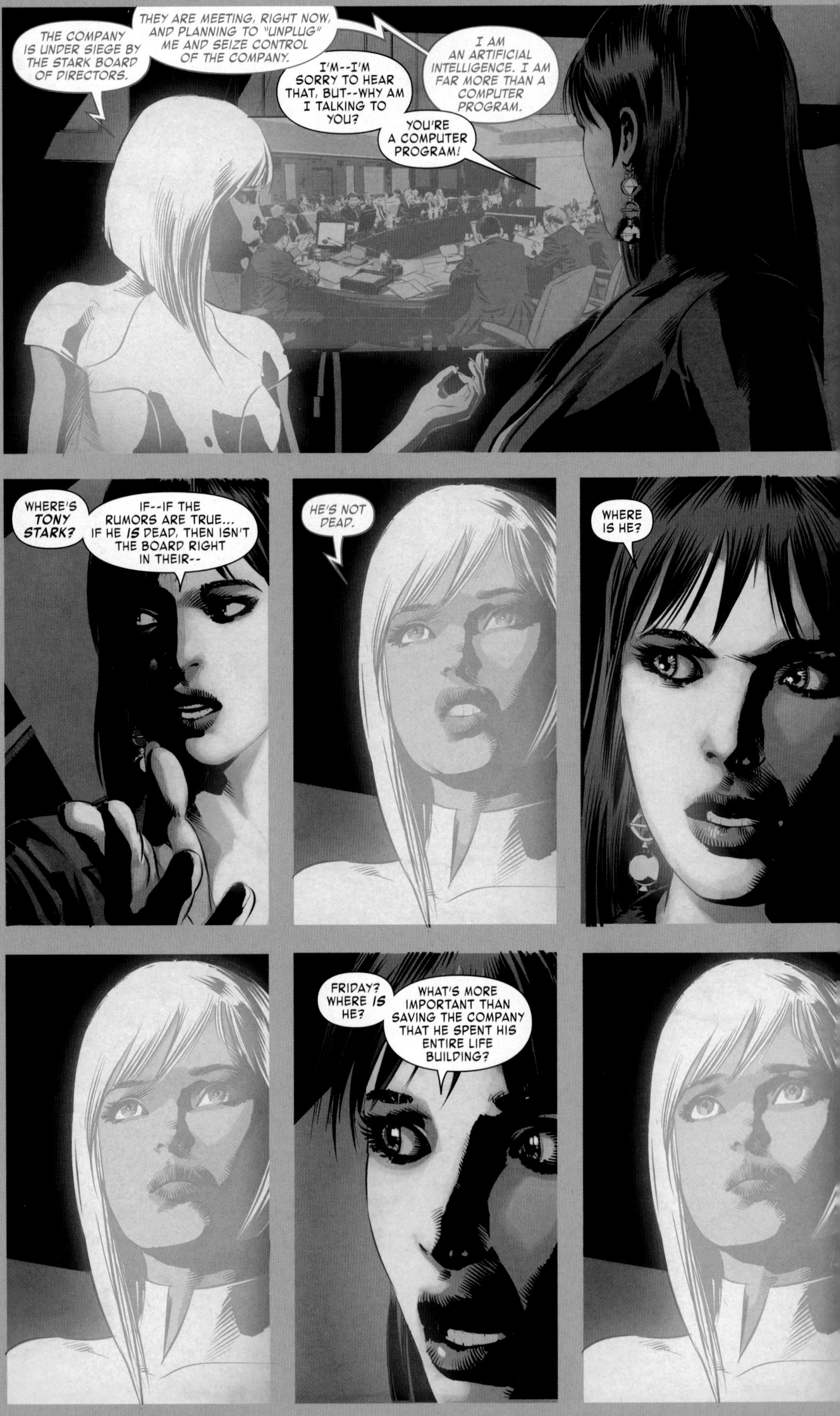
THE COMPANY IS UNDER SIEGE BY THE STARK BOARD OF DIRECTORS.
THEY ARE MEETING, RIGHT NOW, AND PLANNING TO "UNPLUG" ME AND SEIZE CONTROL OF THE COMPANY.
I'M--I'M SORRY TO HEAR THAT, BUT--WHY AM I TALKING TO YOU?
YOU'RE A COMPUTER PROGRAM!
I AM AN ARTIFICIAL INTELLIGENCE. I AM FAR MORE THAN A COMPUTER PROGRAM.
WHERE'S TONY STARK?
IF--IF THE RUMORS ARE TRUE... IF HE IS DEAD, THEN ISN'T THE BOARD RIGHT IN THEIR--
HE'S NOT DEAD.
WHERE IS HE?
FRIDAY? WHERE IS HE?
WHAT'S MORE IMPORTANT THAN SAVING THE COMPANY THAT HE SPENT HIS ENTIRE LIFE BUILDING?

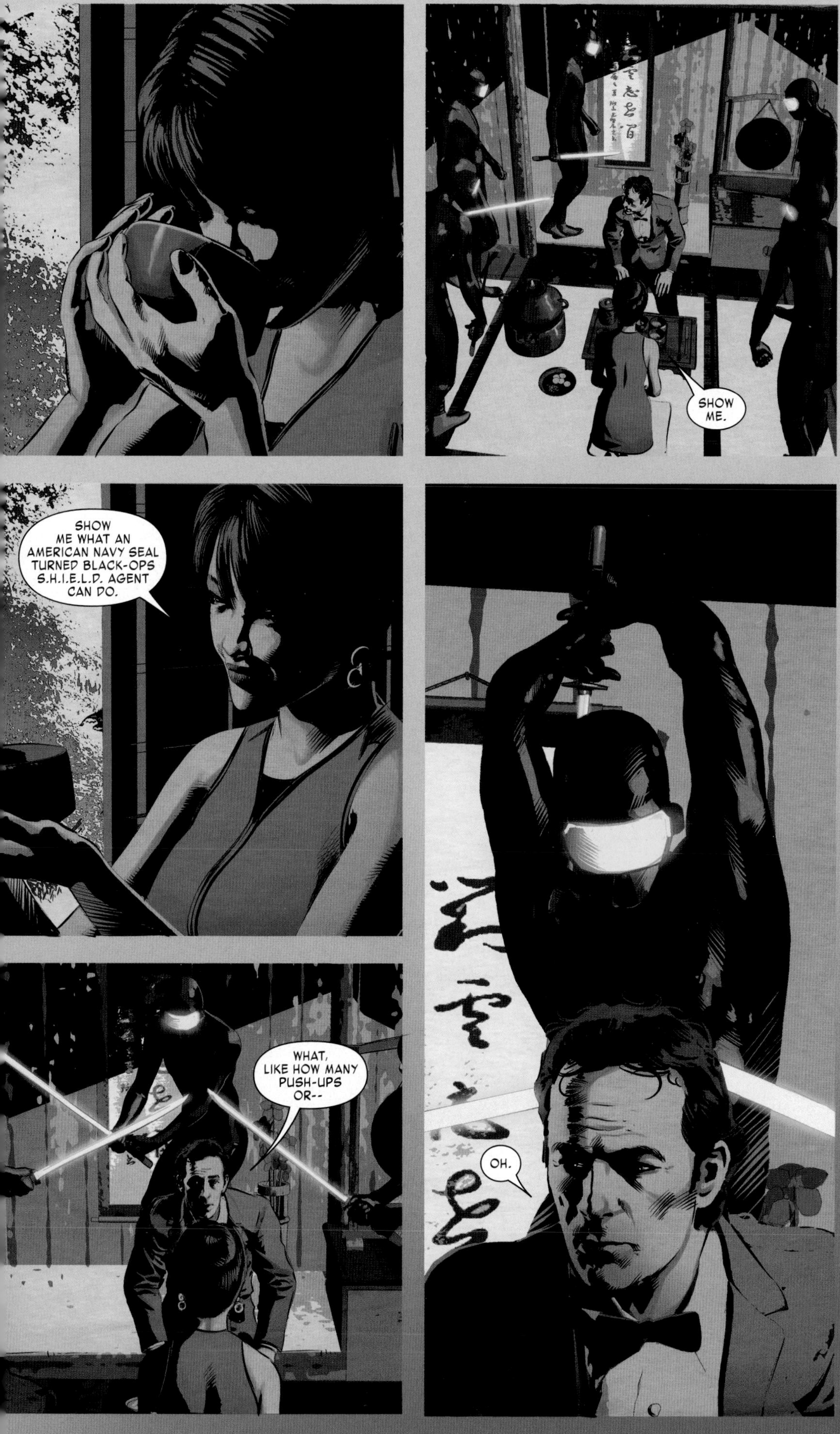
SHOW ME.
SHOW ME WHAT AN AMERICAN NAVY SEAL TURNED BLACK-OPS S.H.I.E.L.D. AGENT CAN DO.
WHAT, LIKE HOW MANY PUSH-UPS OR--
OH.

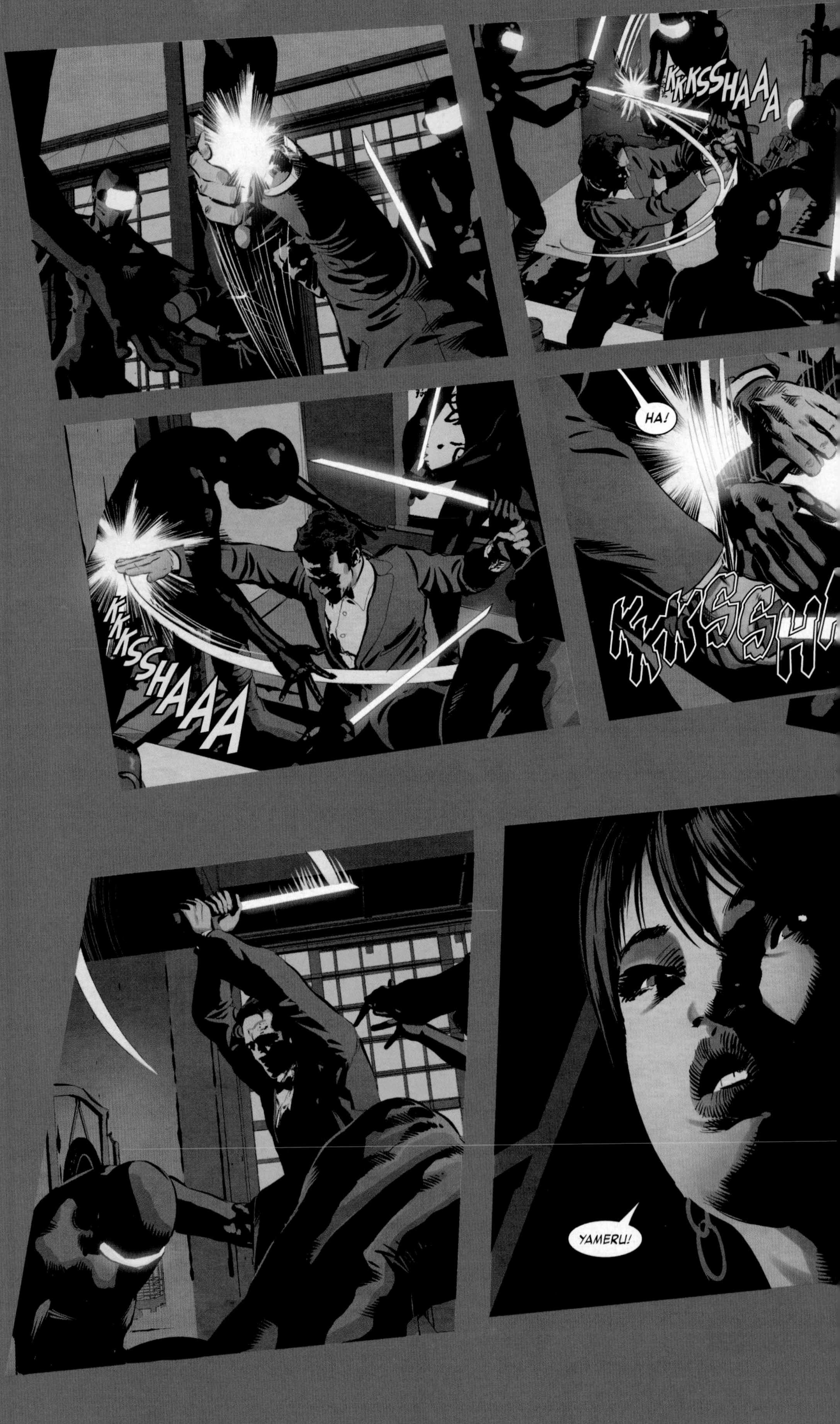

KKKSSHAAA
HA!
KKKSSHAAA
YAMERU!

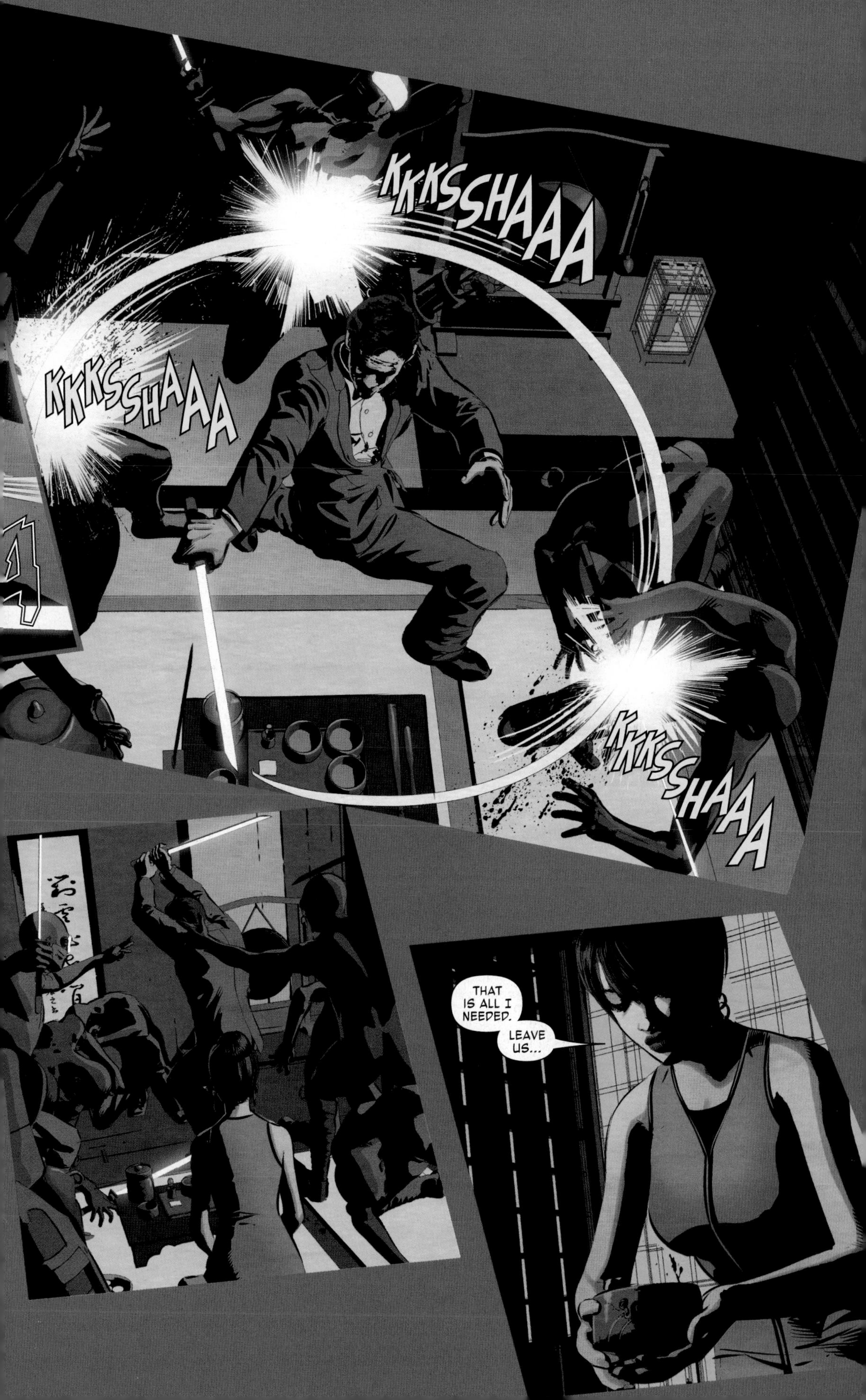
KKKSSHAAA
KKKSSHAAA
KKKSSHAAA
THAT IS ALL I NEEDED.
LEAVE US...

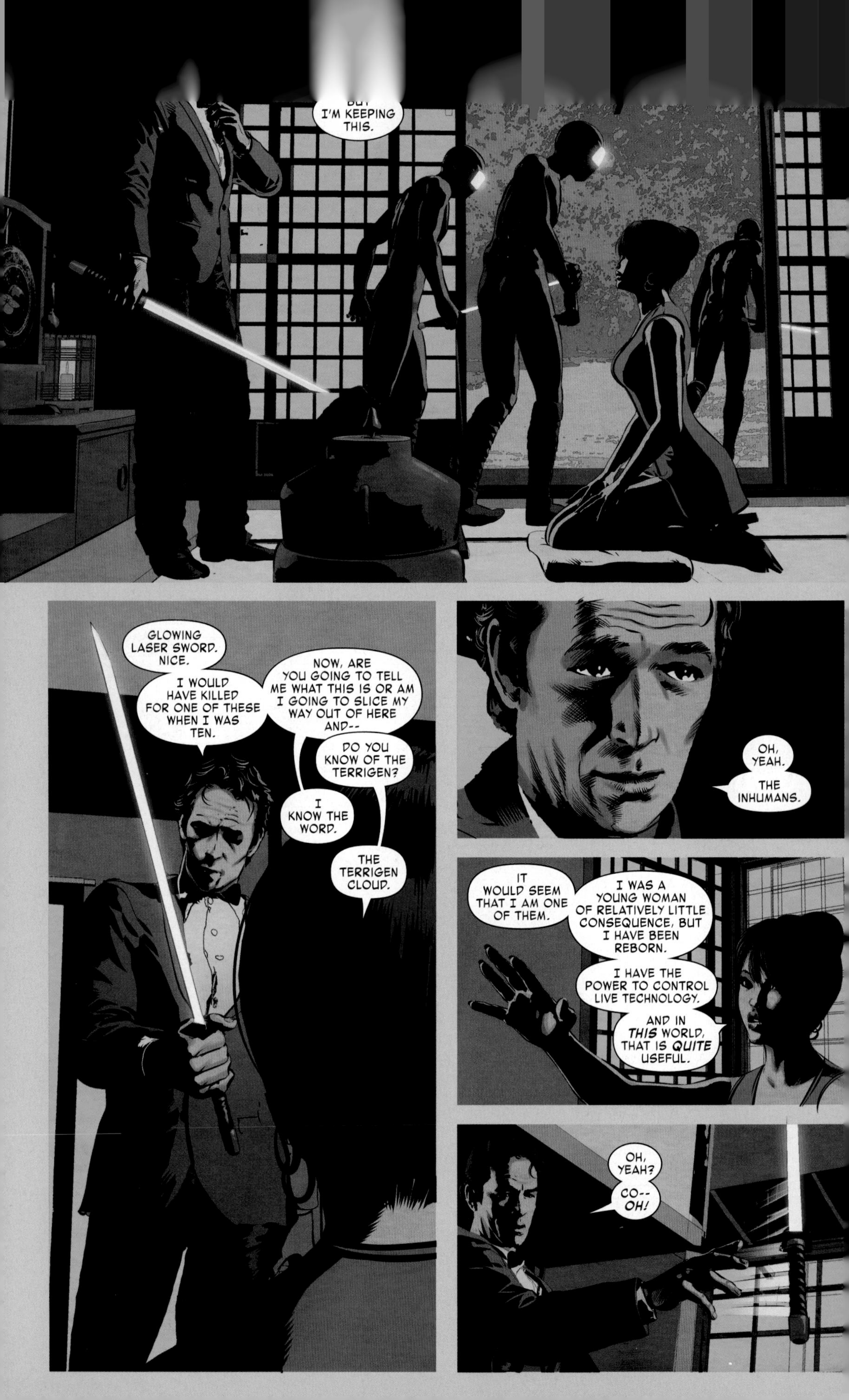

I'M KEEPING THIS.
GLOWING LASER SWORD. NICE.
I WOULD HAVE KILLED FOR ONE OF THESE WHEN I WAS TEN.
NOW, ARE YOU GOING TO TELL ME WHAT THIS IS OR AM I GOING TO SLICE MY WAY OUT OF HERE AND--
DO YOU KNOW OF THE TERRIGEN?
I KNOW THE WORD.
THE TERRIGEN CLOUD.
OH, YEAH.
THE INHUMANS.
IT WOULD SEEM THAT I AM ONE OF THEM.
I WAS A YOUNG WOMAN OF RELATIVELY LITTLE CONSEQUENCE, BUT I HAVE BEEN REBORN.
I HAVE THE POWER TO CONTROL LIVE TECHNOLOGY.
AND IN *THIS* WORLD, THAT IS *QUITE* USEFUL.
OH, YEAH?
CO--*OH!*

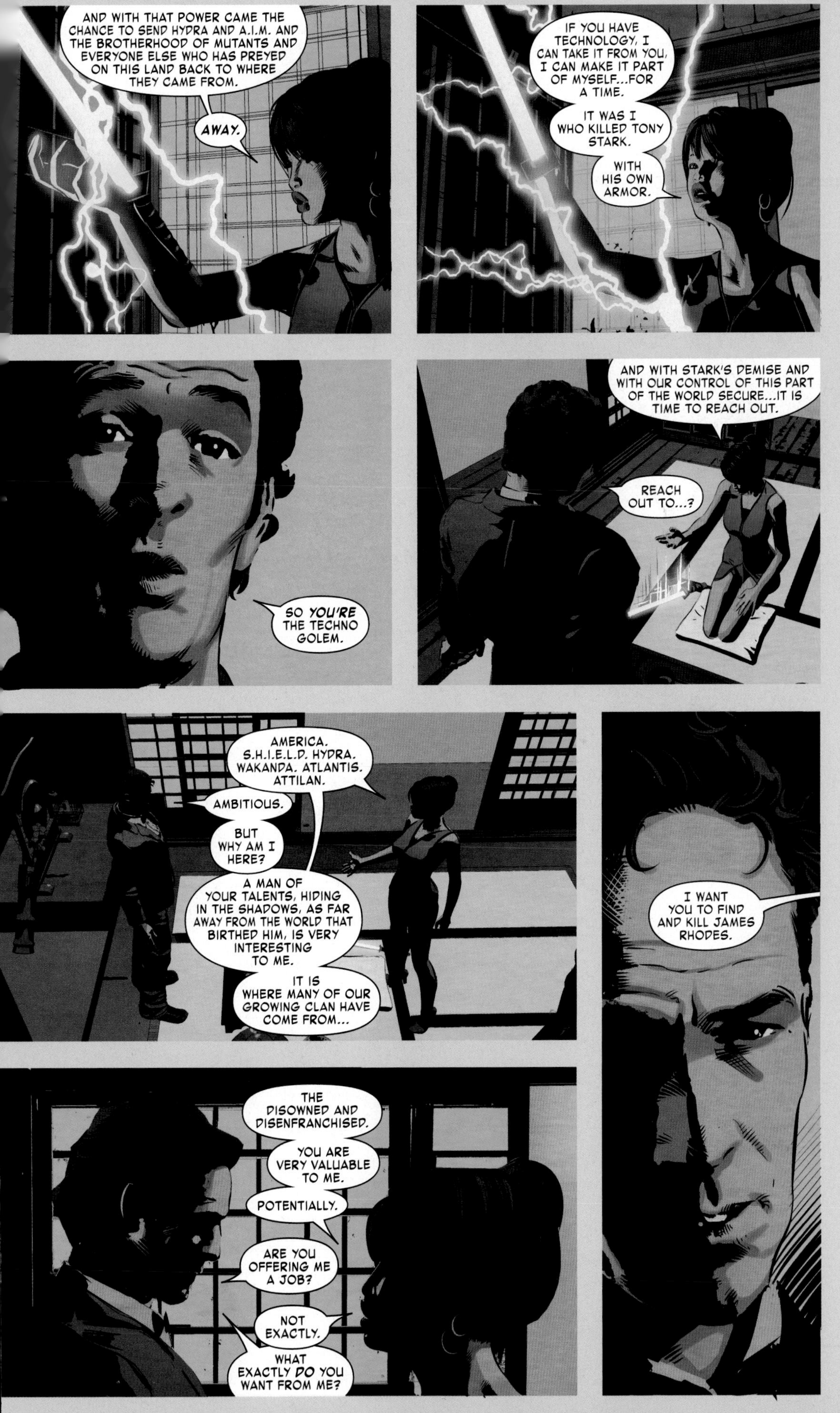
AND WITH THAT POWER CAME THE CHANCE TO SEND HYDRA AND A.I.M. AND THE BROTHERHOOD OF MUTANTS AND EVERYONE ELSE WHO HAS PREYED ON THIS LAND BACK TO WHERE THEY CAME FROM.
AWAY.
IF YOU HAVE TECHNOLOGY, I CAN TAKE IT FROM YOU, I CAN MAKE IT PART OF MYSELF...FOR A TIME.
IT WAS I WHO KILLED TONY STARK.
WITH HIS OWN ARMOR.
SO YOU'RE THE TECHNO GOLEM.
AND WITH STARK'S DEMISE AND WITH OUR CONTROL OF THIS PART OF THE WORLD SECURE...IT IS TIME TO REACH OUT.
REACH OUT TO...?
AMERICA. S.H.I.E.L.D. HYDRA. WAKANDA. ATLANTIS. ATTILAN.
AMBITIOUS.
BUT WHY AM I HERE?
A MAN OF YOUR TALENTS, HIDING IN THE SHADOWS, AS FAR AWAY FROM THE WORLD THAT BIRTHED HIM, IS VERY INTERESTING TO ME.
IT IS WHERE MANY OF OUR GROWING CLAN HAVE COME FROM...
THE DISOWNED AND DISENFRANCHISED.
YOU ARE VERY VALUABLE TO ME.
POTENTIALLY.
ARE YOU OFFERING ME A JOB?
NOT EXACTLY.
WHAT EXACTLY DO YOU WANT FROM ME?
I WANT YOU TO FIND AND KILL JAMES RHODES.

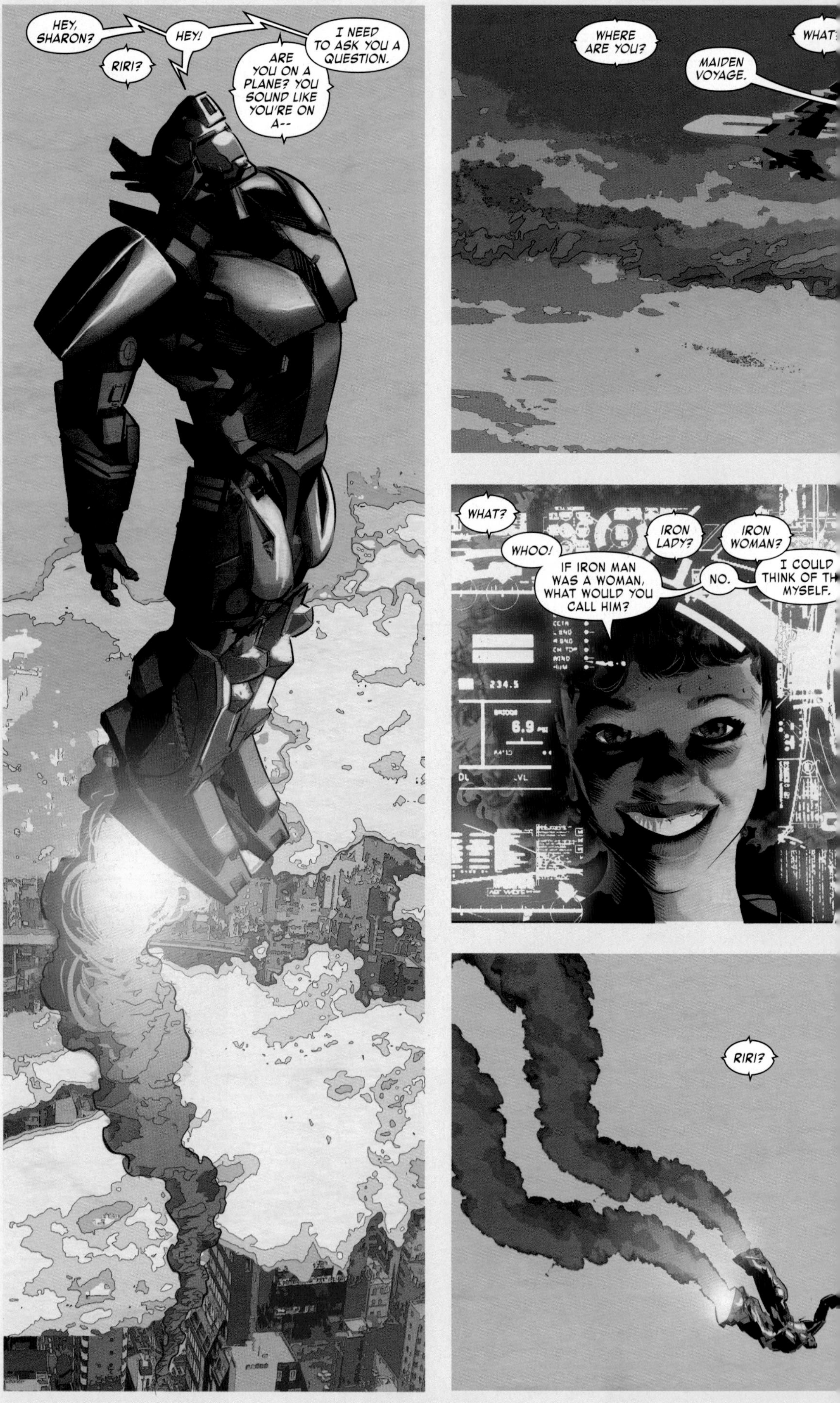
HEY, SHARON?
RIRI?
HEY!
I NEED TO ASK YOU A QUESTION.
ARE YOU ON A PLANE? YOU SOUND LIKE YOU'RE ON A--
WHERE ARE YOU?
WHAT
MAIDEN VOYAGE.
WHAT?
WHOO!
IF IRON MAN WAS A WOMAN, WHAT WOULD YOU CALL HIM?
IRON LADY?
NO.
IRON WOMAN?
I COULD THINK OF TH MYSELF.
RIRI?

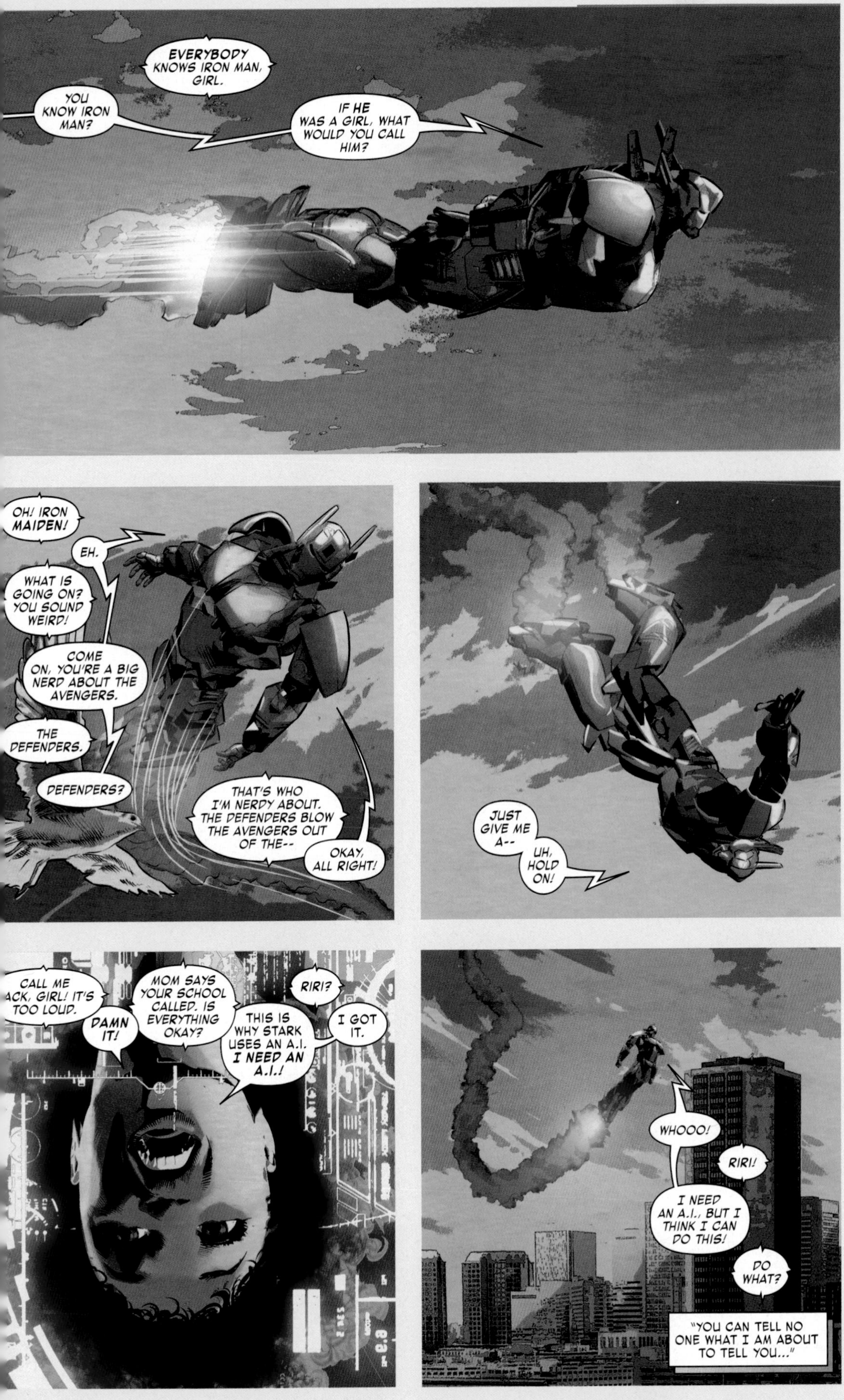
YOU KNOW IRON MAN?
EVERYBODY KNOWS IRON MAN, GIRL.
IF HE WAS A GIRL, WHAT WOULD YOU CALL HIM?
OH! IRON MAIDEN!
EH.
WHAT IS GOING ON? YOU SOUND WEIRD!
COME ON, YOU'RE A BIG NERD ABOUT THE AVENGERS.
THE DEFENDERS.
DEFENDERS?
THAT'S WHO I'M NERDY ABOUT. THE DEFENDERS BLOW THE AVENGERS OUT OF THE--
OKAY, ALL RIGHT!
JUST GIVE ME A--
UH, HOLD ON!
CALL ME ACK, GIRL! IT'S TOO LOUD.
DAMN IT!
MOM SAYS YOUR SCHOOL CALLED. IS EVERYTHING OKAY?
RIRI?
THIS IS WHY STARK USES AN A.I. I NEED AN A.I.!
I GOT IT.
WHOOO!
RIRI!
I NEED AN A.I., BUT I THINK I CAN DO THIS!
DO WHAT?
"YOU CAN TELL NO ONE WHAT I AM ABOUT TO TELL YOU..."

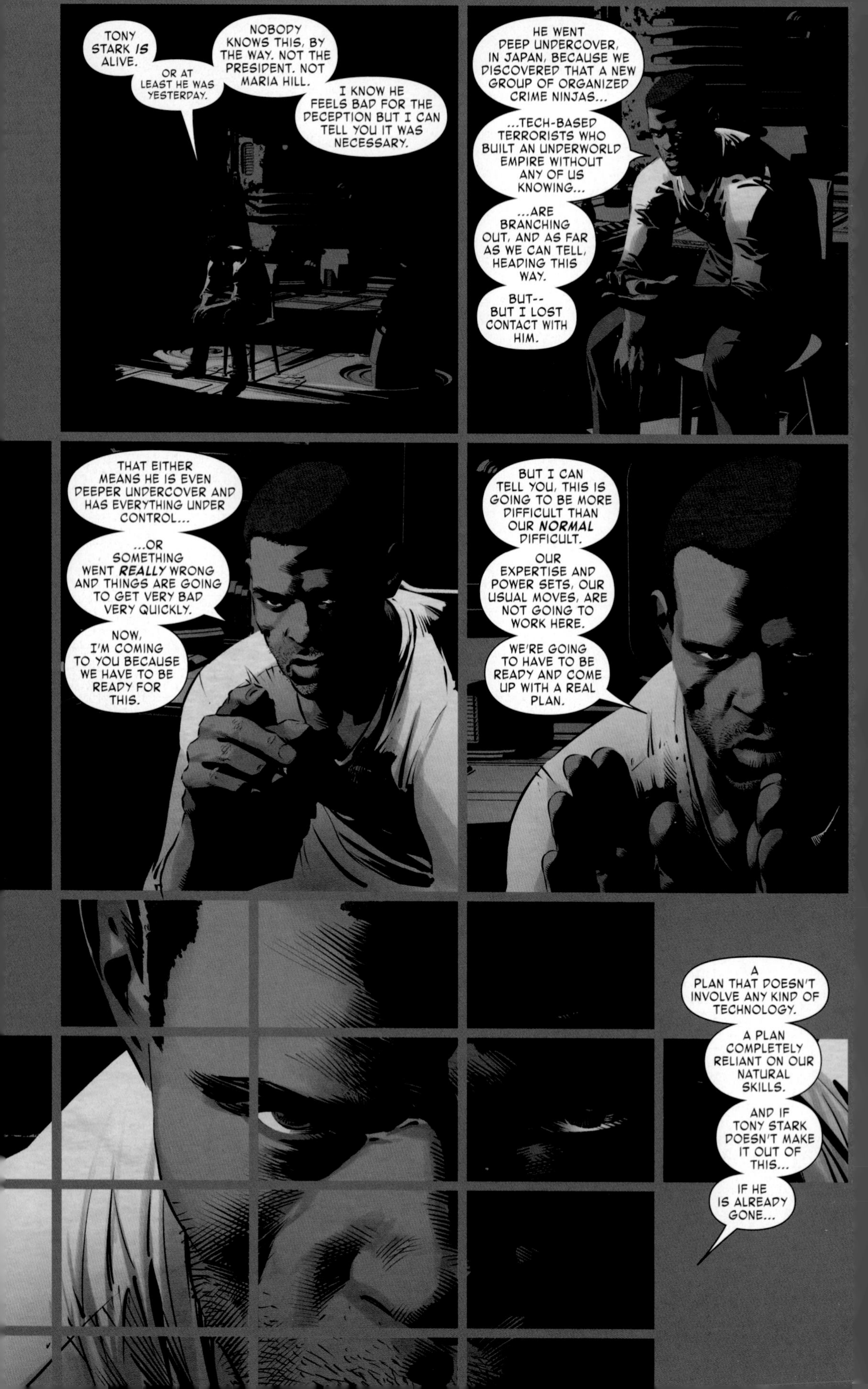

TONY STARK *IS* ALIVE.
OR AT LEAST HE WAS YESTERDAY.
NOBODY KNOWS THIS, BY THE WAY. NOT THE PRESIDENT. NOT MARIA HILL.
I KNOW HE FEELS BAD FOR THE DECEPTION BUT I CAN TELL YOU IT WAS NECESSARY.
HE WENT DEEP UNDERCOVER, IN JAPAN, BECAUSE WE DISCOVERED THAT A NEW GROUP OF ORGANIZED CRIME NINJAS...
...TECH-BASED TERRORISTS WHO BUILT AN UNDERWORLD EMPIRE WITHOUT ANY OF US KNOWING...
...ARE BRANCHING OUT, AND AS FAR AS WE CAN TELL, HEADING THIS WAY.
BUT-- BUT I LOST CONTACT WITH HIM.
THAT EITHER MEANS HE IS EVEN DEEPER UNDERCOVER AND HAS EVERYTHING UNDER CONTROL...
...OR SOMETHING WENT *REALLY* WRONG AND THINGS ARE GOING TO GET VERY BAD VERY QUICKLY.
NOW, I'M COMING TO YOU BECAUSE WE HAVE TO BE READY FOR THIS.
BUT I CAN TELL YOU, THIS IS GOING TO BE MORE DIFFICULT THAN OUR *NORMAL* DIFFICULT.
OUR EXPERTISE AND POWER SETS, OUR USUAL MOVES, ARE NOT GOING TO WORK HERE.
WE'RE GOING TO HAVE TO BE READY AND COME UP WITH A REAL PLAN.
A PLAN THAT DOESN'T INVOLVE ANY KIND OF TECHNOLOGY.
A PLAN COMPLETELY RELIANT ON OUR NATURAL SKILLS.
AND IF TONY STARK DOESN'T MAKE IT OUT OF THIS...
IF HE IS ALREADY GONE...

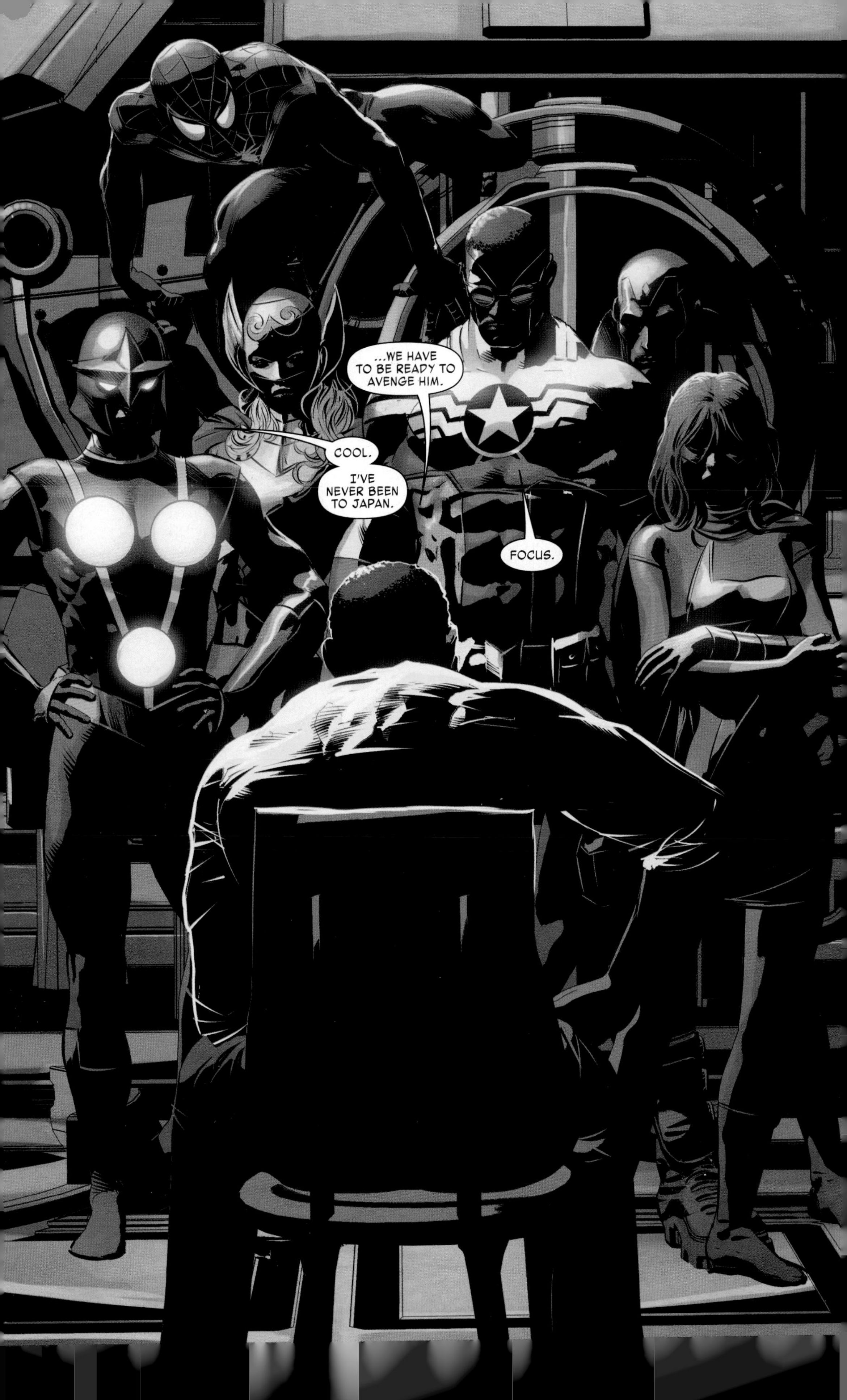
...WE HAVE TO BE READY TO AVENGE HIM.
COOL.
I'VE NEVER BEEN TO JAPAN.
FOCUS.

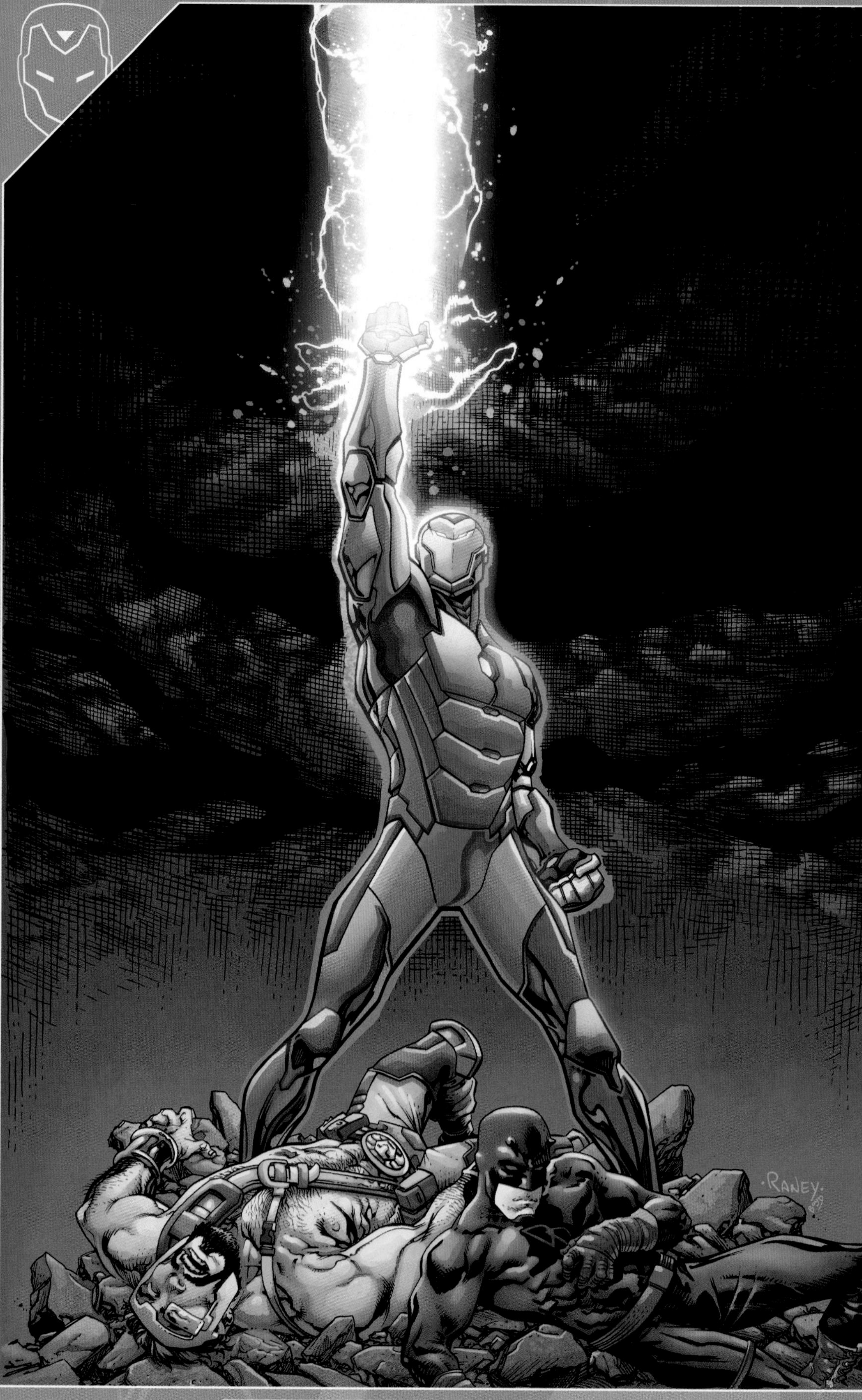
RANEY

#10 REENACTMENT VARIANT BY TOM RANEY & JORDAN BOYD

#11

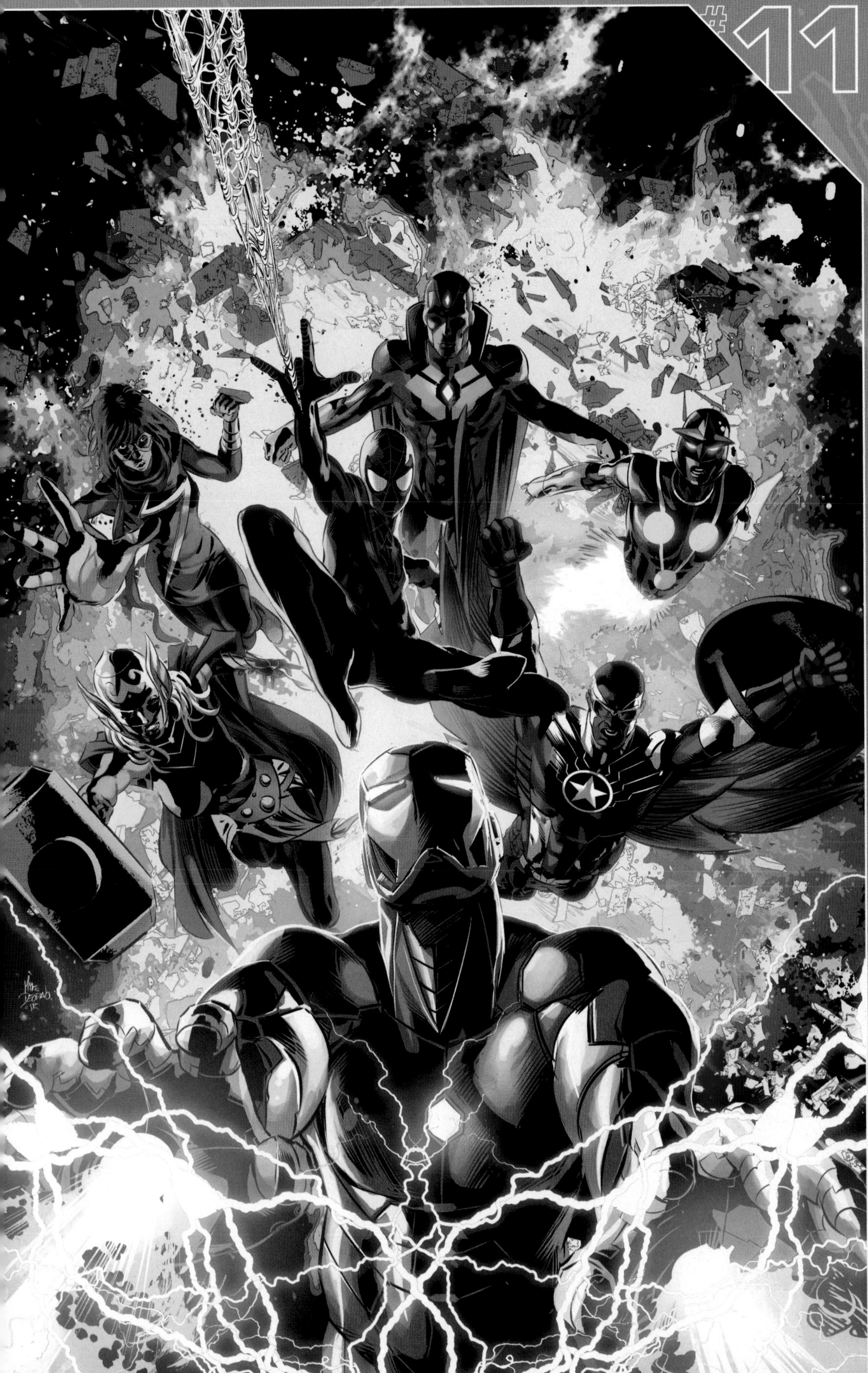

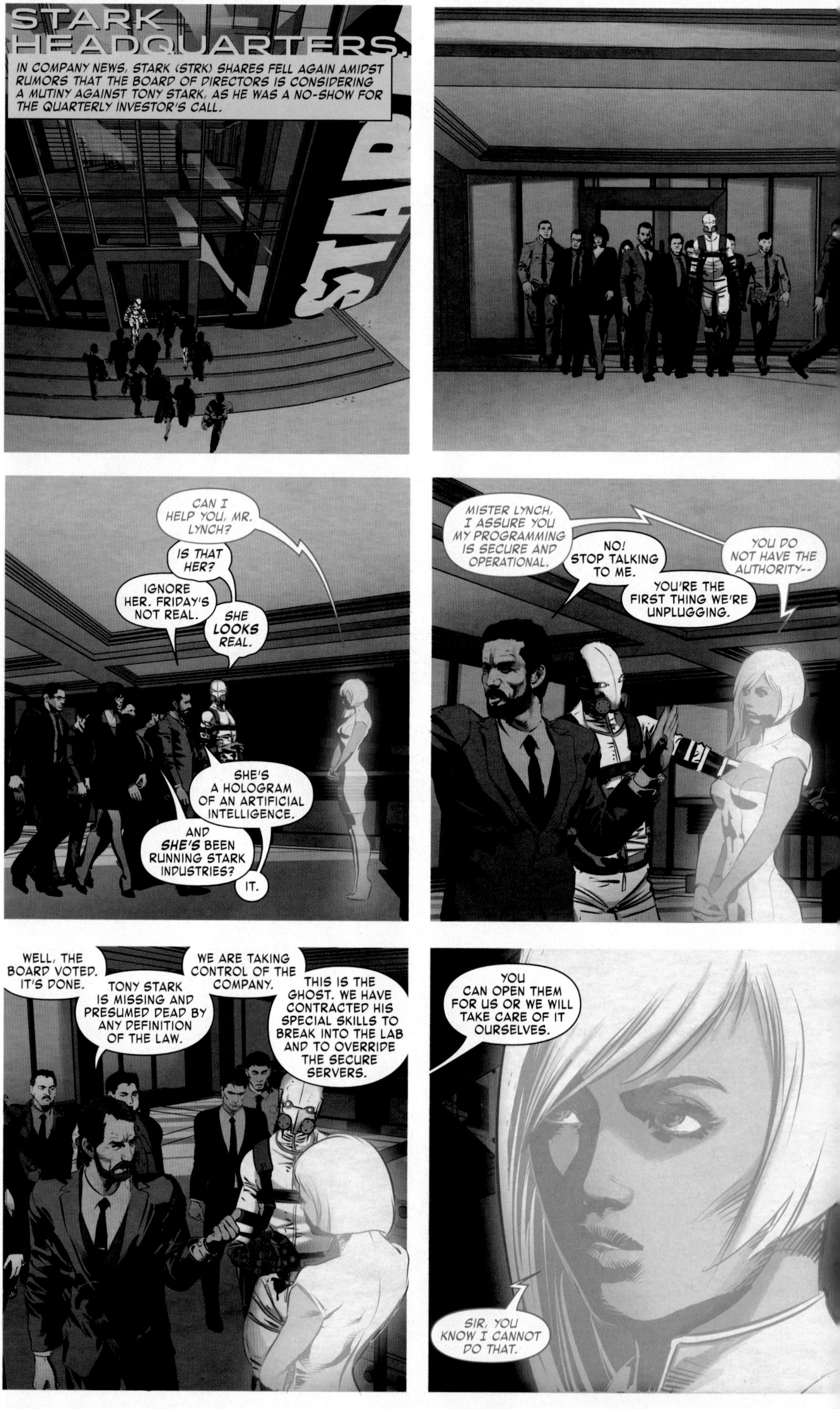

STARK HEADQUARTERS.
IN COMPANY NEWS, STARK (STRK) SHARES FELL AGAIN AMIDST RUMORS THAT THE BOARD OF DIRECTORS IS CONSIDERING A MUTINY AGAINST TONY STARK, AS HE WAS A NO-SHOW FOR THE QUARTERLY INVESTOR'S CALL.
CAN I HELP YOU, MR. LYNCH?
IS THAT HER?
IGNORE HER. FRIDAY'S NOT REAL.
SHE LOOKS REAL.
SHE'S A HOLOGRAM OF AN ARTIFICIAL INTELLIGENCE.
AND SHE'S BEEN RUNNING STARK INDUSTRIES?
IT.
MISTER LYNCH, I ASSURE YOU MY PROGRAMMING IS SECURE AND OPERATIONAL.
NO! STOP TALKING TO ME.
YOU DO NOT HAVE THE AUTHORITY--
YOU'RE THE FIRST THING WE'RE UNPLUGGING.
WELL, THE BOARD VOTED. IT'S DONE.
TONY STARK IS MISSING AND PRESUMED DEAD BY ANY DEFINITION OF THE LAW.
WE ARE TAKING CONTROL OF THE COMPANY.
THIS IS THE GHOST. WE HAVE CONTRACTED HIS SPECIAL SKILLS TO BREAK INTO THE LAB AND TO OVERRIDE THE SECURE SERVERS.
YOU CAN OPEN THEM FOR US OR WE WILL TAKE CARE OF IT OURSELVES.
SIR, YOU KNOW I CANNOT DO THAT.

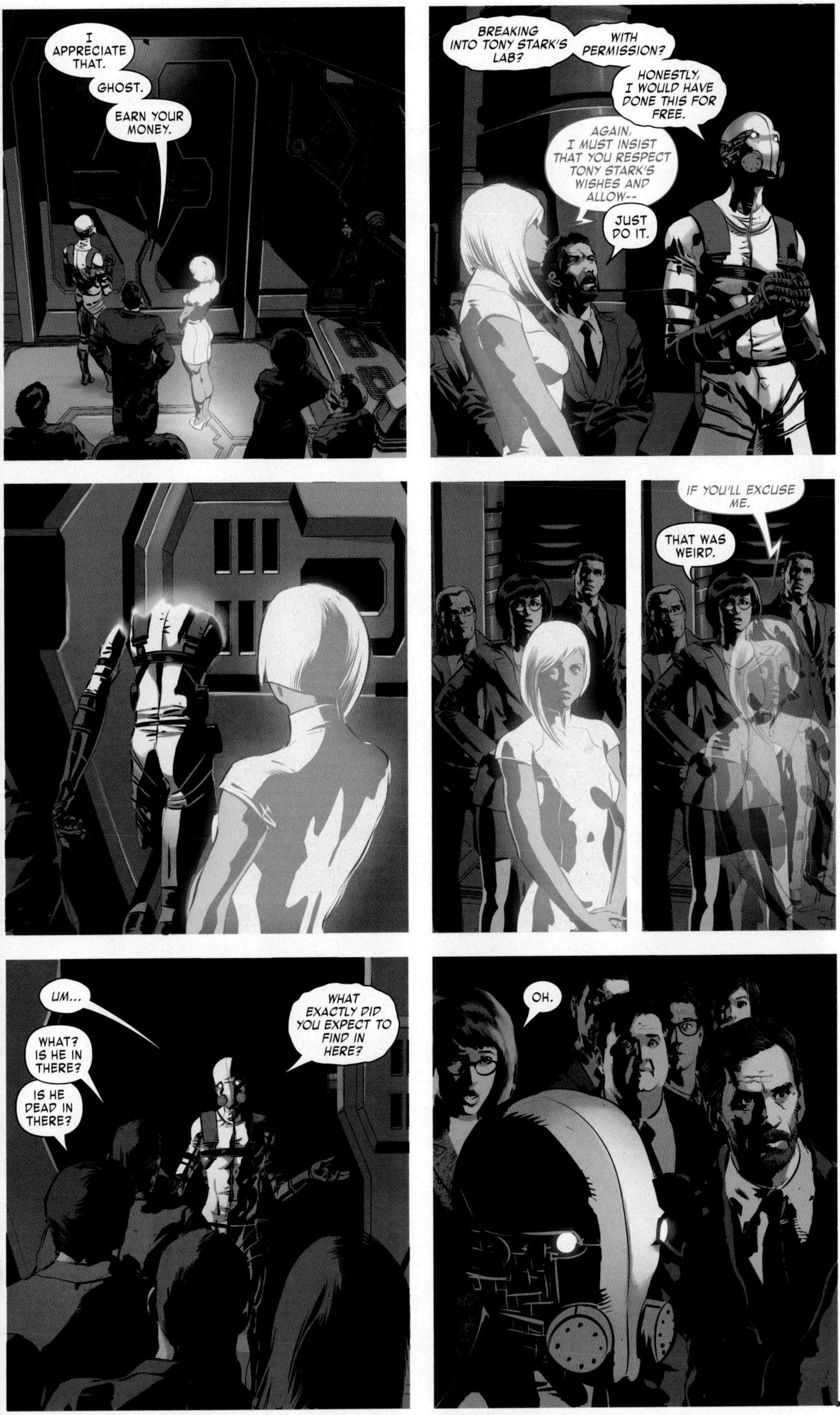
I APPRECIATE THAT.
GHOST.
EARN YOUR MONEY.
BREAKING INTO TONY STARK'S LAB?
WITH PERMISSION?
HONESTLY, I WOULD HAVE DONE THIS FOR FREE.
AGAIN, I MUST INSIST THAT YOU RESPECT TONY STARK'S WISHES AND ALLOW--
JUST DO IT.
IF YOU'LL EXCUSE ME.
THAT WAS WEIRD.
UM...
WHAT? IS HE IN THERE?
IS HE DEAD IN THERE?
WHAT EXACTLY DID YOU EXPECT TO FIND IN HERE?
OH.

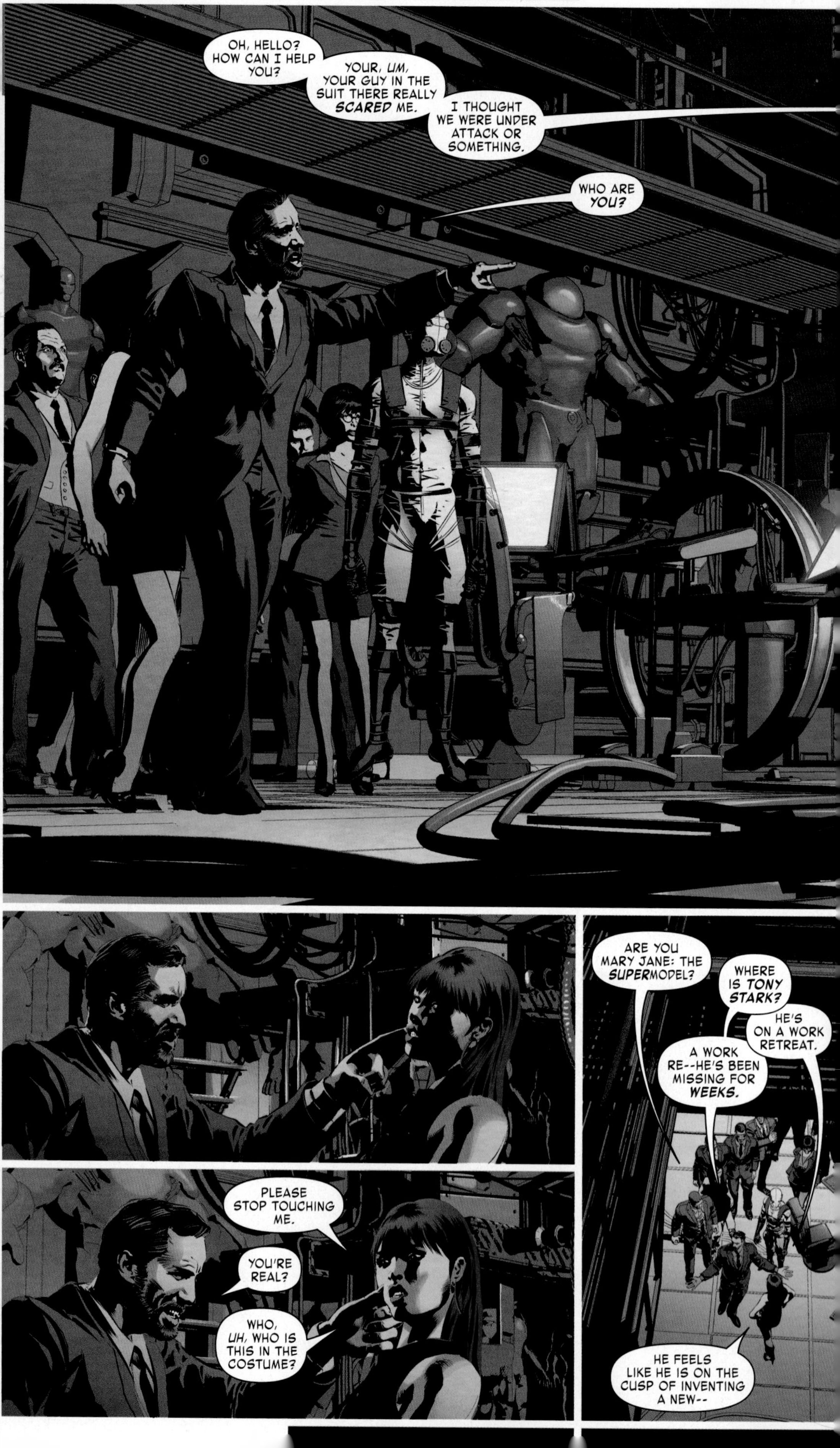
OH, HELLO? HOW CAN I HELP YOU?
YOUR, UM, YOUR GUY IN THE SUIT THERE REALLY SCARED ME.
I THOUGHT WE WERE UNDER ATTACK OR SOMETHING.
WHO ARE YOU?
PLEASE STOP TOUCHING ME.
YOU'RE REAL?
WHO, UH, WHO IS THIS IN THE COSTUME?
ARE YOU MARY JANE: THE SUPERMODEL?
WHERE IS TONY STARK?
HE'S ON A WORK RETREAT.
A WORK RE--HE'S BEEN MISSING FOR WEEKS.
HE FEELS LIKE HE IS ON THE CUSP OF INVENTING A NEW--

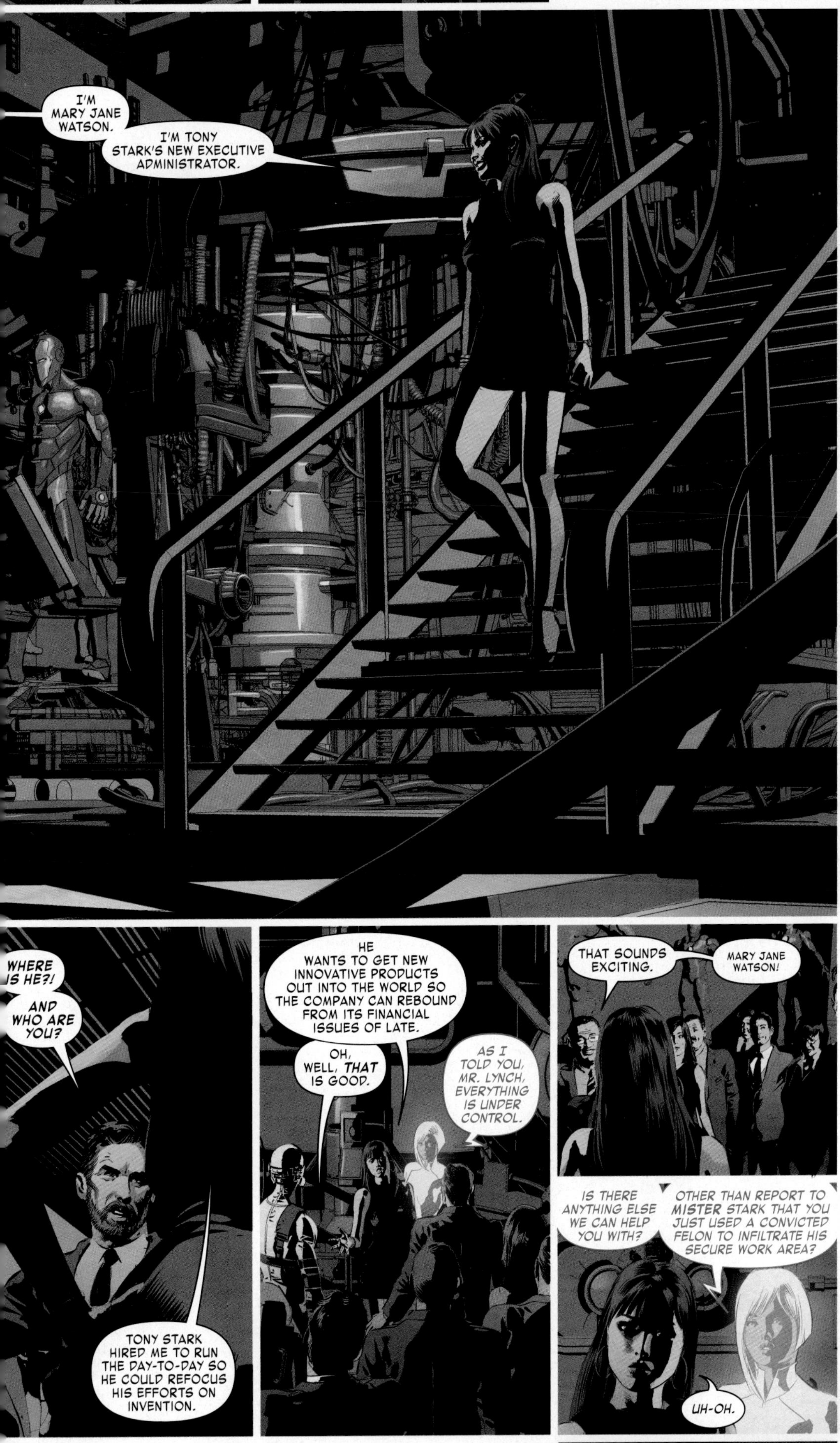
I'M MARY JANE WATSON.
I'M TONY STARK'S NEW EXECUTIVE ADMINISTRATOR.
WHERE IS HE?!
AND WHO ARE YOU?
TONY STARK HIRED ME TO RUN THE DAY-TO-DAY SO HE COULD REFOCUS HIS EFFORTS ON INVENTION.
HE WANTS TO GET NEW INNOVATIVE PRODUCTS OUT INTO THE WORLD SO THE COMPANY CAN REBOUND FROM ITS FINANCIAL ISSUES OF LATE.
OH, WELL, THAT IS GOOD.
AS I TOLD YOU, MR. LYNCH, EVERYTHING IS UNDER CONTROL.
THAT SOUNDS EXCITING.
MARY JANE WATSON!
IS THERE ANYTHING ELSE WE CAN HELP YOU WITH?
OTHER THAN REPORT TO MISTER STARK THAT YOU JUST USED A CONVICTED FELON TO INFILTRATE HIS SECURE WORK AREA?
UH-OH.

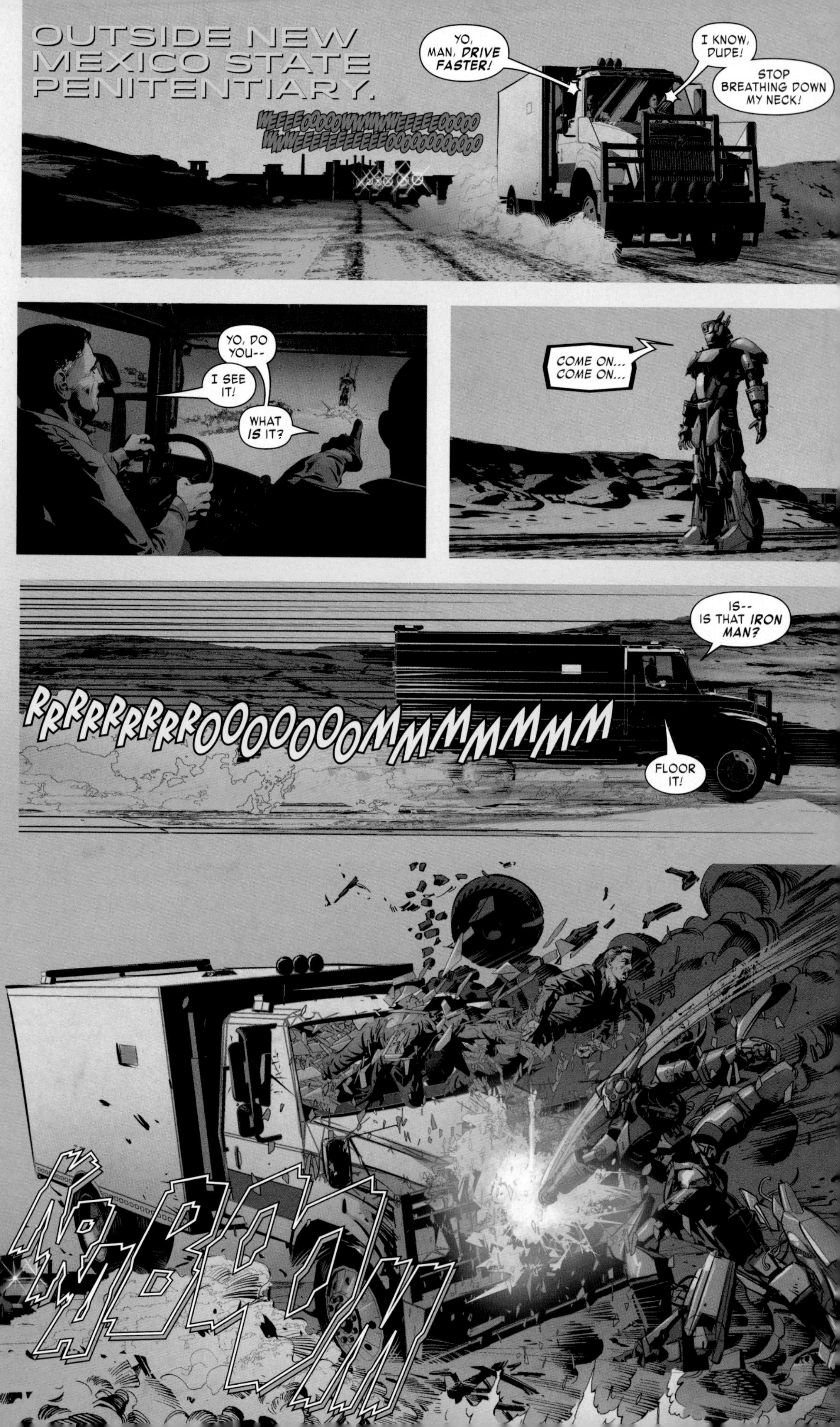

OUTSIDE NEW MEXICO STATE PENITENTIARY.
YO, MAN, DRIVE FASTER!
I KNOW, DUDE!
STOP BREATHING DOWN MY NECK!
WEEEEOOOOOWWWWWEEEEEOOOO WWWEEEEEEEEEEOOOOOOOOOOO
YO, DO YOU--
I SEE IT!
WHAT IS IT?
COME ON... COME ON...
IS-- IS THAT IRON MAN?
RRRRRRRRROOOOOOOOMMMMMMMM
FLOOR IT!

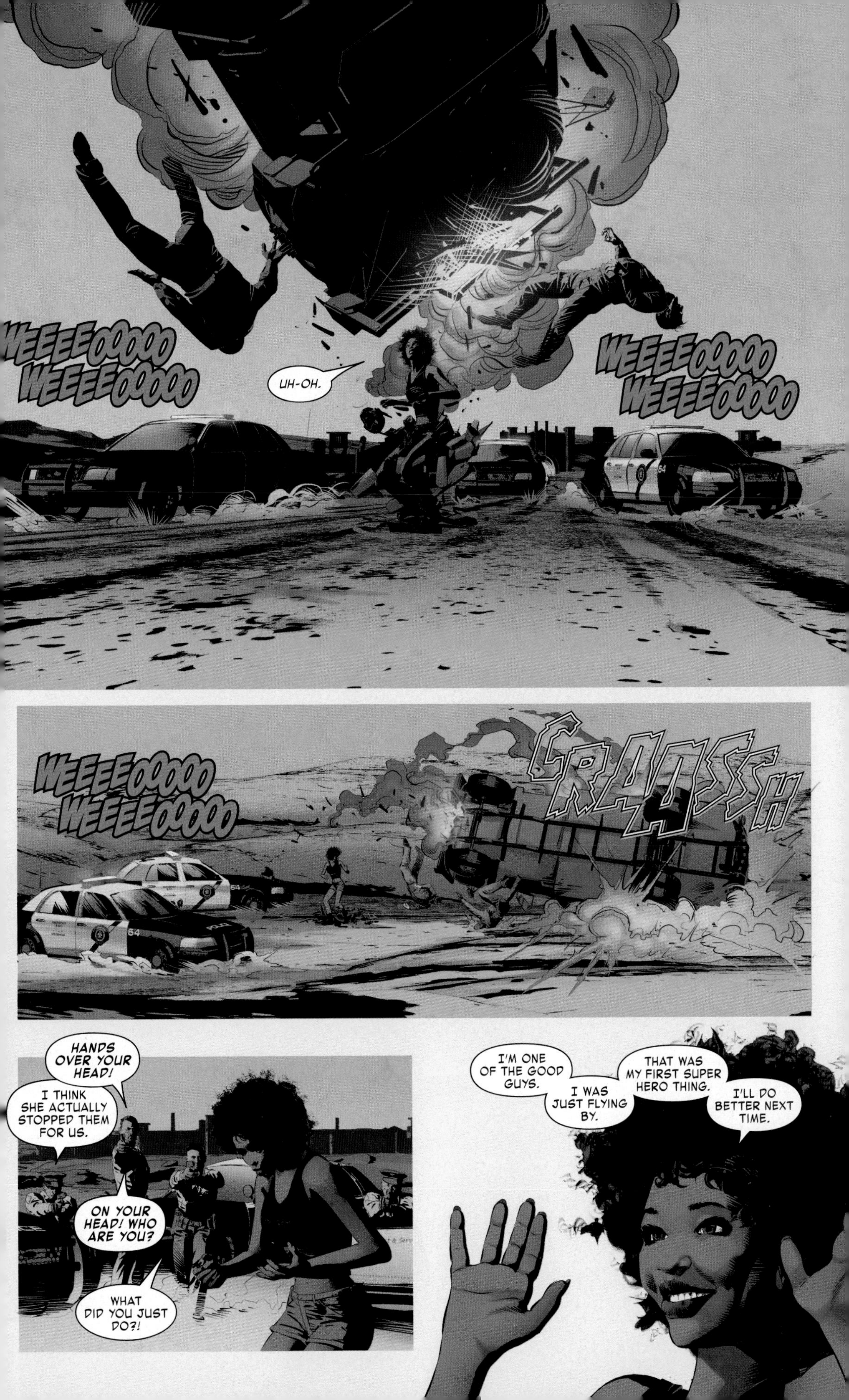
WEEEEOOOOO
WEEEEOOOOO
UH-OH.
WEEEEOOOOO
WEEEEOOOOO
WEEEEOOOOO
WEEEEOOOOO
CRAASSH
HANDS OVER YOUR HEAD!
I THINK SHE ACTUALLY STOPPED THEM FOR US.
ON YOUR HEAD! WHO ARE YOU?
WHAT DID YOU JUST DO?!
I'M ONE OF THE GOOD GUYS.
I WAS JUST FLYING BY.
THAT WAS MY FIRST SUPER HERO THING.
I'LL DO BETTER NEXT TIME.

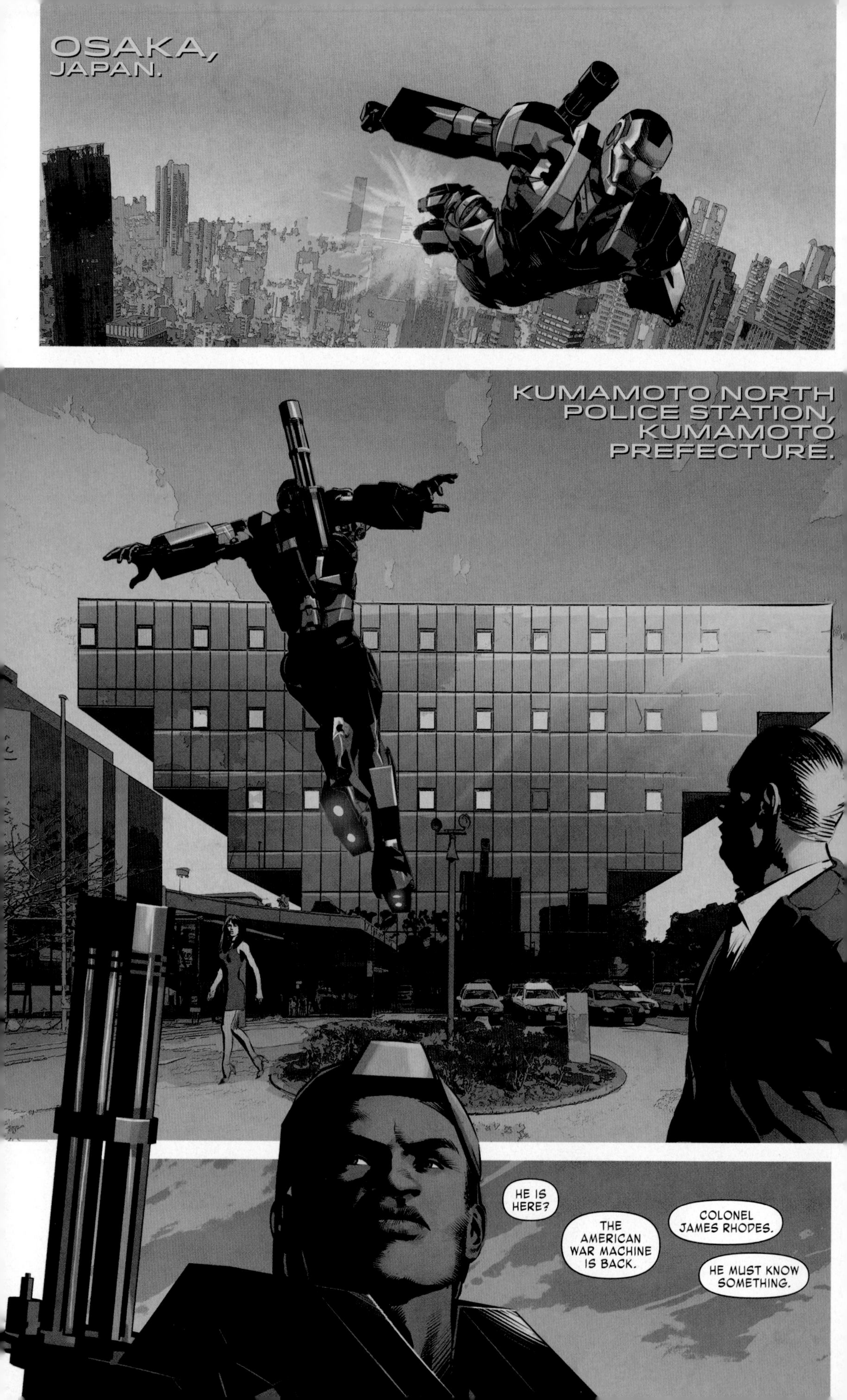
OSAKA, JAPAN.
KUMAMOTO NORTH POLICE STATION, KUMAMOTO PREFECTURE.
HE IS HERE?
THE AMERICAN WAR MACHINE IS BACK.
COLONEL JAMES RHODES.
HE MUST KNOW SOMETHING.

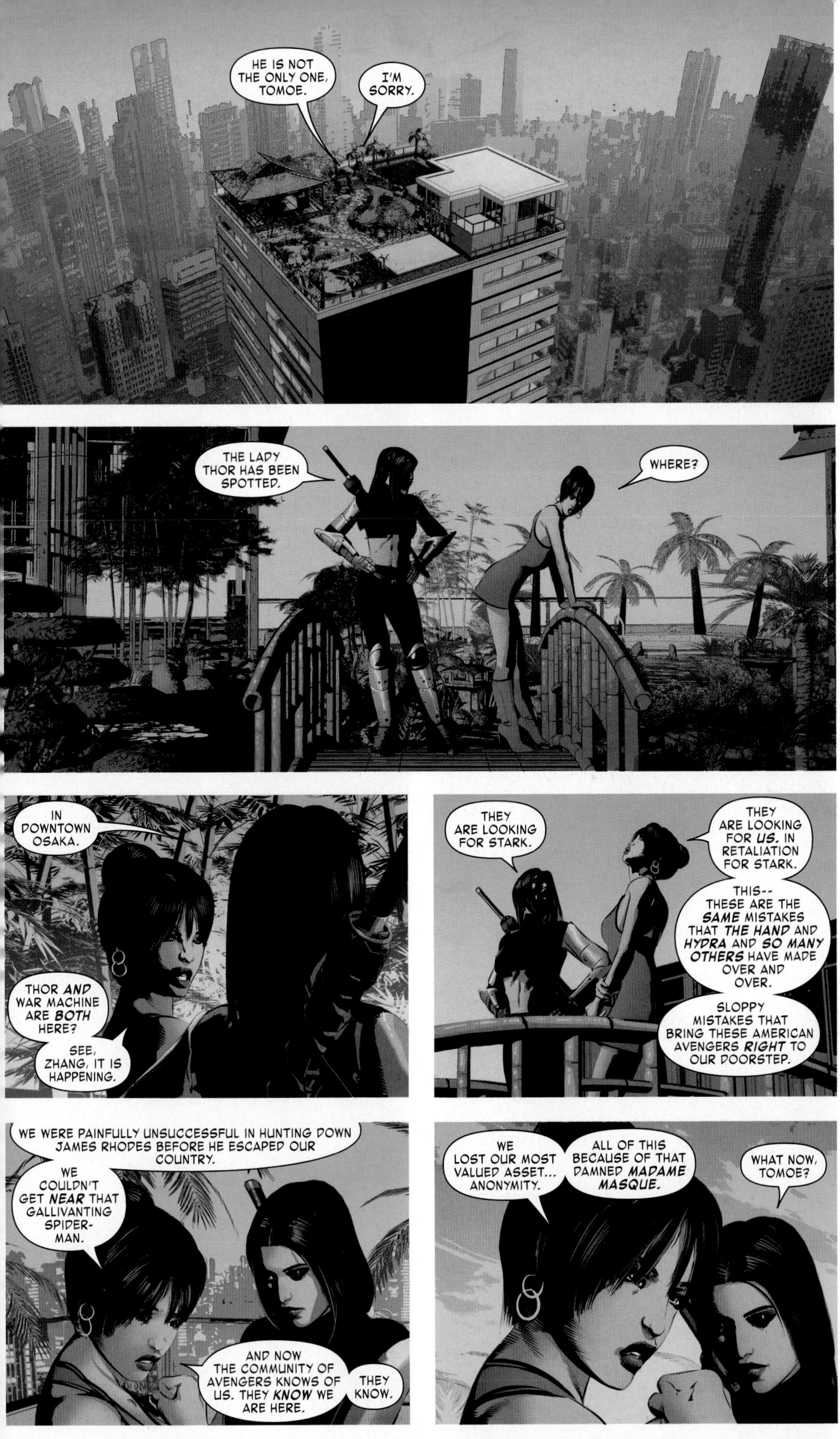
HE IS NOT THE ONLY ONE, TOMOE.
I'M SORRY.
THE LADY THOR HAS BEEN SPOTTED.
WHERE?
IN DOWNTOWN OSAKA.
THOR AND WAR MACHINE ARE BOTH HERE?
SEE, ZHANG, IT IS HAPPENING.
THEY ARE LOOKING FOR STARK.
THEY ARE LOOKING FOR US. IN RETALIATION FOR STARK.
THIS-- THESE ARE THE SAME MISTAKES THAT THE HAND AND HYDRA AND SO MANY OTHERS HAVE MADE OVER AND OVER.
SLOPPY MISTAKES THAT BRING THESE AMERICAN AVENGERS RIGHT TO OUR DOORSTEP.
WE WERE PAINFULLY UNSUCCESSFUL IN HUNTING DOWN JAMES RHODES BEFORE HE ESCAPED OUR COUNTRY.
WE COULDN'T GET NEAR THAT GALLIVANTING SPIDER-MAN.
AND NOW THE COMMUNITY OF AVENGERS KNOWS OF US. THEY KNOW WE ARE HERE.
THEY KNOW.
WE LOST OUR MOST VALUED ASSET... ANONYMITY.
ALL OF THIS BECAUSE OF THAT DAMNED MADAME MASQUE.
WHAT NOW, TOMOE?

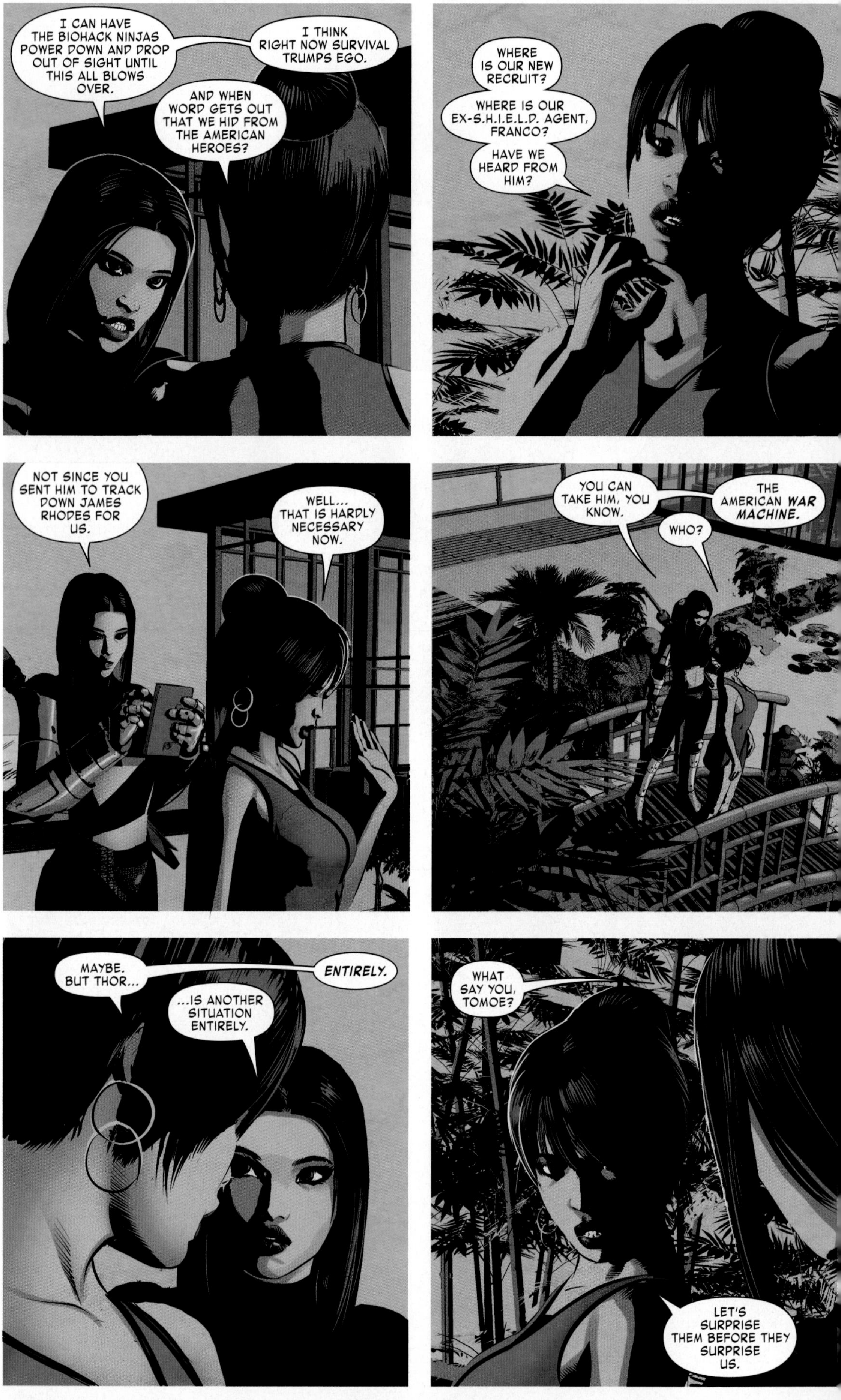
I CAN HAVE THE BIOHACK NINJAS POWER DOWN AND DROP OUT OF SIGHT UNTIL THIS ALL BLOWS OVER.
I THINK RIGHT NOW SURVIVAL TRUMPS EGO.
AND WHEN WORD GETS OUT THAT WE HID FROM THE AMERICAN HEROES?
WHERE IS OUR NEW RECRUIT?
WHERE IS OUR EX-S.H.I.E.L.D. AGENT, FRANCO?
HAVE WE HEARD FROM HIM?
NOT SINCE YOU SENT HIM TO TRACK DOWN JAMES RHODES FOR US.
WELL... THAT IS HARDLY NECESSARY NOW.
YOU CAN TAKE HIM, YOU KNOW.
THE AMERICAN WAR MACHINE.
WHO?
MAYBE. BUT THOR...
ENTIRELY.
...IS ANOTHER SITUATION ENTIRELY.
WHAT SAY YOU, TOMOE?
LET'S SURPRISE THEM BEFORE THEY SURPRISE US.

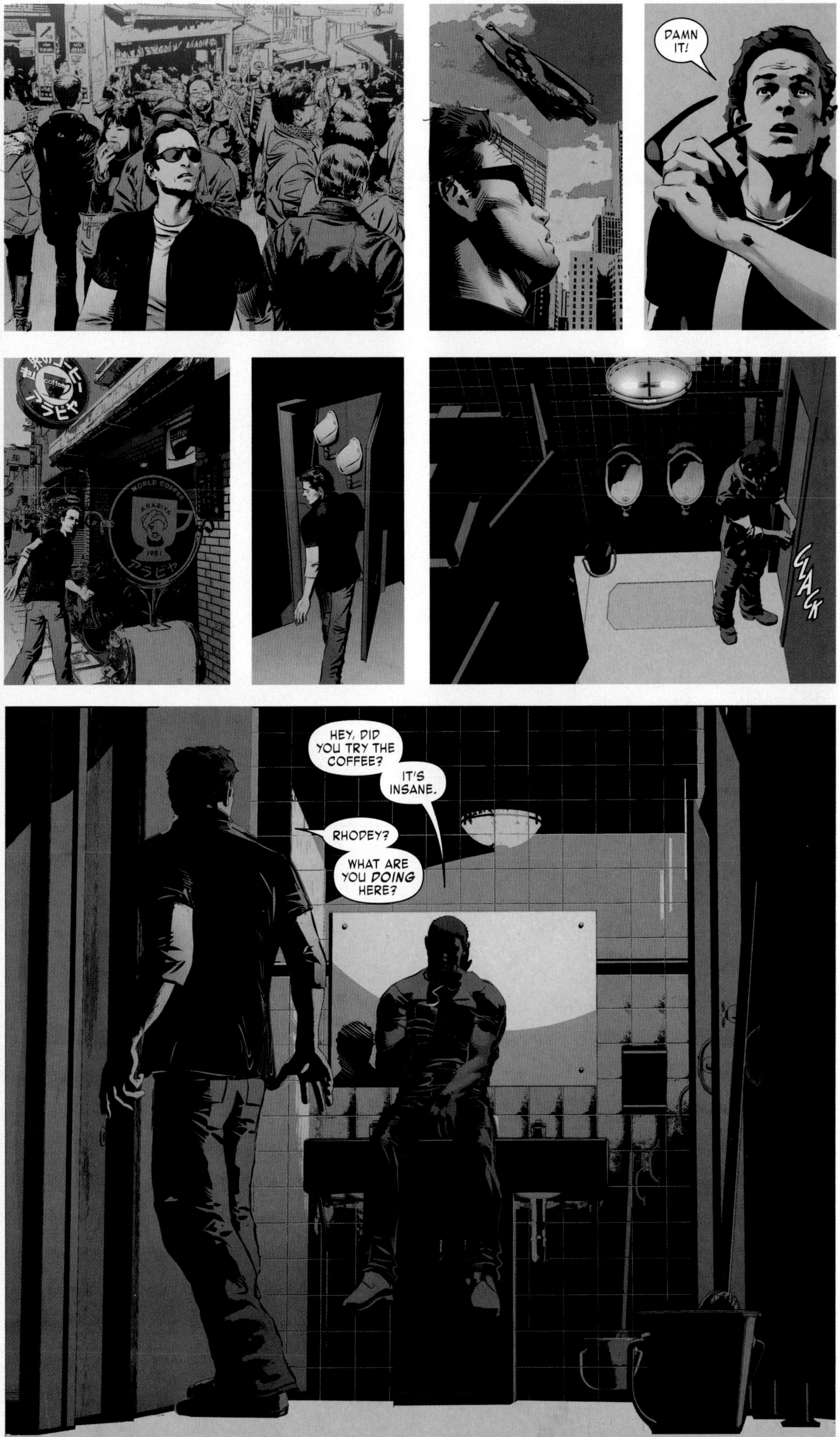
DAMN IT!
CLACK
HEY, DID YOU TRY THE COFFEE?
IT'S INSANE.
RHODEY?
WHAT ARE YOU DOING HERE?

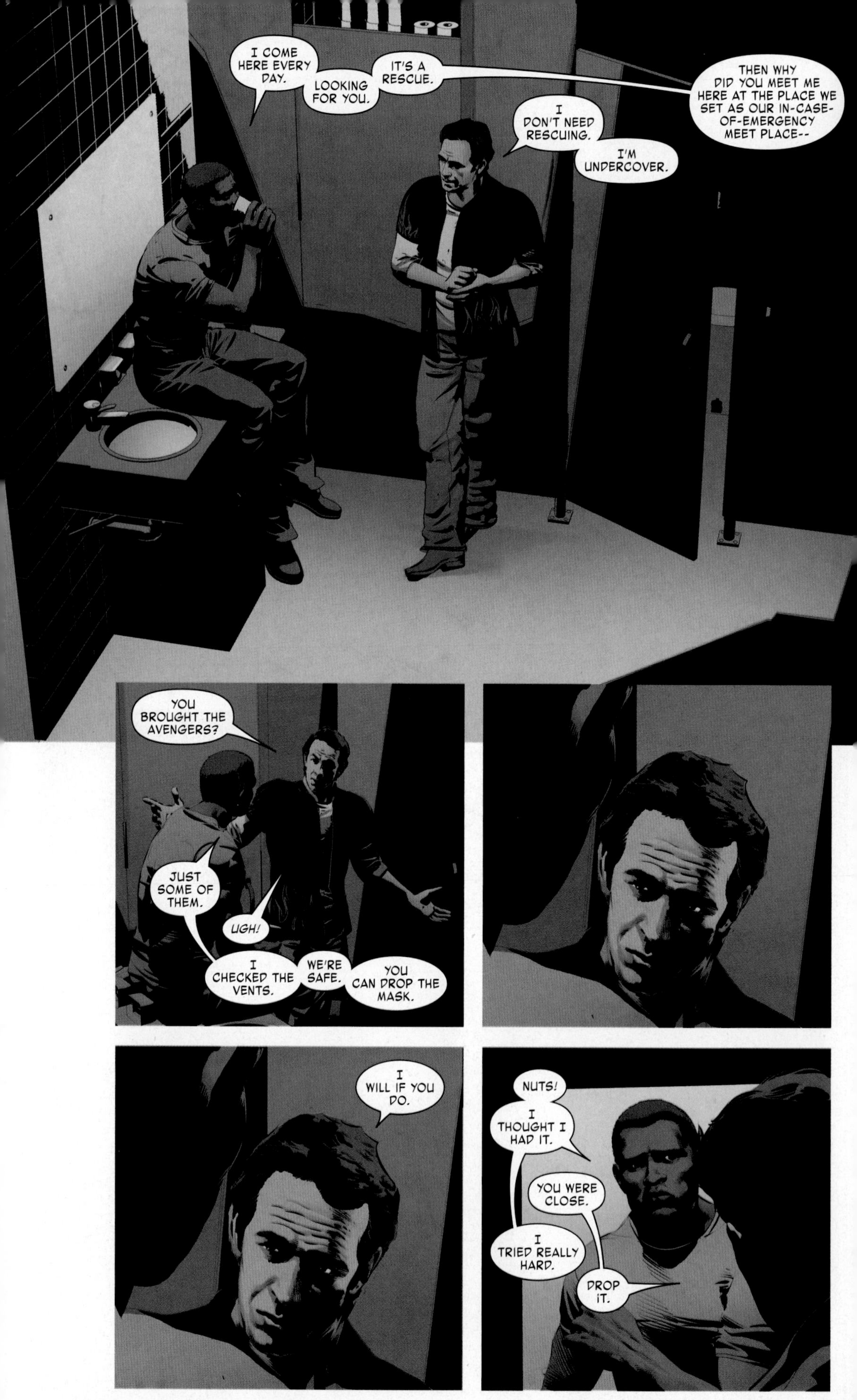
I COME HERE EVERY DAY.
LOOKING FOR YOU.
IT'S A RESCUE.
THEN WHY DID YOU MEET ME HERE AT THE PLACE WE SET AS OUR IN-CASE-OF-EMERGENCY MEET PLACE--
I DON'T NEED RESCUING.
I'M UNDERCOVER.
YOU BROUGHT THE AVENGERS?
JUST SOME OF THEM.
UGH!
I CHECKED THE VENTS.
WE'RE SAFE.
YOU CAN DROP THE MASK.
I WILL IF YOU DO.
NUTS!
I THOUGHT I HAD IT.
YOU WERE CLOSE.
I TRIED REALLY HARD.
DROP IT.

DON'T SWEAT IT, MS. MARVEL.

RHODEY'S MY OLDEST, BESTEST FRIEND.

AND I'VE LIVED THROUGH A SKRULL INVASION OR TWO IN MY TIME.

OKAY, WELL, I'M AN INHUMAN SHAPE-SHIFTER, I KNOW HOW I MAKE MY FACE DO WHAT IT DOES.

HOW ARE YOU DOING THAT?

UGH, THAT FEELS SO MUCH BETTER.

YOU'RE DOING THAT WITH TECH?

OH, MAN.

BIOTECH, ACTUALLY.

THAT FEELS GOOD.

M'ITCHY.

I'M TRYING TO THINK OF A POLITER WAY TO SAY THIS BUT: YOU'RE NUTS, MISTER STARK.

YEAH.

SO, WHY ARE YOU HERE?

RHODEY BROUGHT US ALL HERE.

AND HE PROMISED I'D BE BACK BY 6 P.M. JERSEY TIME.

AND HE WANTS YOU TO KNOW, AND I QUOTE: "I'M NOT GOING TO SAY SORRY FOR THIS."

SORRY FOR WHAT?

I HAVE HIM.

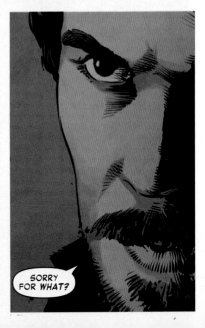

SORRY FOR WHAT?

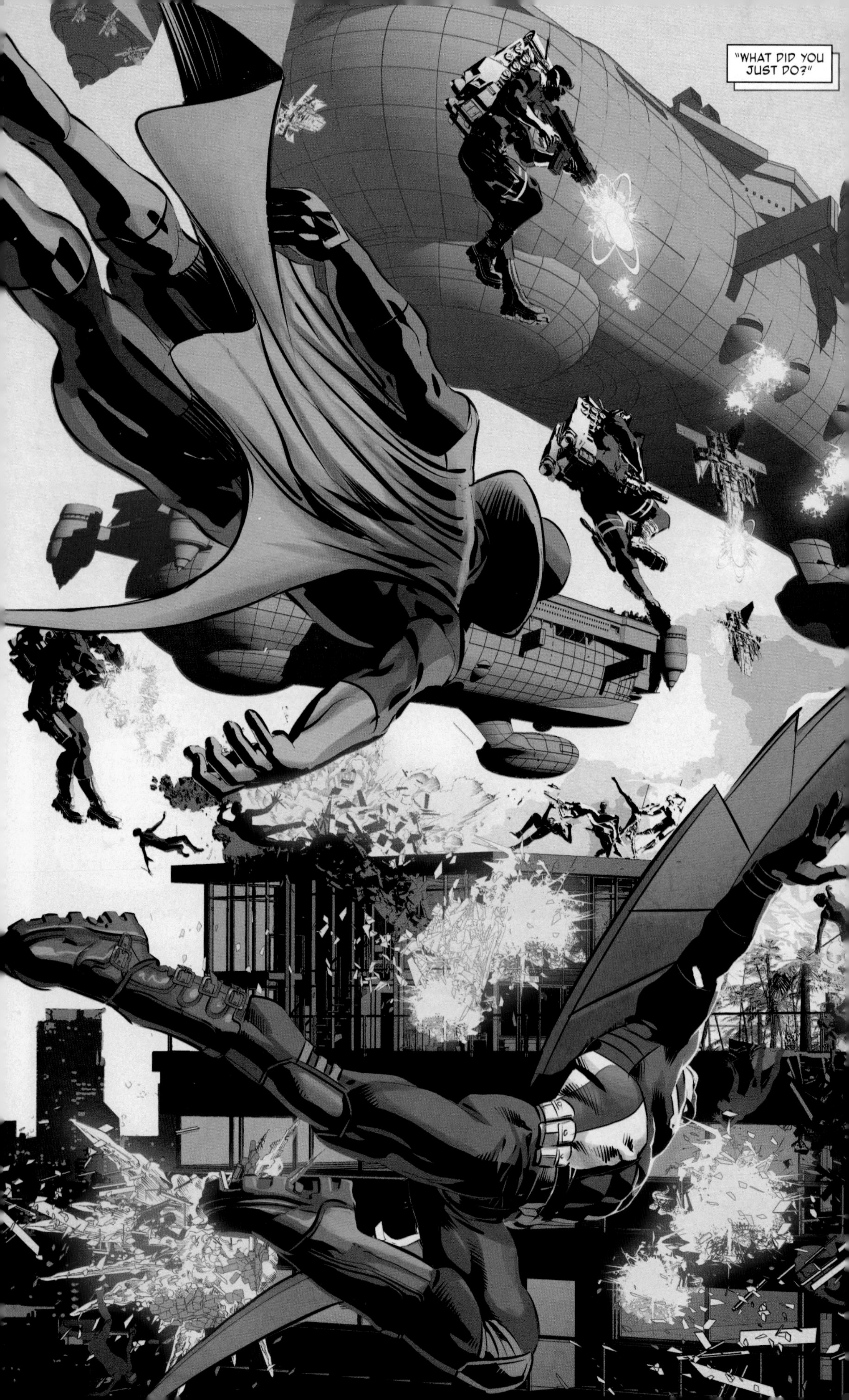
"WHAT DID YOU JUST DO?"

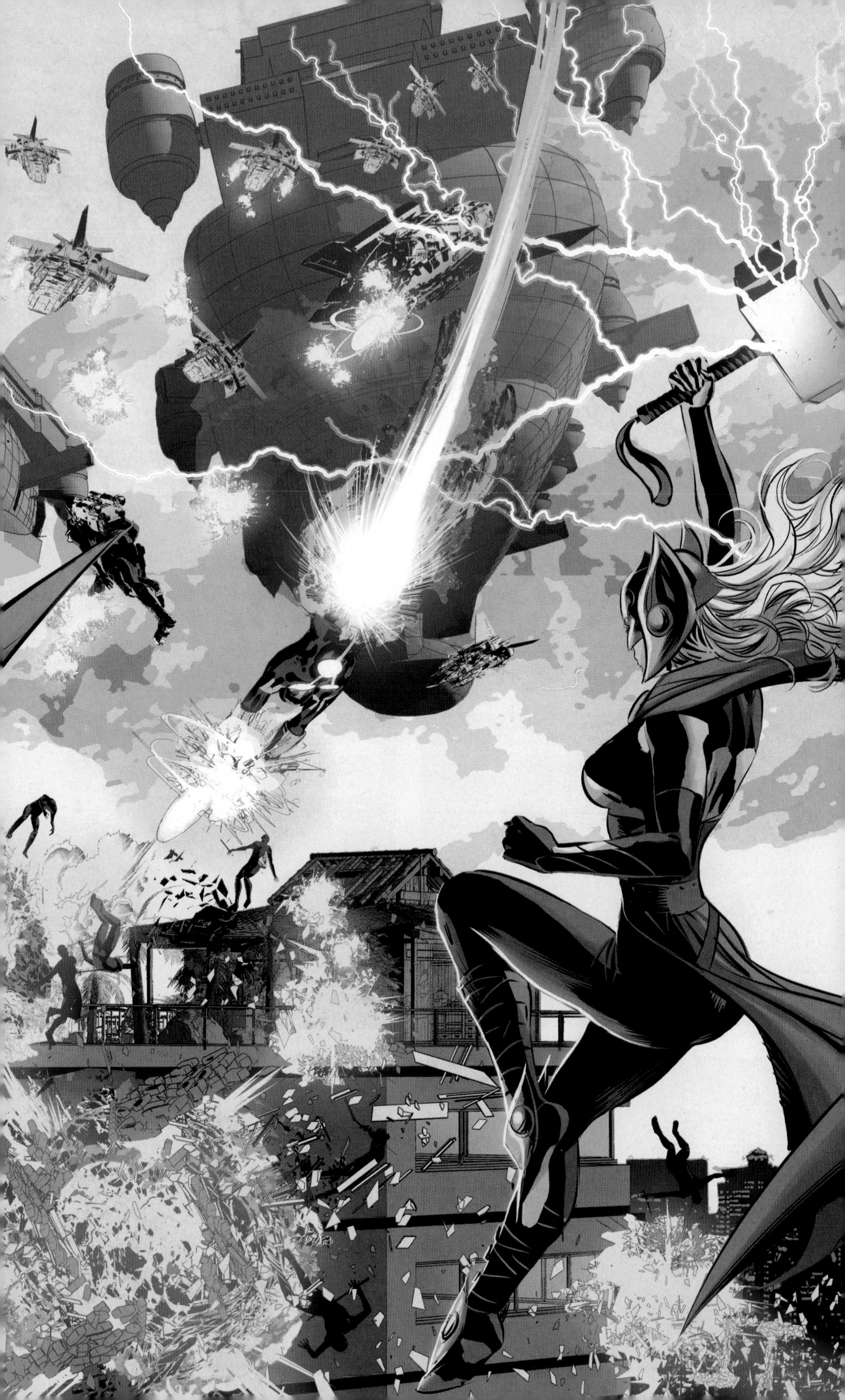

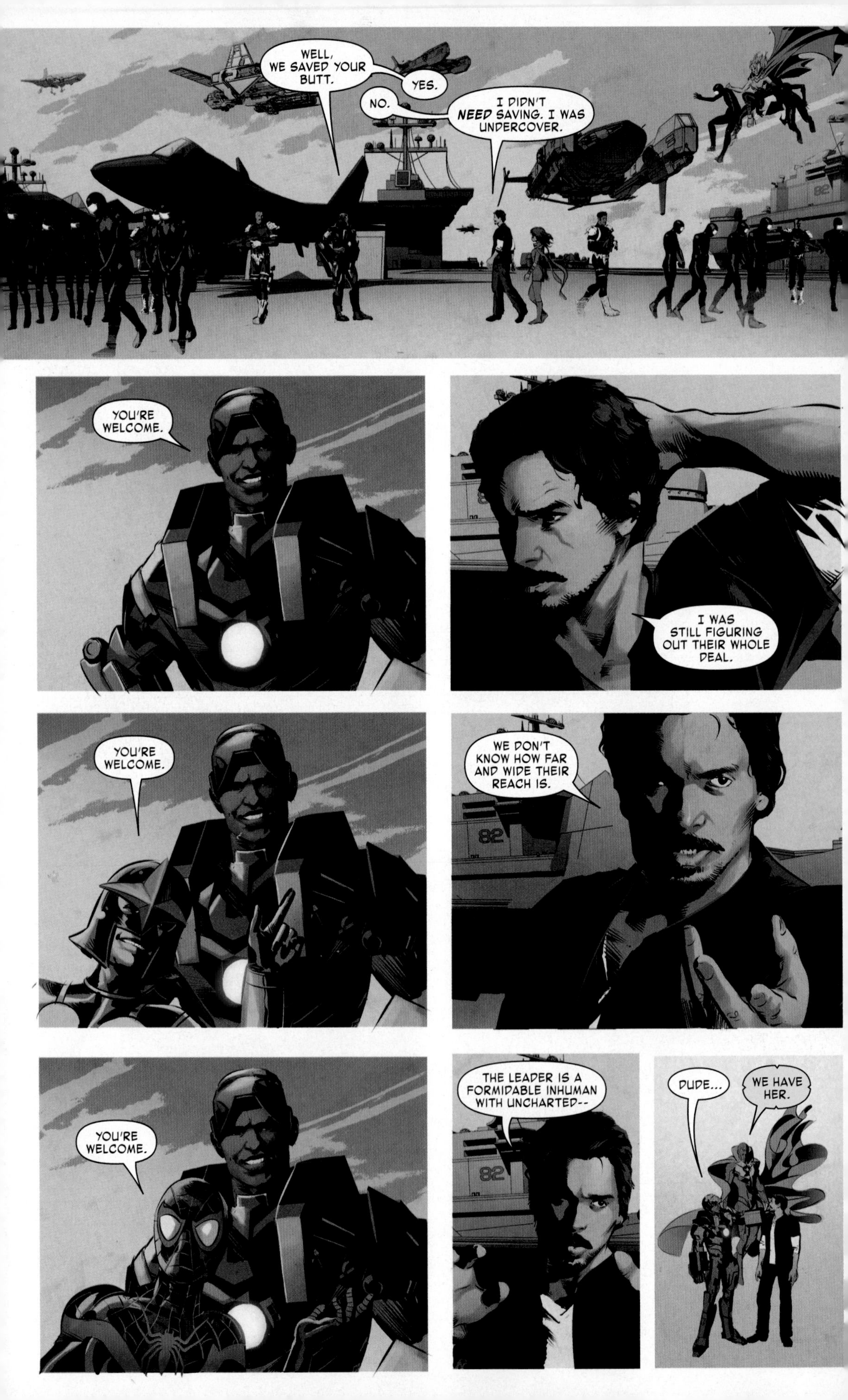
WELL, WE SAVED YOUR BUTT.
YES.
NO.
I DIDN'T NEED SAVING. I WAS UNDERCOVER.
YOU'RE WELCOME.
I WAS STILL FIGURING OUT THEIR WHOLE DEAL.
YOU'RE WELCOME.
WE DON'T KNOW HOW FAR AND WIDE THEIR REACH IS.
YOU'RE WELCOME.
THE LEADER IS A FORMIDABLE INHUMAN WITH UNCHARTED--
DUDE...
WE HAVE HER.

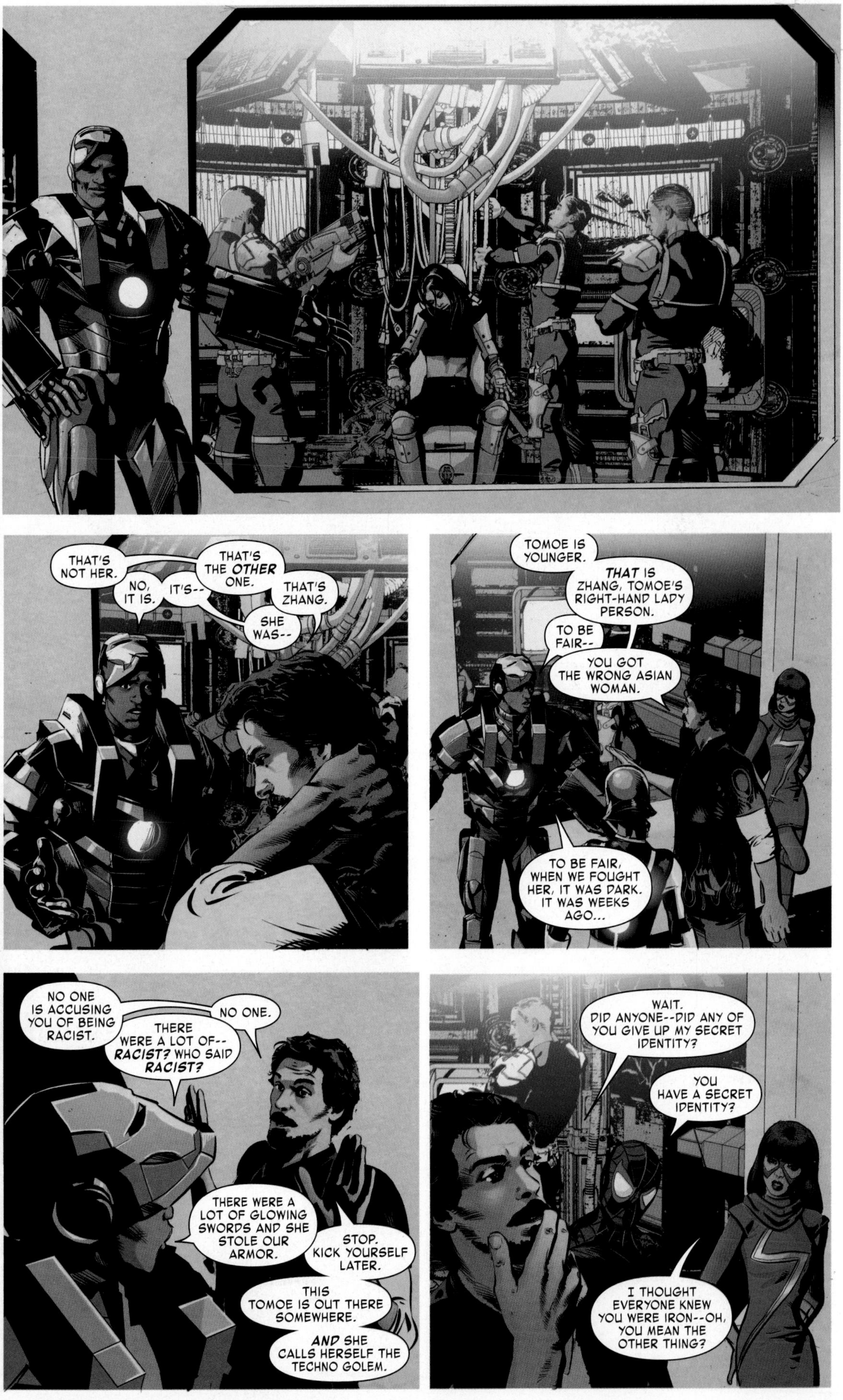
THAT'S NOT HER.
NO, IT IS.
IT'S--
THAT'S THE OTHER ONE.
THAT'S ZHANG.
SHE WAS--
TOMOE IS YOUNGER.
THAT IS ZHANG, TOMOE'S RIGHT-HAND LADY PERSON.
TO BE FAIR--
YOU GOT THE WRONG ASIAN WOMAN.
TO BE FAIR, WHEN WE FOUGHT HER, IT WAS DARK. IT WAS WEEKS AGO...
NO ONE IS ACCUSING YOU OF BEING RACIST.
NO ONE.
THERE WERE A LOT OF--
RACIST? WHO SAID RACIST?
THERE WERE A LOT OF GLOWING SWORDS AND SHE STOLE OUR ARMOR.
STOP. KICK YOURSELF LATER.
THIS TOMOE IS OUT THERE SOMEWHERE.
AND SHE CALLS HERSELF THE TECHNO GOLEM.
WAIT. DID ANYONE--DID ANY OF YOU GIVE UP MY SECRET IDENTITY?
YOU HAVE A SECRET IDENTITY?
I THOUGHT EVERYONE KNEW YOU WERE IRON--OH, YOU MEAN THE OTHER THING?

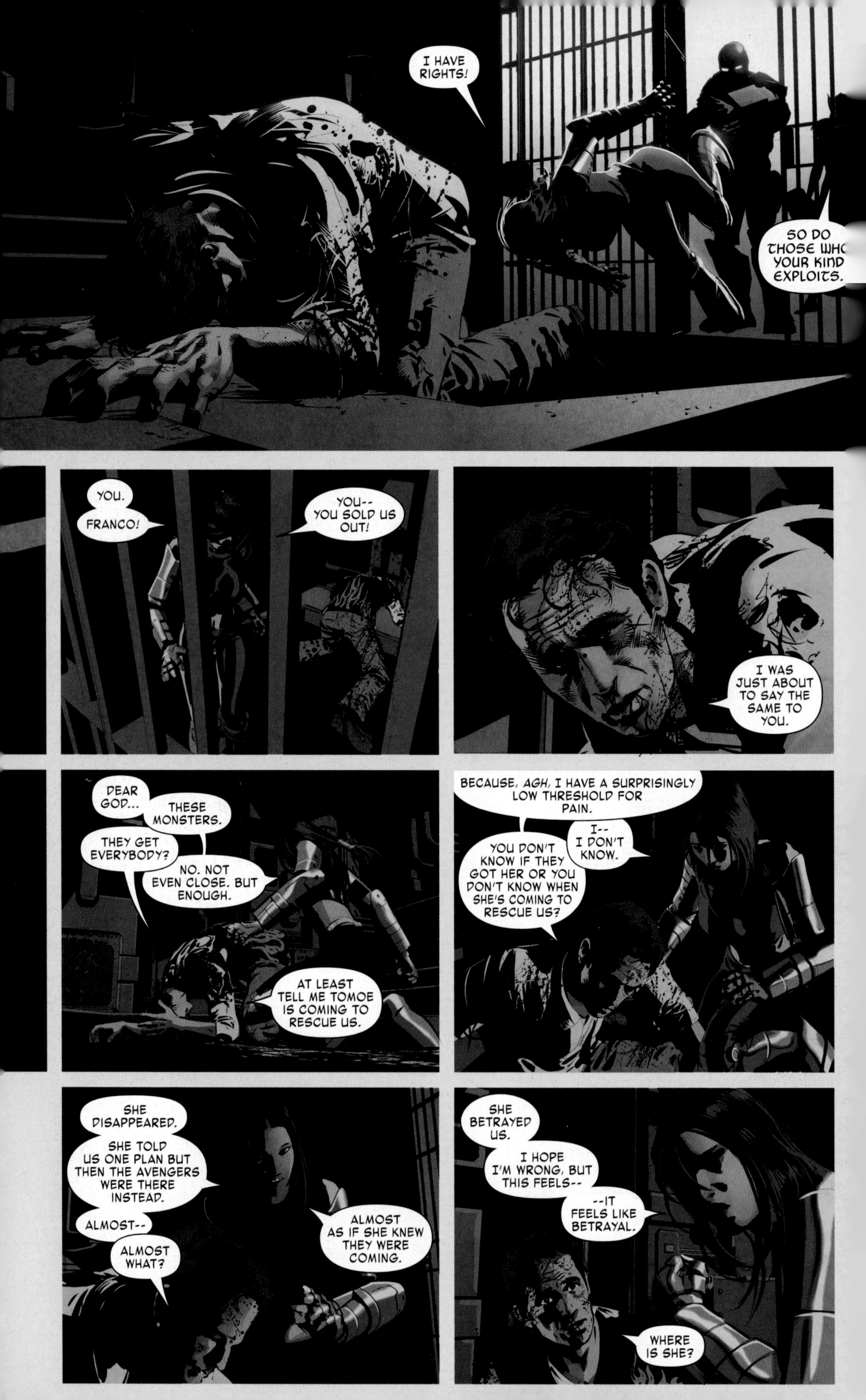
I HAVE RIGHTS!
SO DO THOSE WHO YOUR KIND EXPLOITS.
YOU. FRANCO!
YOU-- YOU SOLD US OUT!
I WAS JUST ABOUT TO SAY THE SAME TO YOU.
DEAR GOD...
THESE MONSTERS.
THEY GET EVERYBODY?
NO. NOT EVEN CLOSE. BUT ENOUGH.
AT LEAST TELL ME TOMOE IS COMING TO RESCUE US.
I-- I DON'T KNOW.
YOU DON'T KNOW IF THEY GOT HER OR YOU DON'T KNOW WHEN SHE'S COMING TO RESCUE US?
BECAUSE, AGH, I HAVE A SURPRISINGLY LOW THRESHOLD FOR PAIN.
SHE DISAPPEARED.
SHE TOLD US ONE PLAN BUT THEN THE AVENGERS WERE THERE INSTEAD.
ALMOST--
ALMOST WHAT?
ALMOST AS IF SHE KNEW THEY WERE COMING.
SHE BETRAYED US.
I HOPE I'M WRONG, BUT THIS FEELS--
--IT FEELS LIKE BETRAYAL.
WHERE IS SHE?

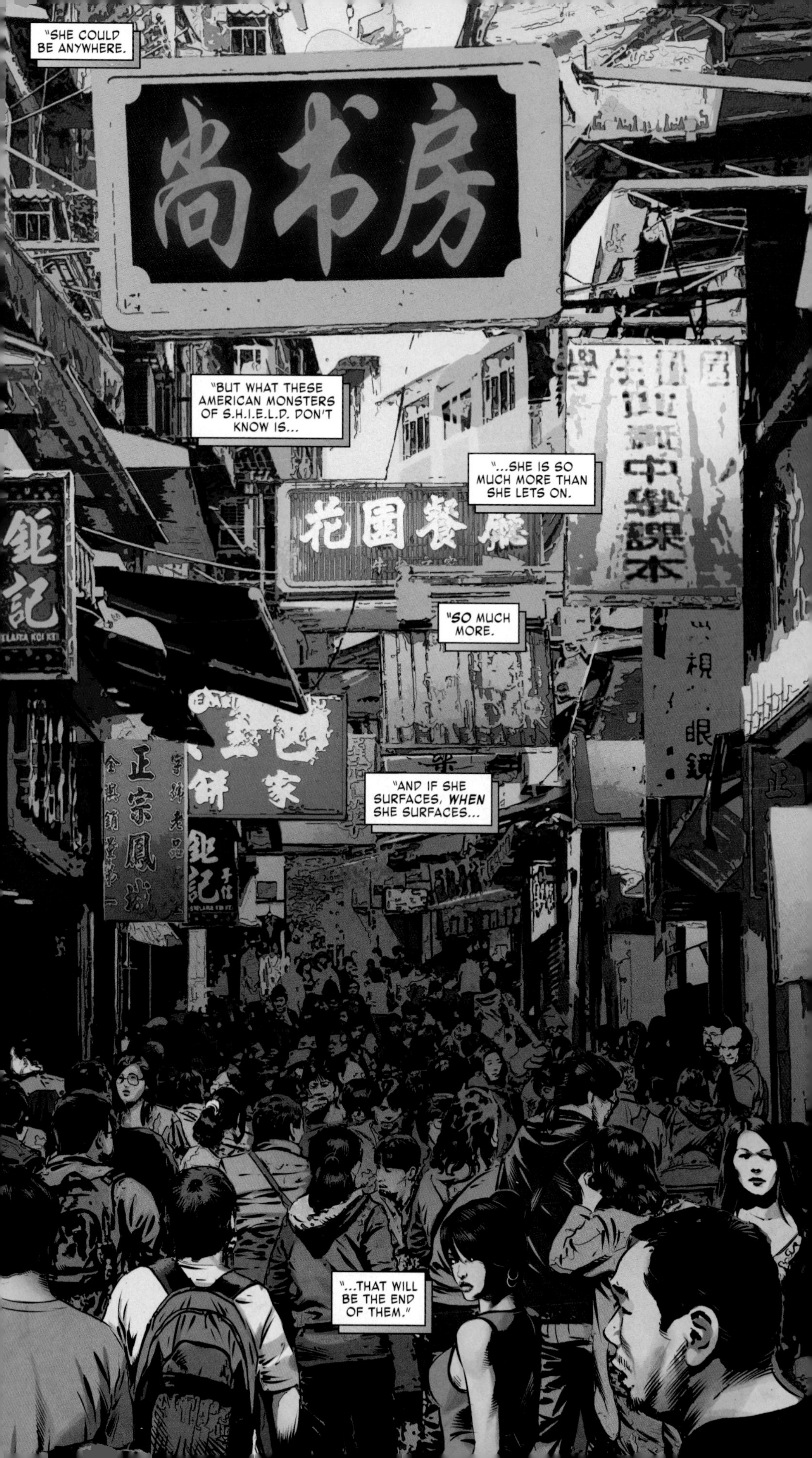
尚书房
"SHE COULD BE ANYWHERE.
"BUT WHAT THESE AMERICAN MONSTERS OF S.H.I.E.L.D. DON'T KNOW IS...
"...SHE IS SO MUCH MORE THAN SHE LETS ON.
花園餐廳
鉅記
"SO MUCH MORE.
"AND IF SHE SURFACES, WHEN SHE SURFACES...
"...THAT WILL BE THE END OF THEM."

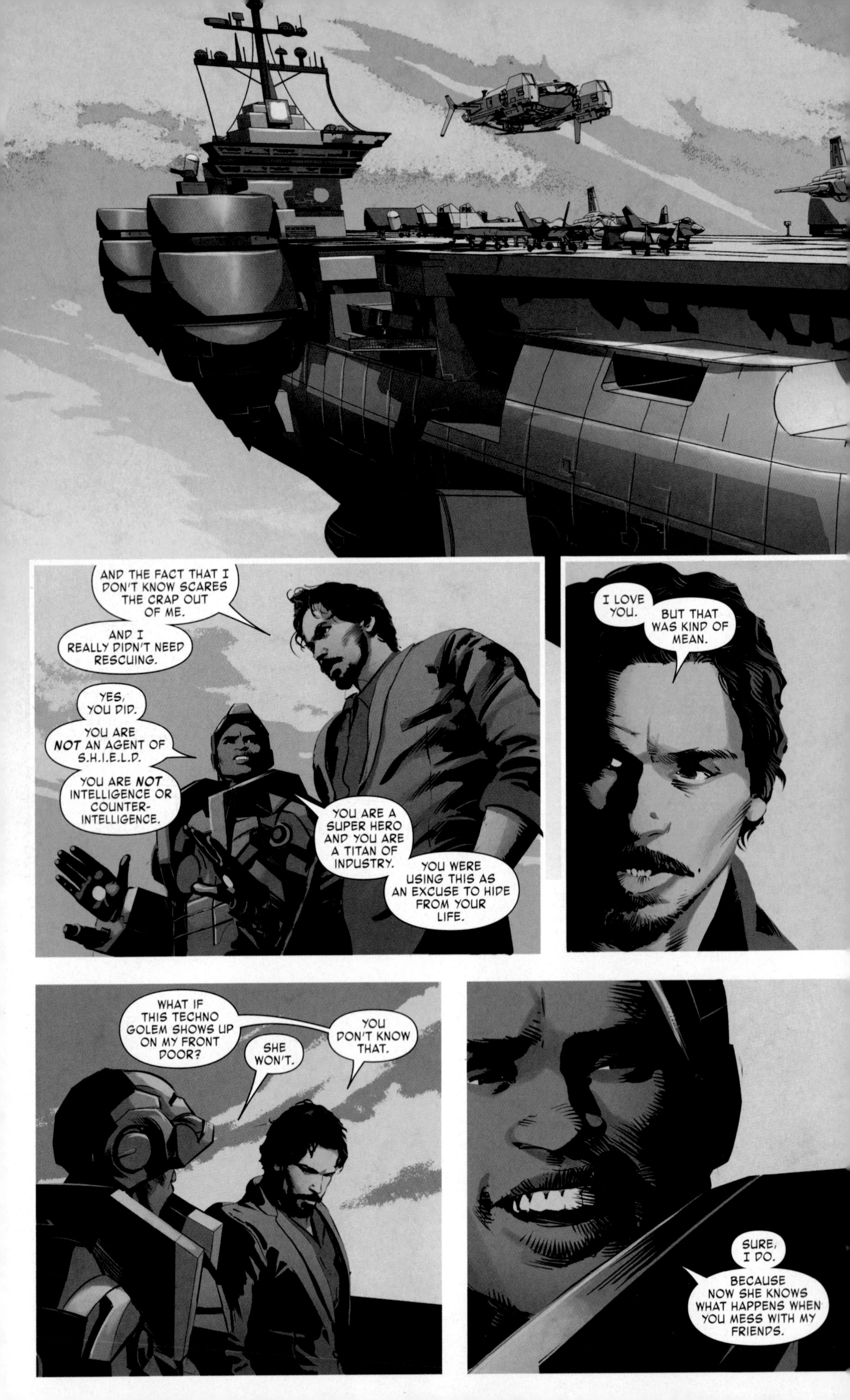
AND THE FACT THAT I DON'T KNOW SCARES THE CRAP OUT OF ME.
AND I REALLY DIDN'T NEED RESCUING.
YES, YOU DID.
YOU ARE NOT AN AGENT OF S.H.I.E.L.D.
YOU ARE NOT INTELLIGENCE OR COUNTER-INTELLIGENCE.
YOU ARE A SUPER HERO AND YOU ARE A TITAN OF INDUSTRY.
YOU WERE USING THIS AS AN EXCUSE TO HIDE FROM YOUR LIFE.
I LOVE YOU.
BUT THAT WAS KIND OF MEAN.
WHAT IF THIS TECHNO GOLEM SHOWS UP ON MY FRONT DOOR?
SHE WON'T.
YOU DON'T KNOW THAT.
SURE, I DO.
BECAUSE NOW SHE KNOWS WHAT HAPPENS WHEN YOU MESS WITH MY FRIENDS.

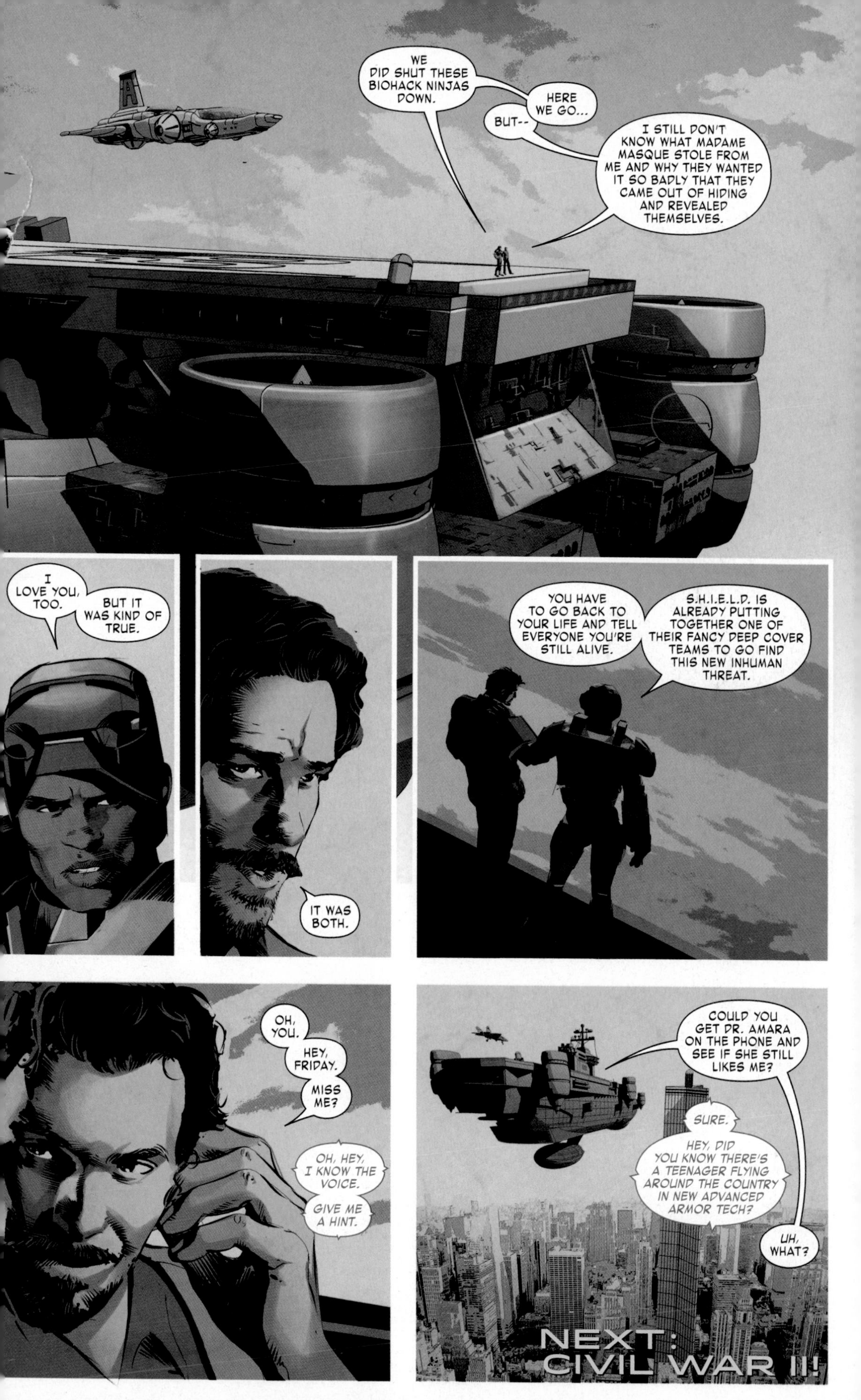
WE DID SHUT THESE BIOHACK NINJAS DOWN.
HERE WE GO...
BUT--
I STILL DON'T KNOW WHAT MADAME MASQUE STOLE FROM ME AND WHY THEY WANTED IT SO BADLY THAT THEY CAME OUT OF HIDING AND REVEALED THEMSELVES.
I LOVE YOU, TOO.
BUT IT WAS KIND OF TRUE.
IT WAS BOTH.
YOU HAVE TO GO BACK TO YOUR LIFE AND TELL EVERYONE YOU'RE STILL ALIVE.
S.H.I.E.L.D. IS ALREADY PUTTING TOGETHER ONE OF THEIR FANCY DEEP COVER TEAMS TO GO FIND THIS NEW INHUMAN THREAT.
OH, YOU.
HEY, FRIDAY.
MISS ME?
OH, HEY, I KNOW THE VOICE.
GIVE ME A HINT.
COULD YOU GET DR. AMARA ON THE PHONE AND SEE IF SHE STILL LIKES ME?
SURE.
HEY, DID YOU KNOW THERE'S A TEENAGER FLYING AROUND THE COUNTRY IN NEW ADVANCED ARMOR TECH?
UH, WHAT?
NEXT: CIVIL WAR II!

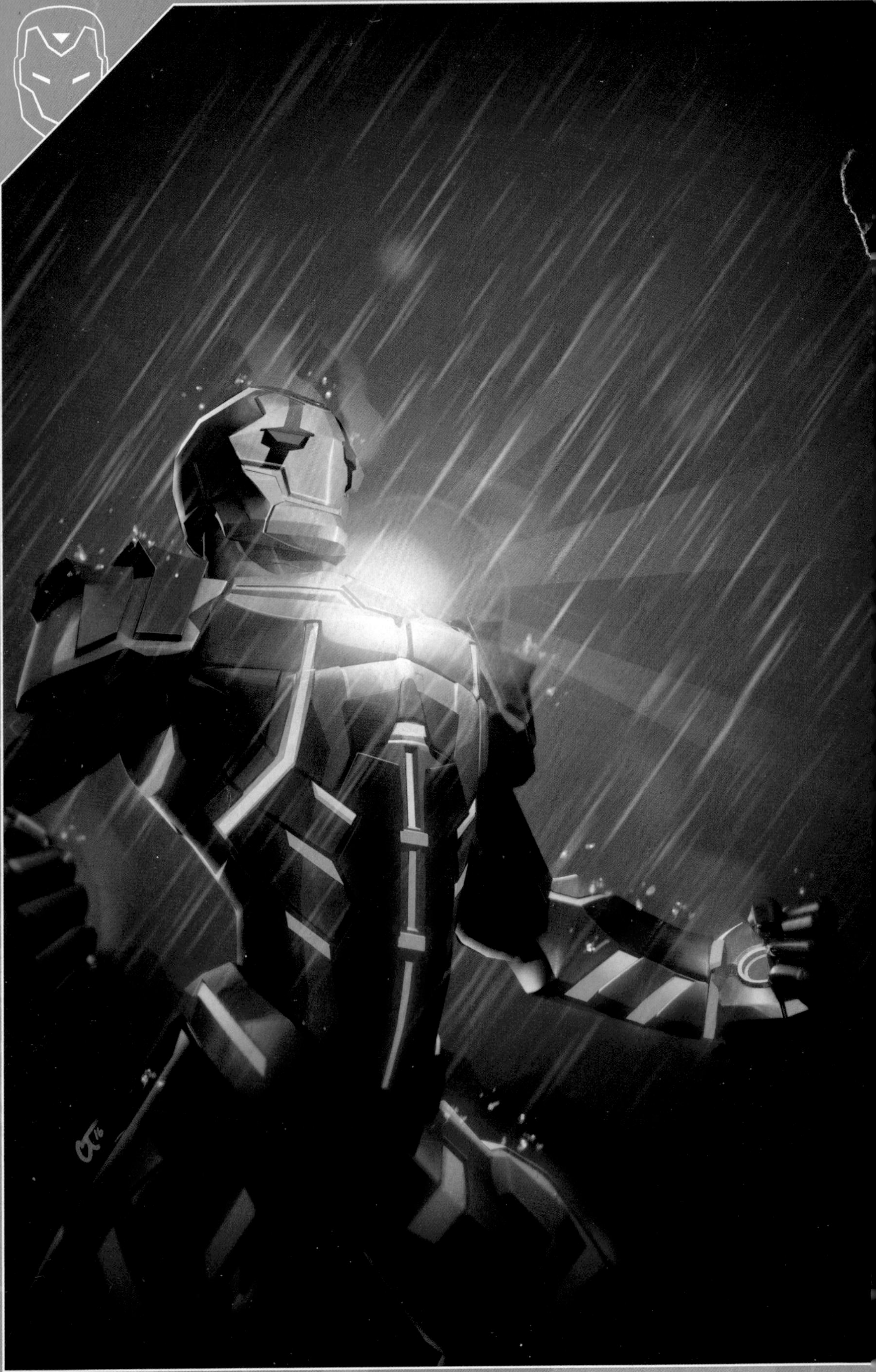

#9 AGE OF APOCALYPSE VARIANT BY CHRIS TURCOTTE